THE RISE OF
POLITICAL LYING

Also by Peter Oborne

Alastair Campbell: New Labour and the
Rise of the Media Class
(1999 and 2004, with Simon Walters)

Basil D'Oliveira: Cricket and Conspiracy
(2004)

THE RISE OF
POLITICAL LYING

PETER OBORNE

First published in Great Britain by The Free Press in 2005
An imprint of Simon & Schuster UK Ltd
A Viacom Company

1 3 5 7 9 10 8 6 4 2

Simon & Schuster UK Ltd
Africa House
64–78 Kingsway
London WC2B 6AH

www.simonsays.co.uk

Simon & Schuster Australia
Sydney

A CIP catalogue record for this book
is available from the British Library.

ISBN 0-7432-7560-8
EAN 9780743275606

Typeset by M Rules
Printed and bound in Great Britain
by Cox & Wyman Ltd, Reading, Berks

To Martine

Contents

PART THREE

Acknowledgements

I have incurred overwhelming debts to hundreds of people while writing this book, so I feel guilty to mention only a few by name. My two researchers, Elizabeth Jones and Tom Greeves, have been immense. Elizabeth has been superb, keeping the show on the road and remaining calm at all times. Tom has proved an outstanding researcher and fact-checker. George Cazenove, James Frayne and Neil O'Brien all did brilliant work towards this book. Tim Knox, Richard Ritchie and Samir Shah have all read and commented on long sections. John Morrison has shared with me his detailed knowledge and acute analysis of the Hutton Inquiry, and showed enormous generosity with his time and understanding. I have derived great enlightenment from discussing the philosophy of lying with Adam Pryce MP. David Morrison has shared his deep understanding of the Iraq War and its aftermath. Greg Rangwala has helped me greatly on British government dissembling during the build-up to the Iraq War. Andrew Sparrow, historian of the parliamentary press gallery, has shared his observations about the techniques used by British politicians to avoid telling the truth. Boris Johnson, editor of the *Spectator*, generously allowed me to go on sabbatical as well as providing instruction about Greek philosophy. Veronica Wadley, editor of the *Evening Standard*, also very kindly allowed me to suspend my weekly column. Thanks are also due to the *Observer* and the *Independent* for their generous permission to publish two articles by the late political journalist Tony Bevins about Tory lying. My publisher Andrew Gordon and agent Gill Coleridge have been great. Finally, my thanks go out to my wife and children, who have paradoxically seen both too much and too little of me during the time this book was written. All failures of fact, understanding or analysis remain, of course, my own.

THE RISE OF
POLITICAL LYING

INTRODUCTION

'Our job is to create the truth' – Peter Mandelson

On 2 December 1997 the government minister Peter Mandelson gave evidence to MPs on government plans to celebrate the millennium. He dismissed critics of the proposed Dome, maximised its advantages, and unveiled an amazing new feature. Mandelson boasted that it would be 'vast, huge in scale'. He divulged few details but described it as an 'interactive attraction which comes under the working title of "Play at Surfball: The New Twenty-First Century Sport".'[1]

Newspapers enthusiastically reported the news. *The Times* stated that 'Mr Mandelson offered the committee a glimpse of the Dome's attractions. The most exciting entertainment would be an interactive computer game called "Surfball", which he described as the sport of the twenty-first century, and a fifteen-minute roller-coaster ride.'[2]

The following week Peter Mandelson was banging the drum again for Surfball. 'The contents of the millennium experience, the Dome, will attract people of all ages,' he told MPs on 8 December, 'although I expect that playing Surfball, the twenty-first century sport, will have an especial appeal to young people.'

3

He was at it again a few days later, writing an *Evening Standard* leader-page article given the headline: 'Don't Panic There's More Than Surfball'.[3] He cited the sport again as he sought to convince the sceptical British public of the merits of the Dome on *Breakfast with Frost* two months later.[4] Soon backbench Labour MPs were joining in. Jim Fitzpatrick, Labour MP for Poplar and Canning Town, declared that the sport would bring 'regeneration' to his con- stituency.'I wouldn't contemplate surfing a ball myself,'he declared. 'I just want to see 1.6 million Surfballers arriving.' City of Durham MP Gerry Steinberg stated that the sport was'quite exciting. Really exciting.Very exciting, in fact. I don't deny that it's very exciting. My secretary will definitely Surfball.'Watford MP Claire Ward, a member of the Commons Culture, Media and Sport Select Committee where Peter Mandelson unveiled the sport, conjured up an image of Surfballers'wearing some kind of virtual millennium headgear that you put on, with gloves that are connected up or a bodysuit, so when you move you feel as if you're part of the balls running in the headset'. Mandelson's political agent Stephen Wallace declared it was the'way forward'.[5]

However, the government was coy about revealing further details of the new sport.When MPs asked Jennie Page, chief executive of the New Millennium Experience Company about Surfball, she told them they were asking for'commercially confidential information which the company proposes to keep to itself for some time yet.'[6] In March 1998 the journalist Richard Heller wrote a letter to Peter Mandelson, asking questions. Was it a team or a solo sport? What referees or umpires did it need? What equipment or playing area? What physical and mental skills were required? Could it be played by either sex, by children and by disabled people? Was it a spectator sport and did it lend itself to international competition? Would it offer possibilities for career development in coaching and management? Heller received an arch reply from Peter Mandelson's private secretary, Rupert Huxter, urging him to curb his impatience until the Dome opened.

The mystery began to intrigue Labour MP Austin Mitchell. Egged on by Richard Heller, he put down parliamentary questions demanding how much had been spent on it, what rights had been acquired and who had been consulted. Only at this point (8 May 1998) did Mandelson come clean.'"Surfball"was a working title,'he imperturbably declared in a written parliamentary answer,'used for illustrative purposes at the end of last year when design proposals were at a very early stage . . . The New Millennium Experience Company does not intend to seek to register the name"Surfball"for any games or features which may form part of the content of the "Serious Play"Zone.' In due course Stephen Bayley, after resigning as creative director of the Dome, revealed the true origins of Surfball. It was invented by a hard-pressed team of consultants making a pitch to the New Millennium Experience Company: 'Engaging the higher cerebral functions for only a fraction of a second, one of their number came up with "Surfball", an apparently new coinage whose components hinted at a combination of the Americanisms so admired by New Labour together with gruffly proletarian reference to a round plaything.'[7]

During its brief but dramatic career, the sport of Surfball was announced in parliament, praised by MPs and written up by journalists. But it never existed. Nevertheless it has its own significance. It is a comparatively early instance of our new public domain, where truth has become indistinguishable from falsehood.

*

Britain now lives in a post-truth political environment.* Public statements are no longer fact based, but operational. Realities and political narratives are constructed to serve a purpose, dismantled, and the show moves on.

This is new. All governments have contained liars, and most politicians deceive each other as well as the public from time to time. But in recent years mendacity and deception have ceased to be abnormal and become an entrenched feature of the British system. This book will show that the rise in political lying as a systemic phenomenon began with the last Tory government, but reached its current fully developed form as the result of the emergence of New Labour.

In 1979, in his famous essay on 'The Power and the Powerless' the Czech playwright and future president Vaclav Havel described how it felt to live within a totalitarian system of government, with 'a world of appearances, a mere ritual, a formal language deprived of semantic contact with reality and transformed into a system of ritual signs that replace reality with pseudo-reality'. Britain is still a democracy, though no longer an especially healthy one, and there are disturbing echoes of Havel's nightmare analysis in our own deceitful public discourse. By no means all inventions are as harmless as Peter Mandelson's Surfball. In 2003 Britain went to war on the back of a fiction: the proposition that Saddam Hussein's Iraq possessed weapons of mass destruction. It did not, but tens of thousands of people died as a result.

This book comes in three parts. Part One, incorporating Chapters

---

* This phrase is borrowed from Eric Alterman, *When Presidents Lie*, p. 305. Alterman applies the phrase to George W. Bush's USA, but it is just as applicable to Tony Blair's Britain.

1–4, will present much of the empirical evidence, and thus help to demonstrate the awesome scale of the problem. Part Two, Chapters 5–8, examines the philosophical, cultural, social and political reasons for the emergence of dissimulation as a defining feature of modern British political culture. The final chapter of this section takes account of the lies told before, during and after the Iraq War of 2003. It shows that these did not come about by chance, but were the inevitable result of the British method of government at the start of the twenty-first century. Part Three analyses the debilitating consequences of our new public mendacity, and then proposes some radical solutions. This section includes an examination of the role of the broadcasting media and the press, so often the vehicle, and to some extent the cause, of government mendacity.

It is important to be clear about definitions. A lie must have two qualities. It must of course contain a falsehood, but must also be uttered with intent to deceive. In other words, a lie is a knowingly false statement. Deception is different. It involves the deliberate creation of a false impression through trickery, omission or a variety of other methods. But it does not necessarily involve falsehood. A series of true statements can be, and often are, put together in such a way that they create a misleading impression in the mind of the listener. Falsehoods can be uttered in good faith, and are not of themselves lies. When a politician makes a statement that in due course turns out to be false, it is quite wrong automatically to assume that a lie has been uttered. There is a parliamentary convention, which has fallen partly into disuse, that where an MP or minister inadvertently puts misleading information into the public domain, he or she should return to the Commons at the first opportunity to correct it.

I have gone to great lengths to make sure that everything in this book is accurate, fair and balanced. This volume is animated by a belief in accuracy, precision, and the virtue of clear and precise statements in both public and private life. It contains a far from comprehensive list of lies. A great many instances have not been included here for reasons of space, or to avoid a tedious, unstructured iteration of deceits and lies. In addition some of the largest episodes of government mendacity – including the 'Cheriegate' affair, the Black Rod episode, and the Ecclestone donation – have been ignored on the grounds that they have been adequately covered elsewhere. It must be assumed, furthermore, that quite a large proportion of the lies and deceits told by government ministers and others have not yet come to light, and may not do so for some time to come. Many other alleged lies have been omitted because of lack of proof. The most famous of these is the frequently repeated story that Tony Blair claimed to have watched the renowned Newcastle striker Jackie Milburn play, overlooking the fact that Milburn left Newcastle when Blair was an infant. Despite hours and hours of research, I have been unable to trace this story to its source, which appears to have been a radio interview conducted in the North East. So the urban myth that Blair claimed to have watched Milburn play has not been included in this volume. Tony Blair's spin-doctor Alastair Campbell once assured me that the story was untrue. There is no reason on this occasion to disbelieve what Campbell says.

This book makes no use of 'private information', the bolthole to which works of contemporary political history inevitably take recourse when they rely on the use of unattributable sources. Everything is transparent. The reader should be able to check the validity of all assertions made in this book through use of extensive notes, which point either to published sources of information, or occasionally to interviews. There are just two partial exceptions. I have made use of an interview given by John Lloyd at the back of his recently published book *What the Media are Doing to Our Politics*. This four-page interview with an unnamed figure, solely defined as a 'member of the present [2004] cabinet,'[8] is helpful for the insights it provides into the state of mind of a senior member of the current administration. All internal evidence suggests that the interviewee is Tony Blair. I asked both John Lloyd and Tony Blair, through the Downing Street press office, to confirm or deny that the prime minister was the cabinet minister in question. Lloyd refused. Downing Street was quite exceptionally evasive and hard to deal with on this matter, at first failing to call back as promised, then giving artful and evasive answers to questions which had not in fact been asked. I was informed, for example, that 'we do not give book reviews'. Doubtless this is the case, but at no stage did I give any Number 10 press officer grounds for believing that I was asking for a book review.

Then, in desperation, I told each of them that I would name Tony Blair as the source. This elicited no response. This reticence is odd in the case of the prime minister since no secrets of state are at stake, and he presumably does not make a practice of giving hole-in-the-corner, anonymous interviews. On the two or three occasions I quote from the Lloyd interview, the assumption is made that Tony Blair is indeed the source, though warnings are attached on each occasion and readers are of course at liberty to make up their own minds.

The second exception to my rule not to use unattributable sources concerns the astonishing remark which, according to the journalist Robert Peston, Chancellor Gordon Brown now 'routinely' says to Tony Blair:'There is nothing you could say to me now that I could ever believe.'[9] Once again, I approached Gordon Brown through the Treasury press office to gain confirmation or, equally helpful, a denial that the Chancellor made this hugely damaging and personal remark to the Tony Blair. Once again I informed the Chancellor that the quotation would appear under his name. Once again, there was no response: no answer whatever to repeated and courteously worded e-mails. In the light of this unsatisfactory state of affairs, Gordon Brown's name is attached in connection with this remarkable statement, but readers can decide for themselves.

Before writing this book I approached five of the main British political parties – Labour, Conservative, Liberal Democrat, SNP and Plaid Cymru asking them to furnish me with examples of the mendacity of their political rivals. All of them obliged, and their contributions were of some use. Some of these allegations were, needless to say, themselves misleading, and all of them needed to be treated with distrust. All allegations of mendacity emanating from political (and indeed any other) sources were carefully checked and verified before they merited inclusion.

PART ONE

1

THE ORIGINS OF CONTEMPORARY POLITICAL LYING

'The truth becomes almost impossible to communicate because total frankness, relayed in the shorthand of the mass media becomes simply a weapon in the hands of opponents' – Tony Blair, *The Times*, 24 November 1987

On 8 March 1994, as a junior reporter on the *Evening Standard*, I heard the Conservative minister William Waldegrave tell the Treasury and Civil Service Committee that it was sometimes acceptable to lie to the House of Commons. Waldegrave maintained that 'in exceptional circumstances it is necessary to say something that is untrue to the House of Commons. The House of Commons understands that and accepts that.' Waldegrave cited as an example the need to protect the pound ahead of a devaluation crisis.[1]

I sprinted out of the committee room, up the stairs to the press gallery, consulted and filed the story. It made the front-page splash in later editions. Ever since I have felt a slight guilt. William Waldegrave was not lying or evading the question when he spoke to the Treasury Committee. Quite the reverse. Waldegrave, a fellow of All Souls, Oxford, was simply attempting in his characteristically agonised and intellectually fastidious way to set out an acceptable moral code for ministers.

And yet his remarks produced a media firestorm. For the best part of a week newspapers condemned Waldegrave's remarks as a fresh instance of 'Tory sleaze'. Labour marched in on the offensive. When reporters tackled Giles Radice, chairman of the Treasury Committee, he declared: 'Frankly, I was amazed. I do not think it right that ministers should justify misleading the House. Questions of procedure make it absolutely clear that ministers should not mislead the House whatever the circumstances are and when they do mislead the House should resign.'[2]

Waldegrave's front bench shadow, Michael Meacher, was more vehement still. He claimed that the 'Waldegrave doctrine exposed just how relative the minister's commitment to truthfulness has become,' adding that 'truth and reliability are at the heart of democracy'. Meacher told me that 'The principle of telling lies or untruths to the Commons is extremely damaging and dangerous. The principle of telling the truth is absolute.'[3]

Soon John Smith, the Labour Party leader, jumped on the bandwagon. 'We don't really need Mr Waldegrave to tell us the Tories don't tell the truth,' he stormed. 'We know they don't tell the truth. And that is why no one will ever believe their promises again.'[4]

There was a great irony at work here. William Waldegrave was doing something very rare for a modern politician and trying to give an honest answer to an honest question. If anyone was guilty of lying, it was his Labour opponents, who set an impossibly high standard of truth telling, and one they had no intention of meeting themselves. It was Waldegrave's misfortune that his remarks played straight into the Labour Party's strategy. Labour was determined to portray Conservative politicians as liars and cheats. This policy was started by John Smith not long after he became Labour leader in 1992, and brought to a climax by Tony Blair after Smith's death in 1994. The policy worked brilliantly, partly because Labour's claims about Tory mendacity contained an element of truth.

Tory Lies, 1979–90

The charge sheet against Margaret Thatcher begins before the 1979 general election. Labour leader Jim Callaghan claimed that the Conservatives would double VAT in order to pay for the income tax cuts they promised. Margaret Thatcher dealt with his accusation by asserting: 'we will not double it'. Her words were strictly true, but disingenuous. The Conservatives jacked up VAT from 8 per cent to 15 per cent within months of taking office, as near to doubling the tax as made no difference. (It was not actually doubled till Norman Lamont lifted the rate to 17.5 per cent shortly after the 1992 general election.)[5]

There is no doubt that Margaret Thatcher lied to the electorate over the sinking of the *Belgrano*, the Argentine cruiser which sank as a result of British military action at the start of the Falklands War, causing terrible loss of life. The ship was torpedoed by the British nuclear-powered submarine HMS *Conqueror*, even though it was outside the 200-mile exclusion zone imposed by the British around the Falkland Islands. Britain had warned that ships breaching the zone would be targeted under British rules of engagement.

Margaret Thatcher justified the action by claiming that the ship had been sailing towards the Royal Navy taskforce. In fact it was sailing away. Mrs Thatcher has always said that she did not know the precise course of the *Belgrano* when she authorised the attack on the cruiser on 2 May 1982. She claims she was only told six months later, just ahead of publication of the Government White Paper on the Falklands Campaign.[6] Her refusal to address the truth about the *Belgrano* in that White Paper led to accusations of lack of candour. In private some Tories were more than happy to own up. An unlikely friendship between the Labour MP Tam Dalyell and the future Defence Minister Alan Clark began one morning in the Commons library when Dalyell strode up to Clark and asked him whether Margaret Thatcher was lying.'Of course she bloody is,'replied Clark. Several months later, however, Margaret Thatcher lied publicly about the *Belgrano* when she appeared on the BBC *Election Call* programme during the 1983 general election campaign. A Mrs Diana Gould asked about the sinking. The prime minister falsely replied that the warship had been heading towards the British taskforce.

The Tory leader's next collision with the truth came with the Westland Affair in 1986. This bitter cabinet row involved the future of the Westland helicopter company. Defence Secretary Michael Heseltine was eager that it should be sold to a European consortium, while Trade and Industry Secretary Leon Brittan was keen that it should find an American partner. Margaret Thatcher backed Brittan in this argument. The grave issue became who authorised the leaking of confidential guidance by the Attorney-General Sir Patrick Mayhew in an unscrupulous attempt to smear Michael Heseltine.

Copies of Patrick Mayhew's letter had been sent to two press secretaries – Bernard Ingham at 10 Downing Street and Colette Bowe at the DTI. While Leon Brittan had everything to gain by leaking Sir Patrick Mayhew's letter, which was very damaging to the European solution Michael Heseltine supported, Colette Bowe did not have the authority to leak such a document without Downing Street consent.

Mrs Thatcher, however, insisted it was Leon Brittan who authorised the leak and that it was arranged by officials at the DTI and Downing Street without her knowledge. She claimed that she had not known the 'full facts' about the leak until afterwards. According to the reporters Magnus Linklater and David Leigh, 'To accept Mrs Thatcher's full explanation it was necessary to believe that both she and Bernard Ingham had behaved entirely out of character; that she had never thought to ask a man in her own office, and with whom she worked in conditions of great intimacy, how a leak of major political significance had been effected.'[7]

The full truth has never been established one way or the other since. The fact that Mrs Thatcher herself seems to have believed, on the eve of the Commons Westland debate, that she might be forced to resign suggests that she may have been guilty. Michael Heseltine in his autobiography, published years later, does not accuse Margaret Thatcher of deceit. Most people close to the story, even if they have no axe to grind, tend to assume that she was implicated.

The evidence that Margaret Thatcher was a liar more or less rests there. In the early 1990s the political journalist Tony Bevins wrote two long and painstakingly researched articles listing alleged Tory mendacity. He cited these two examples – one clearly a demonstrable lie and one merely alleged. But that – a maximum of two lies in ten years – was broadly the extent of the Bevins charge sheet against Margaret Thatcher. The John Major administration presented a different story.

Tory Lies, 1990–97

John Major secured victory in the 1992 general election after a campaign dominated by scaremongering claims that Labour would raise taxes in government. For these charges to retain all their credibility it became essential to deny that the Tories would themselves raise taxes. John Major duly did so, repeatedly stating that 'I have no plans and see no need to increase' VAT.[8] His chancellor Norman Lamont issued the same message, insisting to the House of Commons in his budget statement of 10 March 1992 that 'I have no need, no proposals and no plans either to raise or to extend the scope of VAT.' These pledges were, of course broken by the Tories, who soon raised VAT to its present level of 17.5 per cent.

Unlucky John Major was then driven towards falsehood by his increasingly desperate attempt to sustain the pound within the exchange rate mechanism (ERM). On 10 September 1992 he insisted 'there will be no devaluation, no realignment' of sterling.[9] Within the week he was being forced to suspend British membership of the ERM, and the pound fell precipitously. Major's opponents always made a great deal of the vainglorious words he used in defence of sterling: in fairness to him he did everything possible to keep his word until the matter was taken out of his hands by the currency markets on Black Wednesday, 16 September

1992. His critics were also to make much of the statement he made on 1 November 1993, after the Shankill Road bombings which killed ten people, that face-to-face talks with the IRA 'would turn my stomach'.[10] But the British prime minister went on to authorise such talks with terrorists, and these talks would slowly lead to the IRA ceasefire of 1995. It is true that the prime minister's angry words were thoroughly misleading. But it is easy to understand both the passion with which the words were uttered, and the subsequent need for secrecy when talks were entered into.

It was the Sir Richard Scott inquiry into Arms to Iraq that, as much as anything else, suggested that the last Tory government had lost its moral bearings. Sir Richard found that ministers misled the Commons. His report[11] showed that ministers had issued misleading statements about the secret change in the guidelines surrounding the sale of equipment to Iraq which was agreed by ministers in the late 1980s. Sir Richard demonstrated a contempt for the truth at very senior levels of British government. Nothing exemplified this easy cynicism more vividly than the conversation between the Liberal Democrat MP Sir Russel Johnston and Alan Clark, then Minister for Defence Procurement, on Wednesday 5 December 1990. Sir Russel asked Alan Clark (who, it later emerged, was one of three ministers at the meeting where guidelines were changed) whether he 'was aware of and connived at sales from the United Kingdom to Iraq of equipment which could be used for military purposes'. Clark replied that 'I have a complete and total answer to these allegations, which are rubbish, trash and sensational.'[12]

But Sir Russell Johnston was right, and Alan Clark's answer was lies and bluster. Two years later Clark's confession that ministers had not been straight about arms sales caused the trials of three executives from the arms exporter Matrix Churchill to collapse. He told Presiley Baxendale at the Scott Inquiry that 'I had to indulge in a fiction, and invite them [UK companies exporting to Iraq] to participate in a fiction.'[13]

Alan Clark was by no means the only minister to mislead MPs during the Arms to Iraq affair. The Scott Report concluded that ministers deceived parliament about a change in policy on Iraq. Scott said that letters sent out by William Waldegrave and other ministers were 'in my opinion apt to mislead the readers as to the nature of the policy on export sales to Iraq that was currently being pursued by the government. Mr Waldegrave was in a position to know that this was so.'[14]* But Scott went on greatly to mitigate this criticism, saying that he accepted that Waldegrave 'did not intend his letters to be misleading and did not so regard them.' This qualification was of extreme importance because it meant that William Waldegrave could not be accused of lying, merely of making a mistake in good faith.

But what was in some ways more striking than the conclusions reached by Sir Richard Scott was the response of the John Major government. Rather than apologise, or accept that parliament had been misled, ministers embarked on a mendacious and brazen attempt to assert that they had been vindicated. For the last four years of the Major administration, it was generally held that the government's media management was poor, bordering on helpless.

---

* Today Waldegrave still challenges that conclusion. In an e-mail to the author dated 27 May 2002 William Waldegrave asserts that 'the guidelines certainly did not change in December 1988. Scott believes (wrongly) that they were changed by Ministerial correspondence of late January and February 1989. In fact, as I and others involved at the time believed then and believe now, the Salmon Rushdie fatwah of February 14th ended all discussion without any agreement to change being made.'

The glaring exception was the handling of the publication of the Scott Report in February 1996, hailed at the time as masterly. A press package was produced, with no fewer than thirteen press releases responding, department by department, to Richard Scott's findings. Some of them blatantly misrepresented the Scott Report. One Treasury briefing, appearing under the name of Chancellor Kenneth Clarke, declared, 'Does Scott say Waldegrave misled Parliament? No.' When Labour complained that Scott had said nothing of the kind – in fact Scott had found Waldegrave's statements to MPs and replies to written questions variously 'untrue', 'not remotely arguable' and 'inadequate and misleading' – Ken Clarke blamed a 'drafting error'. The Labour opposition went on to cite a further four cases where they said that government press releases told less than the full story. They said that one Cabinet Office press release lied by saying that there was no policy change on arms sales to Iraq in 1989, and that the government wrongly said that ministers who signed Public Interest Immunity Certificates were required to do so by law, a conclusion that had not been reached by Sir Richard Scott.[15]

Before the debate, Conservative MPs were given a short three-page document. Entitled simply 'Scott', it set out 'key points to make', claiming that ministers had been completely vindicated. Ian Lang, the cabinet minister speaking for the government, asserted that William Waldegrave – found by Scott to have misled the Commons – had nothing to apologise for. In his Commons statement after publication of the report, Waldegrave went to the lengths of demanding a public apology from Labour for having suggested that there was a 'conspiracy' to send innocent men to jail. But the quotations he produced from Robin Cook did not use the word. In due course Sir Richard Scott's spokesman Christopher Muttukumaru despatched a letter to John Alty, principal private secretary to Ian Lang, protesting at the way ministers were using quotes from Sir Richard selectively in their defence.[16]

The Matrix Churchill trial and the Scott Report laid bare a culture of deception and arrogance among senior ministers, while the subsequent handling exposed a readiness to manipulate the facts. On the eve of the vote on the affair of 26 February 1996, writing in the *Sunday Telegraph*, the Labour leader Tony Blair made an appeal to Tory MPs to vote against the government. He asked them: 'Are you really going to send to your constituents the message that you don't mind being misled by ministers and are not prepared to stand up for the principle of ministerial accountability?'[17] Almost all Tory MPs ignored him.

The Arms to Iraq imbroglio and the Westland Affair helped to establish the moral status of the last Tory government. But neither scandal was quite so memorable as the two remarkable liars thrown up by the Conservative administrations of 1979–97: Jonathan Aitken and Jeffrey Archer, both of them impresarios of deceit who operated on an heroic scale.

Jeffrey Archer was a liar and fantasist. His parties at Conservative Party conferences were legendary events, attended by practically all the cabinet. Very few could resist Archer's charm, and yet for years there was abundant evidence that he was a rogue and conman. Though he never held ministerial office, he was nevertheless a member of the intimate circle surrounding both Margaret Thatcher and John Major and, to a lesser extent, William Hague.

Michael Crick, author of a masterly biography of Archer, which does full justice to his extraordinary life story, wrote: 'Any one of those three was surely aware of all the evidence that Archer was a deeply dishonest man, a deeply untrustworthy man, and a man of appalling judgment.'[18] However, Jeffrey Archer was a hugely engaging figure, he was brilliant at raising money for the party; his wit, absurdity and ebullience raised the morale of Conservative activists.

Archer lied about anything. He was born in central London, but passed off his place of birth as Somerset. He attended Wellington, a perfectly respectable Somerset school, but often led people to believe he was an old boy of the more swash-buckling Wellington College in Berkshire. When he applied for a modest schoolmastering job he grossly exaggerated his examin-ation achievements. Another CV listed a fictitious year at Sand-hurst military academy. Archer did manage to take a one-year diploma at Oxford: thereafter he gave the impression that he had completed a full degree course. In the mid-1980s Margaret Thatcher made Jeffrey Archer a deputy chairman of the Conservative Party, a post he soon had to resign because of scandal. Later John Major elevated him to the House of Lords, while William Hague embraced him as the Conservative Party's official candidate to be Mayor of London.

Archer was not officially exposed until 2001, when he was sen-tenced to four years in prison for having lied in the libel case in which he was the plaintiff against the *Daily Star* in 1986. The *Daily Star* had accused Archer of having sex with a prostitute Monica Coghlan – the scandal that caused him to resign as Tory deputy chairman. Archer won the case thanks to the evidence of a witness, Ted Francis, that Archer could not have been having sex with Coghlan at the time alleged because he was having dinner with

Francis. Fifteen years later Francis admitted that he was lying. Archer was found guilty of perjury and sent to prison.

Jonathan Aitken, who was also jailed for perjury, was a more sinister figure than Jeffrey Archer. Margaret Thatcher, who never trusted Aitken, left him loitering on the backbenches for years. John Major swiftly promoted him to the cabinet, but he soon faced allegations that he had taken substantial payments from Saudi businessmen. Aitken resigned in 1995 in order to fight a libel action against the *Guardian* and Granada TV, calling a press conference in which he declared that 'if it falls to me to start a fight to cut out the cancer of bent and twisted journalism in our country with the simple sword of truth, and the trusty shield of fair play, then so be it. I am ready for the fight.'[19]

The action came perilously close to success. It failed when it became clear that an Arab businessman had paid the bill for a weekend's stay at the Ritz in Paris in 1993. Aitken had insisted that his wife had paid the bill and persuaded his daughter Victoria to sign a false witness statement, saying that she and her mother were in Paris on the weekend in question. In fact British Airways receipts made it clear that they were in Switzerland at the time. It was the discovery of these documents right at the end of the trial that brought Aitken down. But he was very largely a lone wolf, operating against rather than alongside the political machine. He deceived and betrayed his own colleagues as well as the world at large.

The same applied to another notorious Tory liar, the MP Neil Hamilton. An exotic figure, Hamilton resigned as Trade and Industry minister in October 1994 after his links with the business tycoon Mohamed Fayed came to light. It was claimed that he secretly accepted cash payments from Fayed in return for tabling parliamentary questions. Though this was later found to be true, it is at least to Hamilton's credit that once he became a minister he resisted approaches from the Harrods owner: it may indeed be the case that Hamilton's very fastidiousness as a minister brought about his downfall. Neil Hamilton was nevertheless a colourful example of a culture of arrogance, greed, sleaze and casual mendacity which had become a settled feature among a group of mainly backbench Tory MPs by the late 1980s. Tory sleaze was a key part of the background against which New Labour emerged in the early 1990s, and the reason why Tony Blair's repeated claims that he would make an honest broker were so appealing.

Tony Blair Claims to Tell the Truth

The falsehoods and sleaze of the Conservatives provided an irresistible target for Tony Blair and his rampant New Labour opposition. The future prime minister and his shadow ministers wasted few opportunities to denounce the Tories as liars, cheats and scoundrels. Later, once he was established in Downing Street, Tony Blair seems to have come to regret this strategy, apparently lamenting to a friendly journalist that 'it was a media tactic which could of course be used against us, and which was distasteful in some ways.'[20] Distasteful or not, at the time he threw the Labour opposition into this strategy with abandon.

At the same time as attacking the Tory Party, New Labour made large, expansive claims about its probity and integrity. No recent Labour leader – perhaps no leader of any British political party since Gladstone led the Liberals – has ever made such dramatic claims about his own moral status as Tony Blair. In his first party conference speech on 5 October 1994, the future prime minister spoke with colossal passion of the responsibility that government ministers must have to the truth. He accused the Conservatives of fostering cynicism about public life, and dramatically promised 'a new politics, a politics of courage, honesty and trust'. Warming to the theme, Blair declared that 'those most in need of hope deserve the truth. Hope is not born of false promises; disillusion is. The British people are tired of dogma ... They are tired of glib promises broken as readily in office as they were made on the soap box.'

I was at that Labour conference, and heard those remarks. Political journalists are supposed to be callous and cynical. We weren't on this occasion. Like almost everyone else present I felt uplifted and exhilarated. As a young and raw political reporter I was convinced that this man would bring honesty back into British politics, and the press coverage at the time shows that most others felt just the same. We believed that we were in the presence of something marvellous, benign and entirely new. Tony Blair presented himself as a new kind of politician or, rather, someone who was not really a politician at all. His youth, honesty and decency put to shame the corrupt, tired and cynical world all around. Pretty well all of us – politicians, journalists, Tories, Lib Dems, and above all the voters – swallowed this whole. It is practically certain that Blair himself believed this version of reality even more than the rest of us.

Tony Blair's claim that he was specially honest – indeed his claim to be honest at all – has turned out not to be true. The strangest thing is that there was importance evidence which shows it wasn't true even at the time. I was a lobby correspondent back in 1994, and the evidence was accessible to me – just as it was available to all of us lobby reporters, and everyone else. But we didn't want to look, and even if we had looked, no one would have wanted to know about it.

The proof was to be found in the very recent past, in the management of Tony Blair's campaign for the Labour leadership. Far from being the open, trusting, decent affair that one might have imagined, it was devious, secretive and mendacious. It was so devious indeed that the future prime minister's main adviser throughout the campaign was kept secret. And he was kept secret not just from the voters and the outside world. His identity was quite deliberately and deceitfully hidden from those who were officially running the Blair campaign.

This extraordinary episode concerned the future cabinet minister Peter Mandelson. According to John Rentoul, Tony Blair's sympathetic and well-informed biographer, Mandelson played the role of 'campaign adviser in chief'.[21] This created a problem because many people in the Labour Party, including many of Blair's own supporters, could not abide the saturnine ex-spin-doctor. Two of Tony Blair's most senior campaign managers, the Labour MPs Mo Mowlam and Peter Kilfoyle, made plain to Blair that they would not work for him if Peter Mandelson had anything to do with the campaign. Today Peter Kilfoyle says: 'I made clear at the outset that I would be involved so long as Mandelson wasn't. I laboured under the misapprehension that Mandelson was not involved. When we sat on the campaign committee his name never came up.'[22]

Blair dealt with the revulsion felt by Kilfoyle and others towards Mandelson in a peculiar way. Effectively he had two campaign teams. There was one formal one, the one that existed in the public eye, which included Mo Mowlam, Peter Kilfoyle, the fund-raiser Barry Cox, the Labour MP Andrew Smith and various others. This team met every morning but, to quote John Rentoul, 'the decisions that mattered – about media strategy and speeches – were taken elsewhere.'[23]

This arrangement was kept secret. Had the role of Peter Mandelson been known, there is every reason to believe that Tony Blair's vote would have been smaller. But Mandelson's involvement did not emerge till after the leadership contest was over, when Blair thanked his supporters at a victory party. He issued 'a particular thank-you to a friend of mine called Bobby, who some of you will know. He played a great part and did so well.' Bobby was the code-name given during the campaign to Peter Mandelson, in order to keep his involvement quiet.[24] This decision to unveil Bobby aka Peter Mandelson after he had won was almost as curious a move as the decision to keep him quiet in the first place: it set apart those who were in the know from those who were not. Tony Blair displayed an unattractive arrogance, demonstrating that he was ready to deceive even his supporters.

The role of Peter Mandelson was not, however, the most misleading aspect of the campaign to elect a man who put 'honesty' and 'trust' at the heart of his public manifesto. Within an astonishingly short space of time, Tony Blair was to turn out to be the most radical and transforming Labour Party leader in history. The changes he brought about were enormously to his credit, and established his reputation as a forceful and charismatic figure. They were implemented so swiftly and effectively that it seems inconceivable that he had not mapped out these changes in his own head in advance. But he communicated none of this as he fought a cautious campaign. John Rentoul captures this wariness and circumlocution nicely, stating that:

Blair's leadership election manifesto, which did not advertise any changes to the Labour Party, turned out to be a misleading prospectus. By the time of the Special Conference, Blair had changed the party's constitution, effectively changed its name and redrawn its policies on tax, inflation, the minimum wage, exam league tables, opted out schools, Northern Ireland, regional government and the House of Lords.[25]

The story of how Tony Blair set about the most powerful and remarkable of these changes – the removal of Clause Four – makes a specially interesting case study. The commitment to the 'common ownership of the means of production, distribution and exchange' had been Clause Four of the Labour Party constitution since it was drafted by Sidney Webb in 1918. Labour modernisers since the 1950s had viewed these words as a monstrous encumbrance, but few dared tackle it. It remains one of Tony Blair's most telling achievements that he had the courage to do so.

Books on New Labour always lazily state that the abolition of Clause Four was announced in the prime minister's inaugural party conference speech in 1994, the same one in which he made his dramatic pledges about truthfulness and honesty. But that is not the case. What actually happened was rather different. Towards the end of his speech Tony Blair embarked on a purple passage, ending with the proclamation: 'Let us say what we mean, and mean what we say.'[26]

Almost at once he declared that he and John Prescott were to propose a new statement of the objectives of the Labour Party to 'take its place in our constitution for the next century'.[27] Tony Blair received a standing ovation, and the great majority of delegates walked out of the conference hall without the faintest idea that anything out of the ordinary had happened at all. This is how the *Guardian* reporter Stephen Bates reported the speech the following day:

> Mr Blair sought to present a new spirit in British politics. He also attempted to commit Labour to changing its constitution, although in language so coded that it received a heavy round of applause from delegates who clearly did not at that stage appreciate that it meant the abolition of Clause Four.[28]

Tony Blair never announced that this innocuous sounding statement of aims meant the end of Clause Four. He left that task to his spin-doctors, who briefed the press and others immediately after the speech. Far from saying what he meant, as he brazenly claimed, Blair quite brilliantly pulled the wool over everyone's eyes. This evasiveness was deliberate, a tactic to avoid a hostile reaction from the conference floor while the speech was being made. It is easy to justify the dodge in its own terms, rather less so to reconcile it with the protestations of honesty and trust which filled up the rest of his speech that Blackpool afternoon. This curious and false episode was to set the tone for Tony Blair's three years in opposition. Very few of us in the hall cared to reflect on this at the time.

Tory Lies – and the Origins of New Labour Dissimulation

The most notorious Conservative Party liars of the 1990s were rogue agents who exploited or abused their positions. Men like

Jonathan Aitken, Jeffrey Archer and Neil Hamilton were acting solely on their own behalf from desire for financial gain, personal ambition or other motives. They fell squarely into a long and dishonourable tradition of villains and imposters, which throughout the twentieth century manifested itself in all parties from Horatio Bottomley to Robert Maxwell. They most certainly deceived the wider public, but they misled friends and colleagues just as much. It might well be possible to argue – and the Labour Party most certainly did – that Aitken and Archer were in some way symptomatic of a wider moral corruption that overtook the Conservative Party towards the end of the last century. But it is impossible to sustain the argument, also made by the Labour Party in opposition, that Tory lies had become embedded in the system of government itself.

New Labour Party lies were sharply different. Certainly there have been a number of cases – such as Geoffrey Robinson's failure to tell the truth over his financial dealings – which fall into the freerider category of deceit familiar from the late Tory period. But the most characteristic form of New Labour mendacity was constructed to serve the party and emphatically not the individual interest.

In this sense Labour lying was more virtuous. The lies were first about getting New Labour elected and thereafter sustaining it in power. When Labour misrepresented the Tory record, misled voters in its election manifesto, or cynically lied to newspapermen – all things which it did in opposition – it was to help the Labour Party and the wider British people that Labour claimed to represent.

New Labour under the leadership of Tony Blair took the view at a very early stage that it was quite legitimate to deceive in order to obtain power. The leadership seems to have felt that the Tories were so disgusting, and the alternative offered by Labour so thoroughly desirable, that almost any tactic short of political assassination was legitimate. Indeed those most closely associated with the New Labour movement seem to have concluded, for reasons that are at the very least understandable, that lying and deception was the only way that a party of the Left would ever regain power once more in Britain.

It is impossible to understand why so many senior Labour figures should have felt this way without going back a generation to the 1970s, when the party was last in power. Ever since the war the Labour Party had been swinging in and out of government, first with Clement Attlee, then Harold Wilson and finally Jim Callaghan. As a result the 1970s Labour Party felt something like a party of government. At any rate it had good reason to believe that it occupied the mainstream part of British public discourse and culture.

In the years that followed, this belief changed. Labour suffered four consecutive election defeats in a row. Time and again it put its case relatively truthfully to the British people. Michael Foot, Neil Kinnock and John Smith – Labour's first three leaders during that eighteen-year-long wilderness period that only ended when Tony Blair reclaimed power in 1997 – were all unusually honest and decent politicians. But again and again they found that the British people turned a deaf ear to what they had to say.

After a while the Labour Party started collectively to conclude that there was something deeply unfair and wrong about the mechanisms of democratic politics in Britain. Some of its most intelligent figures argued that political discourse was constructed in such a way that it would be impossible ever again for a left-wing party to win.

They blamed a number of factors for this. One was the nature of the state. Some, particularly those with training on the far Left, felt that Britain was institutionally conservative. They felt that the machinery of government was no longer, as the textbooks claimed, neutral and disinterested. Instead they argued – most people would say they were mainly wrong about this – that the civil service and other institutions had been captured by the Right.

Labour also blamed the broadcasting media and above all the newspaper press. Practically everyone who mattered on the Left shared, and continues to share, this view. Labour's lowest point, in the early and mid-1980s, coincided with the emergence of a new, self-conscious and brilliant media class. Fleet Street newspapers were suddenly shedding the comparative deference and modesty they displayed in the three decades following the Second World War, and becoming a much more independent and confident force. Neil Kinnock was the first mainstream political victim of this dazzling but mean-hearted newspaper culture.

Both Kinnock himself and those around him came to hate the British press with an intensity that can barely be expressed with mere words. They felt that newspapers like the *Sun*, the *Daily Mail* and the *Daily Express* systematically set out to demonise Kinnock and to misrepresent everything that he and the Labour Party had to say. In the end Kinnock stopped talking to large parts of the British media, because he felt that there was no point telling them what he thought. He knew from his own bitter and ugly experience that they would misrepresent what he wrote, rip it out of context, and then use his remarks against him. Neil Kinnock was prone to an occasional lack of discipline and egregious errors of judgement that were legitimately highlighted by critics in the media and elsewhere.

He often confused reasonable criticism with partisan attack. But there is no doubt that he had a case when he sensed that he was persecuted by the press.

As a result, the Labour Party under Neil Kinnock saw itself as the victim of a malfunction in the democratic system. Although Britain had most of the institutions and freedoms normally associated with a liberal democracy during the time that Kinnock was leader of the opposition, it had one characteristic of a totalitarian state. Only one of the two main political parties – the Tories – was confident of securing a fair hearing in the mainstream media. Many voters there-fore received a biased and distorted account of what the Labour Party was seeking to achieve in office. Labour could not possibly hope to get fair treatment at general elections.

The Neil Kinnock camp thought this situation was outrageous and utterly wrong. But they were split about what to do about it. One group held that the whole thing was insoluble and that the Labour Party had no option except to bash on in the belief that one day the eyes of the British public would open and voters would come to see through all the lies, falsehoods and smears put out by the Tory press. This was broadly the position of John Smith, who succeeded Neil Kinnock as Labour leader after the 1992 election defeat. Smith despised the media, and refused to accept that an institution so venal and worthless could have any true importance.

A second group shared all of John Smith's contempt for the media, but rejected his conclusion. They felt that Smith's refusal to engage, however noble, showed a massive failure in his strategic thinking, and even a dereliction of duty. They thought that he was opting out. They saw with great clarity that the first obligation of the Labour Party was to win power. It could do nothing on behalf of the people it represented – the poor, the exploited, the underprivileged – unless it was actually in government. Hardened and embittered by the experience of the Kinnock years, these critics of John Smith saw the media as the roadblock which the Labour Party must clear if it was ever to escape from opposition.

This group was New Labour, which seized power within the Labour Party after John Smith's death in 1994. New Labour, led by Tony Blair but steered by Peter Mandelson and Alastair Campbell, was a highly intelligent and awesomely successful attempt to solve the problem. It is significant that New Labour has its origins during those anguished Kinnock years. Charles Clarke and Patricia Hewitt, later to become senior members of Tony Blair's cabinet, ran Neil Kinnock's private office. Tony Blair and Gordon Brown were the two brightest members of his frontbench team. Alastair Campbell, later to become Tony Blair's very powerful press secretary and director of communications, was Kinnock's close press ally and confidant. Philip Gould, influential political consultant to Tony Blair, began his engagement with the Labour Party as an adviser to Neil Kinnock.

These men and women judged that political power could never be secured in Britain until the press had been appeased. Peter Mandelson understood the problem best of all. He said: 'Of course we want to use the media, but the media will be our tools, our servants; we are no longer content to let them be our persecutors.'[29] Upon becoming leader of the swiftly renamed New Labour party in 1994 Tony Blair made it his urgent priority to secure the backing of newspaper groups that had previously been loyal to the Conservatives. Tony Blair confided to a friendly journalist much later in his career the thinking behind this:

> Maybe you could say we tried too hard to woo over the mag-
> nates – but if you make that critique you have to take into account
> the power of the media here. You must deal with it. If all the
> papers turned against the government or the Prime Minister –
> more have now than before – it, and he, could in the end be
> destabilised to the point of losing. It could happen. Look at Neil
> Kinnock. Neil said – to hell with them: I hate them and won't talk
> to them. And look what happened to him.[30]

This mission to woo the press was extremely successful. Nevertheless, New Labour retained every last ounce of its original inner
contempt for the right-wing press. A number of sympathetic
journalists were co-opted, in an important transgression of boundaries, as collaborators in the project. But in general New Labour
viewed reporters and journalists as contemptible creatures, born
liars, an obstruction to serious discourse whose only interest was to
twist the truth. Following in the footsteps of the philosopher
Grotius, New Labour concluded that it was permissible to make
misleading statements to those who could not be trusted to tell the
truth. It viewed journalists who complained when they were lied to
as simple hypocrites who would never contemplate telling the truth
themselves. One friendly commentator, the *Guardian*'s political
editor Michael White, reflected this state of mind well: 'Mr Blair,
Peter Mandelson and Mr Campbell,' he wrote, 'largely neutralised
the systemic hostility and misinformation of most of the
Conservative Press by adopting its enemy's tactics.'[31] Writing years
earlier, well before he became Labour leader, Tony Blair put the
matter in more measured terms: 'Our news today is instant, hostile
to subtlety or qualification,' he complained, drawing the lesson that

'the truth becomes almost impossible to communicate because total frankness, relayed in the shorthand of the mass media, becomes simply a weapon in the hands of opponents.'[32]

These words, though not without insight or legitimacy, became a justification for evasion and mendacity. During the opposition years between 1994 and 1997 Tony Blair made repeated assertions that he was as honest as the day is long. He doubtless meant what he said. But paradoxically, he seems to have felt that this very candour and honesty liberated New Labour to tell as many lies as it wished.

Labour's Dirty 1997 Election

In that first speech to the party conference as Labour leader, Tony Blair declared that 'when we make a promise, we must be sure we can keep it. That is page one, line one of a new contract between a Labour government and the citizens of Britain.' This was not just an idle remark. Tony Blair returned to the theme in Labour's 1997 manifesto, writing in the introductory section: 'The Conservatives' broken promises taint all politics. That is why we have made our guiding rule not to promise what we cannot deliver; and to deliver what we promise.'[33]

Yet these claims that Labour, unlike the Conservatives, would keep its promises, would soon turn out to be false. University education was one early example. Just before the 1997 election Labour was emphatic in ruling out university tuition fees. Tony Blair declared that 'Labour has no plans to introduce tuition fees for higher education.' Ten days later Robin Cook told Leeds Student Radio on 24 April 1997 that 'We are also quite clear that the tuition costs must be met by the state.'To drive home this point, Cook produced the dramatic warning that'if the Tories were to get back for a fifth term, you would find that they would start to charge students for tuition'.[34] Yet the 1998 Teaching and Higher Education Act brought in tuition fees of £1,000. Labour would go on and deceive the British people in just the same way ahead of the 2001 general election. The party manifesto pledged that 'We will not introduce "top-up" fees and have legislated to prevent them.' The Higher Education Act of 2004 introduced the very top-up fees that Tony Blair had ruled out three years before.

At the 1996 Labour Party conference Andrew Smith, then shadow Chief Secretary to the Treasury told delighted delegates that 'our air is not for sale'[35], ruling out proposals of a privatisation or sale of National Air Traffic Services. NATS was partially privatised in July 2001.

More important than either tuition fees or privatisation, was taxation. Throughout the run-up to the 1997 general election Tony Blair, eager to avoid the mistake made by Neil Kinnock and scare off middle-class voters, insisted that New Labour would not raise taxes. He did not simply give assurances about income tax, but declared that taxes in general were in no danger of going up. 'We have no plans to increase tax at all,' he told his audience at the Birmingham International Convention Centre in 1995. This was no casual aside. The pledge was deliberately produced to reassure sceptical listeners and at the end of the event John Hawksley, president of the Birmingham Chamber of Commerce, said: 'I think I jotted down the phrase"no plans to increase tax at all". That was very encouraging.' John Kampfner of the *Financial Times* noted the same phrase, and reported Blair's next claim: 'After all the one tax cut delivered since 1992 was the scrapping of the increase in VAT on power which was the result of a Labour motion in the House of Commons.'[36]

In 1996 Tony Blair reiterated this pledge as he took part in a live conference phone-in with readers of the *Daily Express*. One reader asked him if voters had anything to fear from a Blair government. Blair told him to 'judge us on the facts rather than Conservative propaganda', adding 'Our proposals do not involve raising taxes.'[37] In 1997, just to ram home the point, the future prime minister insisted that 'the programme of the Labour Party does not imply any tax increases at all.'[38] These claims, designed to establish Labour as the party of low taxation, were hollow. By 2004 voters had been clobbered by scores of tax increases, ranging from stamp duty to fuel, with taxation up by approaching £5,000 for every household in the United Kingdom.

Similar assurances were offered to business. 'We will not impose burdensome regulations on business,' pledged Labour's 'Business Manifesto', published on 11 April 1997, 'because we understand that successful businesses must keep costs down.'[39] But in February 2005 the British Chambers of Commerce 'Burdens Barometer' estimated that the cost for business of new regulation was £39 billion, with hundreds of new regulations being brought in every year. Tony Blair denied this, insisting in 2001 that 'it's a very considerable exaggeration to say that there is a mass of regulation that has come in now.'[40] Exaggeration or not, Britain was becoming sharply less competitive, crashing from fourth to eleventh in the World Economic Forum's international competitiveness league.[41]

Similar assurances were also offered in the form of 'proper protection for the hard-working majority who save for their retirement.'[42] In practice Labour oversaw a crisis in the pensions industry which led Labour MP Frank Field to declare in September 2004 that 'when Labour came to office we had one of the strongest pension provisions in Europe and now probably we have some of the weakest.'[43]

Pensions was the issue which led to the nastiest example of Tony Blair's mendacity during this period: his warning that the Tories planned to abolish the state pension. The claim came during the one week of the 1997 campaign when it looked as if Labour was starting to wobble, and a rogue ICM opinion poll suggested a mass return to the fold among Tory voters.*

It was fair enough for Tony Blair to attack the Tories' pension proposal. But his assertion that 'there is no doubt, when up and running, the purpose of this is to replace the basic state pension with a private pension' was disgraceful. The apocalyptic warning had its effect. One Labour candidate was out canvassing the following day when she encountered an old lady who burst into tears that the state pension would be abolished. According to the account by *Observer* reporters Andy McSmith and Patrick Wintour, the Labour candidate 'felt moved to explain the Government's Basic Pension Plus proposal, to reassure the old lady that not even the Conservatives would be so heartless as to leave her destitute.' Wintour and McSmith billed the candidate as 'probably to be made

---

* The account of the pensions row is heavily based on Patrick Wintour and Andy McSmith's article 'Election 97: Final round: Polls apart as pensions spark an age-old battle of shouting liar', *Observer*, 27 April 1997. Wintour and McSmith observed that 'Labour can legitimately argue that the Tories' long-term aim is to replace the basic state pension with privately purchased provision, enhanced by a £9 a week rebate from the National Insurance contribution. But the government has always said that the new scheme guarantees a pension at least equal to the current basic provision, uprated in line with inflation.'

a Minister in a Labour government'. They quoted her saying after-wards:'I do feel slightly squeamish about the pensions thing. It has been an incredibly powerful message, which on an individual basis has created a lot of fear. It's part of a major political strategy which has a highly personal impact. We have won it hands down. The Tories are completely on the back foot.'

Tony Blair's words were a gross distortion of the proposals for pension reform launched by Social Security Secretary Peter Lilley on 5 March 1997, just three weeks before the election began. Perhaps it was unwary of Lilley, one of the most cerebral and intel-lectually honest members of the John Major government, to publish complex plans on such an emotive subject so close to an election. But writing in *The Times* on 7 March, Tony Blair had shown no indignation, and even gave the plans an equivocal blessing, stating that'There is no doubt that the government's pension pro-posals are bold. For some commentators that is enough. And in one sense by opening up the debate, they give the next government the chance to conduct the debate more sensibly.' Six weeks later he changed his tune.

The attack on pensions was just one part of a New Labour strategy to distort the facts and mislead the public in order to demonise the Tory Party. This tactic was at work the previous summer when a Treasury paper was leaked to the Labour Party. Then shadow chancellor Gordon Brown insisted that 'this plan amounts to nothing less than the demolition of Britain's welfare state.'[44] He was grandly rebuked by Peter Riddell, political com-mentator of *The Times*, who declared that 'to claim that the document reveals the real Tory agenda for a fifth term is absurd. It does not even represent an options paper for ministers.'[45]

An essential part of the Labour strategy in opposition was to diminish the Tory economic achievement. Labour had a problem as the election approached. Although it was embarrassing to admit as much, the British economy was recovering extremely fast from the recession at the start of the 1990s. In order to create a different impression, Tony Blair manipulated some of the facts. A convenient way of demonstrating this syndrome is by examining the party document 'New Labour, New Life for Britain', published in 1996. In the introduction to this work Tony Blair claimed that a Labour government would follow 'high principles of conduct and governance' and rule with 'a moral purpose and direction currently lacking'. But the manifesto itself was full of half-truths and distorted statistics. It was determined to present the Thatcher/Major period as an economic disaster – a paradoxical thing to do since Labour fought the 1997 campaign on the basis that it would retain the Thatcherite free-market, low-tax economic framework.

The manifesto stated that 'the British economy is not stronger than its main competitors in Europe and elsewhere. We have fallen from 13th to 18th in the world league of national income.'[46] In fact, according to the OECD Economic Survey of the United Kingdom for 1996, Britain's national income topped one trillion dollars in 1994, ranking it fifth in the world behind the United States, Japan, Germany and France – up a place since 1979 thanks to the collapse of the Soviet Union.[47] Likewise 'New Labour, New Life for Britain' asserted that 'Our growth rate has lagged behind our main competitors over the 17 Tory years.' In fact, according to World Bank figures, Britain had achieved an annual growth of 2.3 per cent per head since 1979, secondly only to Japan among G7 countries. 'New Labour, New Life for Britain' claimed that 'people are having to work harder to stand still'. This was untrue. In the previous ten years, median real wages in Britain had increased by 19 per cent, and even the lowest paid workers enjoyed a 10 per cent increase.'New Labour, New Life for Britain'claimed that Britain 'had the worst job creation record of any major industrial economy since 1979'. In fact, according to the OECD, Britain provided jobs for a higher proportion of its working age population in 1995 than Germany, France or Italy. The OECD's 1996 Economic Survey concluded that'In short, the United Kingdom's policy of maintaining an economic environment conducive to job creation has paid off in a better jobs and unemployment record than in many Continental European countries.'

These distortions and abuses of evidence were a result of one key problem Labour faced as the 1997 general election approached. The British economy was probably in a healthier state than at any period since the end of the Second World War. Labour seems to have thought it was essential to blacken this benign economic situation. It chose to do so through misleading use of official statistics. On 5 April 1995 the shadow employment secretary Harriet Harman told *The Times* that Labour'wants to tell the truth about employment – unlike this government'. In practice shadow ministers were keen to discredit figures produced by the Office for National Statistics.[48]

The Emergence of a New Labour Epistemology

These false pledges on education, privatisation, taxation and business regulation came about because New Labour was so desperate to get elected that it would do or say practically anything. This led the future prime minister to degrade himself by saying many things that he fundamentally did not believe. The worst case of this deceit involved Europe. Tony Blair has rarely made any secret, when talking in private to pro-Europeans, of his passionate support for the European idea, or the single currency. He insisted to the 1994 Labour Party conference that 'under my leadership I will never allow this country to be isolated or left behind in Europe.'

But he had a problem. During the 1997 general election campaign he was desperate to gain the support of tabloid British newspapers, above all the *Sun*. The tabloids were obsessed with Europe, and Tony Blair felt the need to feed this obsession, and present himself as a Eurosceptic too. This is what he told the *Sun* when interviewed on St George's Day: 'On the day we remember the legend that St George slayed a dragon to protect England, some will argue that there is another dragon to be slayed: Europe . . . Let me make my position on Europe absolutely clear. I will have no truck with a European superstate. If there are moves to create that dragon I will slay it.'[49] In an article in the same paper a week earlier he wrote: 'I know exactly what the British people feel when they see the Queen's head on a £10 note. I feel it too. There's a very strong emotional tie to the Pound which I fully understand. Of course there are emotional issues involved in the single currency. It's not just a question of economics. It's about the sovereignty of Britain and constitutional issues.'[50]

Tony Blair was not exactly lying when he produced these words. But he was certainly sending a very different message to *Sun* readers than to the Labour Party or his pro-European allies. When he found himself alone with Eurosceptic journalists in these early days, he would go much further. He told Paul Dacre, editor of the *Daily Mail*, that 'I agree with so much that you say about Europe.' He shamelessly informed Dacre that it was 'obscene' that the British people should pay 40 per cent tax to the British state. He would flatter Dacre by informing him that the *Daily Mail* was 'the only authentic voice on Fleet Street', comparing the paper favourably with the *Guardian*.'If the *Guardian* approved of me something must be wrong,' the future prime minister told the *Daily Mail* editor.[51] Pretty well none of this reflected Tony Blair's private views about a man he would later apparently denounce as a man 'who has the kind of prejudices and beliefs no one knows about' and as 'accountable to no one'.[52]

There is a natural explanation for this kind of dissimulation as the 1997 election approached. New Labour justified the deception of Dacre and other tabloid journalists as an act of moral justice, and felt that they were treating the editor of the *Daily Mail* in exactly the way that they considered he would behave to others. This attitude liberated Tony Blair from the need for candour. It validated his declaration of love for the pound, made in the *Sun* newspaper. It legitimised the large, strategic silences in his manifesto for the Labour leadership, the falsehoods in the 1997 Labour manifesto; later the same kind of reasoning would account for the lies and evasions during the Iraq War.

All these deceits were washed away: they suddenly became virtuous and were transmuted instead into manoeuvres necessary to secure political power. Tony Blair's remark 'Let us say what we mean and mean what we say' was nothing more than words, pure falsehood. Blair's special gift is in saying what he does not mean, and meaning what he does not say. Tony Blair is an artful politician who has rarely addressed any objective by direct or straightforward methods.

This point was especially well understood by the political journalist Anthony Bevins, a keen student of New Labour. Shortly before his death Bevins wrote two admiring essays about Tony Blair's tradecraft. Bevins stressed the purity of the prime minister's motives. 'Blair's ends are entirely principled: social justice; quality public service, equality of opportunity and a reassertion that citizens have responsibilities as well as rights.'[53] But they were not matched by candour of means. Bevins stressed that Blair would 'never identify the destination'. There was an overwhelming reason for this: 'By defining his destination, or lack of it, he would be offering his opponents the opportunity to sabotage his plans. He therefore keeps mum; moving towards his goal by stealthy step and crabwise movement.'[54]

Bevins's two articles, the first in the *New Statesman* and the second in the *Daily Express*, are extremely helpful. They explain why New Labour has from the start been prepared to use feint, manoeuvre, artifice and sleight of hand to attain its objectives. It had a dark horror of disclosing its true identity, or its real target. New Labour, to an extent consciously, sees itself as comparable to a guerrilla army operating deep behind enemy lines, and not as a conventional force. This has made it sharply distinct from a mainstream political party of the kind that has been familiar in Britain for the last century. Of course the Old Labour Party of Clement Attlee or Jim Callaghan, and the Tories from Stanley Baldwin to Margaret Thatcher indulged in their stratagems and their ruses. But neither of these parties manifested the deep, inbuilt terror of candour and systemic preference for deceit that is New Labour's most singular and most defining characteristic.

So it has become useful to talk of a specific New Labour epistemology, with its various gradations of truth, and methods of telling
it. It distinguishes between two kinds of knowledge. One is considered safe or appropriate for public utterance or display, and then
there is the private kind of knowledge that dare not be uttered
except among the most trusted devotees.

New Labour, having experienced the fatal consequences of truth-
telling in the 1980s, vowed to learn from the past. It judged that a
feigned conformity to the prejudices of its tormentors was the price
of survival, and it was more than ready to pay it. There are far too
many instances to mention: its manifestly false public statements on
Europe and tax are just two of the most spectacular examples. In an
illuminating article written just six months before the 1997 election
the sympathetic *Guardian* columnist Polly Toynbee set out the
matter in precise terms:

> Labour is taking no risks. After four defeats, they have abandoned
> their view of the voter as a decent sort and adopted the Tory
> model of the voter as selfish, lying bastard. Soon after the last
> [1992] election I talked to a deeply depressed Labour shadow
> cabinet member who cursed the voters bitterly and concluded:
> 'the only way we can win is to lie and cheat about taxes the way
> the Tories do.' So let us hope that is their secret strategy.

Toynbee went on to wonder: 'how will we ever persuade people
that government is essentially good, healthy and necessary if no
reputable politicians ever dare stand up and say so?'[55]

New Labour was the solution produced by the Left to deal with
the malfunction in British democracy that – so the Left considered –

had generated a one-party state in the 1980s. New Labour felt at liberty to deceive and to cheat in order to gain power in the face of what it understood to be a twisted and bitter media. It is now the moment to examine how it took forward this damaged belief system into government.

2

NEW LABOUR IN POWER

'To lie like this – telling stupid, boastful "whoppers" which can be definitively exposed for what they are – is a travesty of effective politics . . . Labour must save its big lies for when it really needs them' – Labour MP Sion Simon

More Honesty Pledges – and the Strange Case of Chris Patten and MI6

Tony Blair returned to his favoured theme of honesty, trust and truth within hours of winning his famous 1997 election victory. Standing outside Downing Street on that gorgeous, sunlit, hopeful morning of 2 May, the new prime minister promised to lead 'a government that seeks to restore trust in politics in this country'. He pledged that would give 'people hope once again that politics is and should be always about the service of the public.'[1]

Four days after the election Tony Blair called Labour MPs together at Church House, Westminster, to bang the drum again. 'We are not here to enjoy the trappings of power,' he told them, 'but to do a job and uphold the highest standards in public life.'[2] I remember reporting the event, and noticing with keen interest that the new prime minister seemed not to have forgotten the solemn pledges that he had made in opposition. Two months later he was at it again, calling on all his ministers to 'uphold the highest standards of honesty and propriety which the British people fairly expect of those in public life.'[3] The following year he went even further. 'We have to be very careful,' he proclaimed 'that we are purer than pure.'[4]

Tony Blair could have kept his word. He could indeed have run an honest government that made clear, accurate, truthful statements. When he arrived in Downing Street with his massive landslide in 1997, he could have put aside the techniques New Labour had used to such great effect in opposition. It is a tragedy for New Labour, for Britain and personally for Tony Blair that he did not adopt this course of action. Had he done so, he would have been a different kind of prime minister, and Britain would now be a different kind of country, with a more decent kind of politics.

But New Labour could not make that transition. It was too nervous and too paranoid. It continued to believe, even after sweeping to power with its massive majority, that it was surrounded by enemies. In reality there was overwhelming goodwill, but New Labour could not see it. It brought with it into government the bruised, suspicious mentality that had been beaten into it during the long Kinnock years of defeat and humiliation. It felt irrationally under siege, and continued to use all the tricks that it had developed and polished in its brilliant years of opposition. It felt the same urgent compulsion to control the news agenda. To achieve this it continued to manipulate and deceive. Only now that it was in power it was able to bring to bear the resources of the state and the authority that comes from government as well.

The first really important indication of this new state of affairs came just three months after the general election, with the chain of events that followed news that the Foreign Secretary Robin Cook had been keeping a mistress, Gaynor Regan. This was the moment New Labour must have been dreading, the first 'sleaze' scandal that could be compared to the years of Tory decline. The new government's handling of this affair was very interesting.

On the one hand it displayed a briskness, competence and clinical brutality that had often been absent from the John Major administration. At the first whiff that the *News of the World* was on his case, the hapless Robin Cook was obliged to make an instant, life-defining choice between wife and mistress. This may have been a heartless, inhumane process, but Cook's decision to leave his wife at once and set up home with his secretary Gaynor Regan played a large part in bringing 'closure' (a favourite word among New Labour press handlers) to an unhappy story.

At the same time, but less obtrusively, New Labour launched an operation to distract attention from Robin Cook by placing other dramas on the front pages. That weekend of 2 and 3 August a number of eye-catching stories marvellously appeared in the newspapers. Like a summer snowstorm they came and went in a flash, and did not settle.

The first of these concerned a surprising, eleventh-hour change of plan from the government about the Royal Yacht *Britannia*. The poor old Royal Yacht had been ditched by the incoming government, and even the most fervent monarchists had given up real hope. Then, quite out of the blue, it seemed to be in business again. Several Sunday papers – including the *Telegraph*, the *Independent*, the *Express* and the *Mail* – provided authoritative reports that the paymaster-general Geoffrey Robinson had drawn up a plan to save the vessel.[5] In retrospect these reports can be seen to have had no real substance, and to have been more appropriate for an April Fool's Day joke. But the salvation of the Royal Yacht made the front page even of a stern broadsheet like the *Independent on Sunday*.[6]

These empty Royal Yacht stories can perhaps be dismissed as a piece of innocent amusement. Not so the second wheeze put to use by New Labour to spare Robin Cook from a roasting in the media. This was the claim that MI6 had launched an investigation into Chris Patten, the former Tory Party chairman who had recently stood down as governor of Hong Kong. This suggestion first appeared in the *Sunday Times* under the byline of political editor Andrew Grice. Grice wrote that 'the former Hong Kong Governor is under investigation by M16, Britain's overseas security service, which has found evidence that intelligence reports were passed to Jonathan Dimbleby, the writer and broadcaster, who enjoyed "unprecedented access" to Patten while writing *The Last Governor*, a book about his five-year term in Hong Kong.'

Grice was a famously close contact of Peter Mandelson, so favoured by the New Labour movement that he was offered the job of Tony Blair's press secretary ahead of Alastair Campbell. But his article, though coy about precisely naming sources, went to some considerable lengths to dispel any illusion that might have existed in anyone's mind that Andrew Grice's friends in the Labour Party or the government had anything to do with his report. Grice laboriously suggested, without quite saying so in terms, that disaffected Foreign Office sources were behind it. He blandly informed readers of the *Sunday Times* that 'Government ministers distanced themselves from what one source called "an unseemly squabble among the Tory grandees in the Hong Kong club".'[7]

Perhaps government ministers really did distance themselves from Andrew Grice's story, as he thoughtfully reassured his readers. But the following Sunday morning they became exceptionally keen to help it along. The events which followed are extraordinary and disgraceful – nothing less than an attempt by the British government of the day to feed an unfounded media smear against a major public figure of unblemished integrity.

The smear started late on the Saturday night, just hours before the *News of the World* front-page splash about Robin Cook's affair was to hit the streets. A Labour spin-doctor rang Jon Sopel, the senior BBC journalist (and the first biographer of Tony Blair), to try and persuade him to look into the report that Patten was being investigated. Sopel was reluctant, saying that it was hard to take the story seriously, unless it came with official confirmation from the Foreign Office. Since this was not forthcoming, Sopel took the suggestion no further.

The following morning, the same spin-doctor rang Sopel again, urging him to run the story. Once again Sopel, acting with exemplary propriety, demurred. He describes his predicament today as follows: 'I thought this was bonkers. You can't casually abuse a man of integrity like Patten. So I told them: look, I'm not just going to run this as "Whitehall sources." I'm not going to run the story unless I can put a proper fingerprint on it. Well, they went away and obviously thought about this,' remembers Sopel. 'And then just before the Sunday lunchtime news, they came back to me and told me that I could source the story about Patten being investigated to Downing Street.' Sopel was also told that Peter Mandelson was to go on *The World This Weekend* that Sunday lunchtime, and that if the interviewer asked Mandelson about Chris Patten, 'he would confirm on air that an enquiry was taking place'.[8]

Mandelson was good as gold when asked about the investigation on air. 'All I know is that the issue – the matter, rather than the individual – is under investigation by the authorities.' He told *The World This Weekend* that 'I'm not going to speculate on the outcome of that. But it would be irresponsible for the government not to take the action when there appears to have been a leak of intelligence material.'[9] Mandelson's words were carefully chosen. They added little, but produced enough noise to enable the newspapers to take the story on.

By Monday morning, however, the tone changed. Whether government press handlers had concluded that the Patten story had done its job, or for some other reason, a decision was made to play the story down. Early on the Monday morning Tim Allan, the Downing Street deputy press secretary, rang up Kevin Marsh, the editor of *The World at One*. It was a routine call. 'Is there anything we can help you with?' asked Allan. 'There's a couple of stories we're looking at,' replied Marsh, and cited the Royal Yacht *Britannia*. 'No, that's rubbish,' replied Allan. Marsh mentioned Chris Patten and MI6. 'If you knew where that came from you would know that was rubbish as well.'[10]

Today the victim of this British government-inspired smear, Chris Patten, now the chancellor of Oxford University, looks back on the episode with bafflement. He says that he was never questioned about the book by anyone in government in any way. 'Nobody ever asked me for an interview or any questions about the Dimbleby book,' he says. Jonathan Dimbleby was not asked either. 'I was rather looking forward to the prospect of meeting my first MI5 officer or first Special Branch officer with a warrant to search my premises. To my disappointment neither showed up. Not even a phone call.'[11]

Chris Patten recalls how he was 'down in France one Saturday evening when I was phoned up and asked whether I knew that it was being said that I was going to be prosecuted for breach of the Official Secrets Act.

'That Saturday morning Robin Cook had famously arrived at the VIP lounge at Heathrow Airport to be faced by the *News of the World* revelation.' Patten recalls that the government spin-doctors 'then decided they had two stories in store that would compete for the front pages, first that they were going to save the Royal Yacht, the second that I was going to be prosecuted under the Official Secrets Act. Peter Mandelson deliberately put himself about on *The World at One* and gave one of his ambiguous answers, which did not commit but gave the story fresh legs. I was in France. But it was exceptionally unpleasant for my wife and kids. Then the story went away.'

Patten notes with irony that at the start of the following year he was invited by the British government to lead a highly sensitive report into the future of policing in Northern Ireland. 'Here was this chap who was about to be sent to the Tower of London for breach of the Official Secrets Act,' remembers Patten, 'and now they were asking me to do this. It was like bringing Blake back from Moscow to carry out an inquiry into MI6. Completely absurd.' He judges that it was 'an extremely unsavoury example of how they were going to behave but I didn't take too tragic a view of it'.[12]

There probably was a tiny fragment of truth embedded in the story that Patten was under investigation. To his lasting credit, he had created a number of enemies inside the Foreign Office for his strong stand in favour of democracy and human rights while he was governor of Hong Kong. There may well have been some grumbling from various senior figures who emerged with damaged reputations from Dimbleby's scrupulously researched work. But nothing material ever emerged, and it was wholly reckless and irresponsible of the new Labour government to use its media clout to convert what was at most a minor Whitehall whispering campaign into a fully fledged Official Secrets Act investigation. It was disreputable to diminish the reputation of a leading public figure for the narrow ends of short term media management. Jonathan Dimbleby today calls it a 'disgraceful episode in which a public figure was smeared – dirty politics'. This Chris Patten episode showed how New Labour from its earliest days in power was ready to smear, cheat and distort the facts for purposes of news management.

Numerous people in the future were to suffer from the same kind of treatment. The victims would range from political opponents, to innocent bystanders briefly caught up in the political battle, to out-of-favour cabinet ministers.*

Manipulation of Statistics

New Labour faced a problem when it first entered office. Despite many attempts to dampen expectations, hopes still ran very high

---

* For instance Mo Mowlam records how 'The Times reported that a "very senior colleague" had said I was about to have a nervous breakdown . . . What I couldn't or didn't want to see then, but it is so clear to me now, was that I was being forced out of the cabinet. I was too popular to sack, so I had to be "persuaded to leave". I desperately didn't want to believe there had been a campaign, and denied it to myself even when the evidence was staring me in the face. I have now accepted it and dealt with the anger at what they did to my life.' By the end Mowlam concluded that 'this had become a government that I no longer wanted to be part of.' Mo Mowlam, Momentum, pp. 353–4.

that it could deliver the radical transformation of public services that it had promised in opposition. But there was one difficulty. In practice there was little it could do. The reason for this was the pledge by the new Chancellor Gordon Brown that he would match Tory spending plans for Labour's first two years in office.

While in opposition this pledge had seemed a good idea. It gave New Labour enormous credibility in the City, made it look responsible, above all gold-plated the pledge not to raise taxes. Once in office, however, the pledge put the new government in a strait-jacket, completely unable to deliver the huge boost in spending which many Labour supporters craved.

It is the way New Labour set about solving the problem that is so fascinating. It could have shrugged its shoulders and told its supporters to wait. It could have broken the pledge, though that would have been hugely controversial and led to accusations of bad faith. It took neither of these two courses of action. Instead New Labour resorted to sleight of hand. This seems to have been the idea, or at any rate the responsibility, of Chancellor Gordon Brown, who is by and large a far less mendacious politician than his next-door neighbour Tony Blair. Brown resorted to double, or even treble, counting government spending figures so that he could boast that he was spending far more than was actually the case.

An early example of this deceit came when the chancellor unveiled his Comprehensive Spending Review on 14 July 1998.'On the 50th anniversary of the NHS the Government will now make the biggest ever investment in its future,' announced Gordon Brown to a tumultuous response from the Labour benches.'Under the previous Government the increase for the last three years was

£7 billion. For the coming three years I am announcing an increase in health service funding of a total of £21 billion.'

There was £19 billion extra for education, and equally remarkable increases in other areas. His package was greeted with rapturous headlines.'The Gord Giveth £56 Billion' trumpeted the *Daily Mirror* headline, while the *Daily Mail* announced that 'Brown Goes on a Summer Spree'.[13] Most other papers, encouraged by exuberant Treasury public relations, took the same line.

The account of events propagated by the Chancellor – and swallowed virtually wholesale by a gullible press the following day – was completely misleading. As virtually everyone now accepts, Gordon Brown was actually being incredibly stingy. Under Brown's much-vaunted plans, spending on the NHS was to rise by annual stages from just £37 billion in the financial year 1998/9 to £46 billion in 2001/2. To an ordinary, common-sense observer that meant a £9 billion increase. But to the Chancellor – and to credulous journalists who didn't look behind his incredible figures – the sum was £21 billion. He created his conjuring trick by adding the extra £3 billion for 1999/2000, the extra £6 billion for 2000/1 and the extra £9 billion for the year after that to make £18 billion. After adding in extra money for Scotland, Wales and Northern Ireland that made £21 billion.

The figure for £19 billion extra spending on education was produced in an identical way. In the months that followed government ministers parroted the Treasury line. A shameless Tony Blair told the Commons on 3 November 1999 that 'the £40 billion for schools and hospitals is extra money over and above the present allocation'. But the figures were bogus. John Ford, an economist at the British Medical Association, politely observed that Gordon Brown had done his sums 'in an unconventional way'.[14] One newspaper pointed out that the 'Institute of Fiscal Studies says health spending will actually increase in real terms by 3.6% a year over the five years of this Parliament. Under John Major it increased by 2.5% a year, so Labour is spending more – but not much more. That 1.1% is the equivalent of £460 million a year or £2.3 billion over the lifetime of the Parliament, about a tenth of the figure the chancellor announced.'[15] In the end even the government's own supporters started to work out there was a problem. This is what the Labour MP Sion Simon wrote about Gordon Brown's spending claims after the wool fell from his eyes: 'To arrive at an expenditure figure of £18 billion extra on health by counting a single £3 billion tranche twice and another three times is not creative accountancy or statistical chicanery. It is plain untruth.'

Simon added that 'the lie was as unnecessary as it was stupid', before concluding that:

> . . . when Labour does lie to the electorate, as all governments do all the time, it should make sure that it does it deliberately and well. To lie like this – telling stupid, boastful 'whoppers' which can be definitively exposed for what they are – is a travesty of effective politics. The Opposition can invent all the numbers it wants, because there is no reality against which they can be checked. The ship of state, however, sails on a sea of statistics, and ministers are accountable for them all. So claims to spend twice as much as is really the case will always rebound painfully. When the true sum would have made an ample boost anyway, this is incompetent. Labour must save its big lies for when it really needs them.[16]

In fact the Chancellor had told no actual falsehoods. Other ministers did so, however, as they tried to make credible spending commitments in the very straitened post-1997 environment. On 15 February 2000, in the wake of the Waterhouse report into child abuse in North Wales, John Hutton, a health minister, promised an extra £400 million to improve services for children. The *Today* programme interviewer John Humphrys asked whether it was 'one of those things that has been announced half a dozen times before'. Hutton replied 'No, it's new money.' It soon emerged, however, that Hutton was talking about a £375 million grant that had already been promised in 1998.[17]

Soon Home Secretary Jack Straw was joining in the deception. At his Labour Party conference speech in autumn 1999, Jack Straw told delegates that the police would be able to recruit 5,000 more officers. He said: 'We will be giving the police the money they need to recruit 5,000 more officers. That's 5,000 more officers over and above the police service's recruiting plans.' He went on to insist that his was 'not the sort of hollow promise the Conservatives used to make'. This pledge made headlines in several newspapers.[18] I have found no evidence that the Home Secretary did anything to correct the impression that there would soon be 5,000 extra police on the streets.

But it duly emerged that Jack Straw was being disingenuous. A leaked letter from Alan Milburn, then chief secretary at the Treasury, revealed that the impression created by Straw that there would be '5,000 more officers' was misleading. The Milburn letter read: 'The package does not provide for 5,000 "additional" police officers. It provides for the recruitment of 5,000 officers. Since police forces are already planning to reduce the number of officers – despite their own existing plans to recruit 11,000 new officers over the next three years – the effect of the 5,000 new officers under this package is most likely at best simply to stabilise total numbers.'[19] Defending Jack Straw in the House of Commons on 20 October 1999, Tony Blair insisted that his Home Secretary had said 'exactly the truth'.

There were indeed more police officers over and above existing plans. But Jack Straw gave a misleading impression that overall numbers would increase. The rate of attrition among officers is so great that the 5,000 increase would do no more than keep numbers stable. Police officers reacted angrily. 'This is a complete betrayal of the people and the police officers of this country,' said Glen Smyth, a spokesman for the Metropolitan Police Federation. 'We have now discovered that the announcement appears to be untrue. We are very unhappy; that is an understatement.'[20]

As the 2001 general election approached more and more ministers felt that they were licensed to make dubious claims of this kind about government figures. One of the most egregious examples of this practice concerns child poverty. Ministers repeatedly stated that over a million children had been lifted out of poverty since 1997. The claim was made in the House of Commons by Treasury minister Dawn Primarolo, and asserted in a Treasury press release and by the Chancellor of the Exchequer.[21] Yet the claim was extremely doubtful. Even the government's own figures suggest that 500,000 fewer people lived in poverty by the time of the general election than in 1997.[22] An official report, the Households Below Average Income Survey, showed that the number of children living in poverty, after housing costs, fell from 4.4 million in 1996–7 to 3.9 million in 2000–1. When the sharp discrepancy was later revealed, cabinet minister Alistair Darling tried to get the government out of trouble by denying that the government had ever made the claim in the first place. 'What we said,' claimed Darling, 'was that if we had remained with the policies we inherited, there would be more than one million extra in poverty.'[23] But this was not true either.

Exactly the same kind of bogus claim was made about the £3 billion New Deal programme aimed at returning young people to the job market. Minister for Work Nick Brown declared that the project was a huge success, declaring that 'We are fast approaching 350,000 young people who have found work through the New Deal.'[24] However, the first independent report to study how the project was faring concluded these figures were massively wrong. The National Audit Office praised the New Deal for showing 'small beneficial impact', and suggested that no more than 20.000 extra people found jobs as a direct result of the programme in the first two years.*

Labour Party Deceptions

This readiness to manipulate and thus to deceive was buried deep in the heart of the New Labour political method, as shown by a thor-

---

* See The New Deal for Young People, Report by the Comptroller and Auditor General, HC 639, 28 February 2002, summary and recommendations, para 8: 'The New Deal for Young People achieved its stated target of helping 250,000 young people into work in September 2000. But the economic impact of the programme cannot be measured simply in terms of the number of young people placed into jobs. For example many of them would have found a job anyway because of natural labour market turnover and the general expansion of the economy.' Para 9 stated that 'research commissioned by the Employment Service into the first two years of the programme's operation estimated that the New Deal for Young People had reduced youth unemployment by 35,000 and increased youth employment by 15,000.' See also Jill Sherman and Gary Duncan, 'New Deal has helped only 20,000 to find jobs', The Times, 28 February 2002.

ough piece of academic research carried out by Danny Dorling, Heather Eyre, Ron Johnston and Charles Pattie.[25] The research was published in 2002, but dealt with the period before the 2001 election.

Dorling and his colleagues studied the constituency pages – headed 'What's Labour done in your constituency' – of the Labour Party website. These included a set of statistical indicators for each of the 641 parliamentary constituencies in England, Wales and Scotland. The purpose of these constituency profiles is mainly to allow Labour Party organisers and activists to boast about the government's achievements. Information about each constituency was accessible either by clicking on the name of the relevant constituency or simply typing in your postcode. Data was provided in a number of different categories: the economy, families and children, pensioners, the NHS, schools, unemployment, and law and order.

In many of these cases Labour had genuinely performed extremely well. What struck the researchers as abnormal was that every single indicator in every single constituency had improved. But, according to the Labour Party website, they had managed precisely that. According to Dorling, Eyre, Johnston and Pattie:

> . . . it is extremely unlikely (if not impossible!) that all of the above indicators have improved for all constituencies. However, the Labour Party reported them in such a way as to make it appear that they did. For example, if an indicator had not improved for one timescale then the timescale was changed for that constituency to one during which conditions had improved. Indicators are also reported at different spatial scales. If conditions

hadn't improved at the constituency scale, for example, then a larger scale was deployed at which things had improved: in the case of crime figures, for example, for some constituencies indicators are given which are averages for the whole of England and Wales if these constituencies are in police force areas and regions where crime had increased. Thus, on the Labour Party website crime had fallen under Labour everywhere and police numbers had similiarly risen everywhere, even though to show this both the spatial and temporal scales had to be altered to ensure universal improvement.[26]

In the case of unemployment statistics:

> ... figures are reported for constituencies except in three cases, where those for the standard region in which the constituency is situated are deployed: Bosworth, Newcastle-under-Lyme, Stoke-on-Trent South. Actual unemployment counts by constituency are available in the House of Commons Library, and these confirm that unemployment had risen in these three constituencies . . .[27]

Likewise the researchers discovered that falls in school class sizes were 'reported as a constituency specific figure in all cases except one: Hammersmith and Fulham, for which figures are reported for England and Wales, because they did not decrease in that constituency'.[28]

The *Political Quarterly* researchers stress that 'nothing presented on the Labour Party website is untrue in the strict sense of the word. It is just that the way in which the statistics have been put together –

mixing and matching years and areas to present the best possible picture of improvement – is disingenuous overall.'

These little distortions and white lies, without significance in themselves, were forming part of a menacing and novel pattern, as I shall demonstrate in the next chapter.

3

FROM TRUTH TO FALSEHOOD

'I don't think I've got anything to lose by being honest at this stage in my political career . . .' – Peter Mandelson, on taking up his job as British Commissioner in Brussels

Invention of the Truth

It is impossible to identify a precise moment when the New Labour government started to lie. It just fell into the habit. It did so without realising it, or admitting to itself it what was doing. In its own mind it remained honest, truthful and a standing reproach to the lying Tory government which had preceded it.

It was almost as if there was a parallel world. One was lived in by ministers, their spin-doctors and spokespeople, while the other was inhabited by everyone else. Their remarks may have contained a special logic of their own, but were otherwise disconnected from real events. Ministers ceased to state what was really the case. Instead they made statements based on what they would like to have been been the truth.

A minor manifestation of this came as the government began to prepare for the 2001 election, with the publication of its Annual

Report in July 2000. On page 47 it claimed that 'As part of the delivery of this vision, this year saw the opening of the UK Sports Institute, providing world-class facilities, coaching and support in Sheffield and national and regional centres around the UK.'

This claim was grand, but quite fallacious. No such sports institute had been opened. After several months ministers came under pressure to acknowledge as much. Culture Secretary Chris Smith stated the following October that the assertion that there was a national sports institute based in Sheffield 'could have been misleading, and certainly did not give a full picture of progress in the development of the UK Sports Institute.'[1] A week later the prime minister grudgingly acknowledged there had been a mistake, but in terms that gave the entirely false impression that Sheffield was still destined for the role as headquarters of the UK Sports Institute.*

But the corrections were churlish and, for years afterwards, this Sheffield HQ has continued to enjoy a phantom existence. Sports Minister Richard Caborn's official profile claimed as late as February 2002 that one of his most notable distinctions was making' Sheffield the key site in the UK Sports Institute Network'.[2] In the summer of 2003 hapless reporters were still paying handsome tribute to Caborn's efforts in making 'Sheffield the key site in the UK Sports Institute Network'.[3] Even at the start of 2005 Caborn's ministerial web page was still boasting about his involvement in 'the successful bid to make Sheffield the key site in the UK Sports Institute Network'.[4]

---

* The prime minister said that the original claim in his annual report should have read: 'As part of the delivery of this vision, this year saw the opening of the UK Sports Institute, which will provide world-class facilities, coaching and support in Sheffield and national and regional centres around the UK.'

An example of this kind of invention came from Jack Straw on 7 March 2000 when the then Home Secretary introduced his Criminal Justice Bill into the House of Commons: This bill set out to remove the right of trial by jury in all criminal cases. In the preamble to his speech Straw asserted that the bill 'enjoys the active endorsement of the Lord Chief Justice, Lord Bingham, and of the vast majority of the High Court Bench of nearly 100 senior judges . . .'

The problem with this assertion is that it certainly does not seem to have enjoyed the Lord Chief Justice's active support, at any rate not in its entirety. Lord Bingham had indeed supported the bill at an earlier stage. Now he had developed reservations. He wrote to the Home Secretary two weeks before the debate to express his concern about the proposal to strip magistrates of the broad discretion to take the circumstances of the accused into account. It is hard to square this with Jack Straw's claim that the bill enjoyed Lord Bingham's 'active endorsement'.

When the bill came before the Commons for its third reading on 25 July 2000, the Labour backbencher Bob Marshall-Andrews declared that 'there is not the slightest doubt that the Home Secretary's statement on Second Reading, either wilfully or otherwise, misled the House. When invited by the Deputy Speaker to 'rephrase' his comments, he said that Jack Straw's comments on 7 March were 'manifestly inaccurate', though he did not suggest they were deliberately so.[5] The Marshall-Andrews intervention sets out the circumstances surrounding Straw's statement with great detail. So far as can be told Jack Straw's defence seems to depend on a casuistical interpretation of the word 'it'. I wrote to Jack Straw asking him to explain himself, but he failed to reply.

Here is another example of invention: on 4 July 2001 Andrew

Smith, then chief secretary to the Treasury, was asked for evidence of cost and efficiency savings resulting from the Private Finance Initiative. In his written answer he claimed that a National Audit Report on 'PFI and Value for Money' had 'found an average cost saving of 20%, or just under £1 billion in total.' This answer was soon found to be a fabrication, and the National Audit Office confirmed that it had never published, and was not aware of, such a report. A week later, to his credit, Andrew Smith made an apology.

A much more grievous manifestation of this disconnection between ministers and truth came in March 2001, as the Foot and Mouth outbreak, with all its tragic consequences for farmers' livelihoods, struck the British countryside. On 11 March Agriculture Minister Nick Brown appeared on the BBC *Breakfast with Frost* programme and made a number of reassuring comments to the effect that the disease was under control. He stressed that he was 'absolutely certain' this was the case.[6] Nick Brown was talking complete nonsense, as experts at once pointed out. National Farmers' Union deputy director Iain Gardiner said, 'I think this week will see the rate [of outbreak] going faster. Yes, the disease is spreading. There have been more sheep movements than anybody expected and one of the problems is that it's spreading across the face of Britain, it's not just in one area.'[7] When the independent report on the Foot and Mouth tragedy was published the following July, it concluded that the minister's comments 'did not reflect the situation on the ground. The disease was, at this stage, out of control by any reasonable measure.'[8] Nick Brown's hopelessly misleading remarks may have reflected what he hoped was the case, or might have preferred to be the case, especially with a general election looming in the imminent future. But they were a catastrophically false description of what was really going on.

Often the truth is invented as a matter of political convenience. A telling example was the announcement of so-called euro 'roadshows' in the summer of 2003 to sell the case for the euro 'around the country'. On 10 June 2003 Gordon Brown and Tony Blair held a joint press conference on the euro. It came the day after the Chancellor, to the reported disappointment of the prime minister, had ruled out British entry to the euro for the time being 'in the national economic interest.' The press conference was partly designed to show that, despite this setback, the government was still bravely pressing forward with the single currency proposal. But the 'roadshows' were a fictitious enterprise, as *The Times* discovered when two months later it asked the Foreign Office how they were going. According to reporter Melissa Kite, 'the roadshow had not yet begun, but would start after the summer recess'. She went on: 'Denis MacShane, the Minister for Europe, said that it was never meant to be a literal roadshow; that was just a figure of speech.'[9] Kite also quoted 'one senior minister' saying that 'he believed the idea had most likely been dropped because it was "naff".' However, a Treasury official asserted that 'the roadshows have already started. It's been happening for quite a while. The Chancellor has done stuff and various ministers have been out and about.' But when asked to give the first day of the programme, the official said, 'It's one of those things. I don't think there was a specific date.' The road shows – in the sense of a well-advertised series of public meetings in which the prime minister and the chancellor took the case for the euro directly to the British people – do not appear to have existed. They were announced by the prime minister and his Chancellor in June 2003. They were written up by reporters. They were – perhaps – awaited by the British public. The chances are that they never were intended to happen, and that the June announcement was a political device to save the Prime Minister's embarrassment after being forced to climb down on the single currency.

This disconnection between truth and reality has persisted right up to the present day. A troubling example came on 5 November 2004 when Defence Secretary Geoff Hoon informed *Today* programme listeners that Iraq was now 'more secure', thanks to the coalition invasion of April 2003. He even repeated this bizarre assertion when challenged by John Humphrys. Hoon's remark was the exact opposite of the truth. As he spoke, even the brief journey from Baghdad airport to the comparative safety of the 'green zone' in the centre of town was fraught with peril, while foreigners found it impossible to travel through much of the rest of the country except at extreme personal risk. Once again, ministers were starting to create their own world of virtual reality. Jack Straw showed a similar sort of dislocation when he told GMTV in September 2004, at the time when Kenneth Bigley was being held hostage in Iraq, that 'we've made it clear we have a policy which we adhere to strictly always, that we don't negotiate with hostage takers.'[10] This claim was open to question. Four years previously Afghan gunmen had seized a Boeing 727 on an internal flight and flown it to Britain. The *Guardian* recorded the following day that 'Negotiators working to free more than 150 hostages held on board have begun discussing "issues" which could lead to an end to the crisis, police disclosed this morning.'[11]

A far more culpable case of a minister inventing the facts to suit his purposes came from Denis MacShane, Minister for Europe, an engaging figure who brings colour and vitality to the Blair government. Even more than many politicians, MacShane likes to operate by trashing the characters and misrepresenting the motives of his opponents. In the summer of 2004 he gave an interview to the *Daily Telegraph* in which he accused Eurosceptics of fomenting 'xenophobia' and 'hatred'. He accused tabloid newspapers and the Conservative Party of validating 'a kind of Orwellian hate language against other European countries that diminishes Britain's greatness.'[12]

In the wake of these remarks MacShane was invited on to the *Today* programme. He used the opportunity to denounce Eurosceptics for telling 'lies' about Europe. He went on: 'By all means let's have a political ding-dong, but let's do it on the basis of facts and not on these myths.' Presenter Ed Stourton then pressed MacShane to justify his dramatic claims. He answered: 'Do you remember in the winter there was all this hysteria from Poland or Hungary coming into the country? They were described in one of our papers as a "murderous horde" – a "murderous horde". These are nannies and hospital workers from Poland, they're European citizens, they're paying taxes here. When is somebody going to stand up to that kind of language?'[13]

Afterwards I consulted a database to try and discover which newspaper had used such inflammatory language. Nothing came up, so I rang the news department of the Foreign Office, which promised to get back with an answer. Five minutes later, to my surprise, MacShane himself came on the line. When I asked about the 'murderous horde' he became vague, and after wriggling for a while denied that he had ever used the phrase. 'I never said it', he insisted. But he had.

A huge number of people were listening to that *Today* interview. They heard a senior government minister making a charge of some gravity. He said it twice. Listeners were entitled to assume that he was telling the truth. In fact the Minister for Europe had made up the quote.

Rewriting History

As New Labour entrenched itself in power, it did not merely invent the present, it started to mould the past to suit its own purposes. Communist regimes used to do this. In the novel *Nineteen Eighty-Four* the job of the hero Winston Smith, as he worked away in the Records Department of the Ministry of Truth, was to change past newspapers so that they agreed with the latest Party line.

Jack Straw's 2001 Criminal Justice Bill provided a sinister example of this falsification of the truth. By March, with the general election looming, the bill was running out of time. With only 90 out of 132 clauses debated, the government brought discussion to a standstill and moved a motion which stated that the 'Bill shall be deemed to have been reported to the House, as amended by the Committee, and as if those Clauses and Schedules the consideration of which had not been completed by the Committee has been ordered to stand part of the bill.'[14]

This legal language was being used to make an incredible statement. It asked MPs to vote on a motion which stated that 42 clauses of the Criminal Justice Bill had been considered in committee, when they hadn't been considered at all. Jack Straw was using Labour's Commons majority to turn fiction into fact.

Very few MPs cared. But there was a small, honourable rebellion in the Commons. It took place four days later in a mainly empty house at 1.20am in the morning, and was led by the Conservative backbencher Richard Shepherd. He asked on 12 March 2001:

> Why am I concerned about the motion? It does not take any great feat of imagination to think that it reinvents history. Four days ago the House failed to do something. The Government have moved a motion that states that it has done something. Stalin rewrote history. I am concerned about the rewriting of history by deeming things to have happened that have not . . . the Order Paper now suggests that what is not true is true.

The official *Hansard* record shows several interruptions, suggesting that Shepherd was shouted down several times as he spoke, and of course the Home Secretary had his way.

The following year deputy prime minister John Prescott tried to rewrite history in an equally flagrant fashion. Prescott's Orwellian moment came when the environmental pressure group Friends of the Earth drew to public attention a pledge he had made some five years earlier. 'I will have failed,' he said in June 1997, 'if in five years' time there are not many more people using public transport and far fewer journeys by car. It's a tall order, but I urge you to hold me to it.'[15] Prescott had indeed made these comments, at a reception for environmentalists at the Royal Geographical Society in London. Furthermore he had confirmed the pledge when questioned in the House of Commons by the MP Tom Brake on 20 October 1998. Brake quoted the pledge, then asked whether 'the Government will keep their election promises and reduce traffic levels overall, not merely the growth in traffic?' Prescott replied: 'I agree to keep that commitment: judge my performance in five years.'

Five years duly passed and then Prescott was reminded of the pledge. The Department of Transport spokesperson initially responded that 'The quote [that Friends of the Earth attributed to Mr Prescott] is not true and has never been true.'[16] Later on, the Department of Transport passed all queries about Mr Prescott's remarks to the Office of the Deputy Prime Minister, whose spokesman said: 'More journeys are now being made by public transport and fewer by car. That is being proved around the country.'[17] Prescott himself made the following statement: 'It was never possible to expect an absolute cut in motor traffic with a growing economy and more than one million people back in work.'[18]

Just two months after the government falsely denied that John Prescott had ever made his pledge about car travel, Downing Street was engaged in a truth reconstruction exercise concerning asylum figures. The *Daily Express* embarrassingly revealed that the government had dropped its promise to deport 30,000 'bogus' asylum seekers a year. In an attempt to head off unwelcome publicity government officials concocted a claim that the U-turn had actually come twelve months before, contriving a speech by Home Secretary David Blunkett in order to spare the government's blushes.

The *Daily Express* story appeared on 22 July 2002. In response to questions the government official spokesman insisted the U-turn was a year old, a move which had the effect of deterring other newspapers and broadcasters from following the story up. This is how the No 10 website records the conversations:

> He [the prime minister's official spokesman] reminded journalists that David Blunkett had underlined on 24 June 2001 that the target was not attainable . . .
>
> Asked by the *Express* if the Prime Minister was concerned that the Government had missed its 30,000 target for asylum removals, the PMOS said that as he had pointed out this morning, the Home Secretary himself had acknowledged in June 2001 that we were not going to hit the 30,000 target.

In fact Blunkett had said nothing about immigration targets on 24 June. He had indeed spoken on the subject in the House of Commons three days later, on 27 June. But, according to *Hansard,* he had confirmed the target and strengthened it. This is what he actually said:

> The Labour manifesto said that in excess of 30,000 people who had not justified their claim would be removed by 2003–4, which is about 2,500 people a month. We have decided that target must be met by early next year, which enables us to have a commitment to reach and exceed the 30,000 removals by 2003.

The Downing Street official spokesman had rewritten history by attributing to the Home Secretary remarks he had not made. This false and misleading account of events had the fortunate effect of stopping journalists from following up an embarassing story.[19]

Just four weeks later came another example of Orwellian reinvention of the truth. This came from Foreign Secretary Jack Straw as he campaigned for the euro on 27 August 2002. Jack Straw claimed that the government had made the political case for the euro ahead of Chancellor Gordon Brown's assessment of the so-called five economic tests for entry. 'We in the UK government have already made the political case. We put it to the British people not on one occasion but two elections. We believe in principle the euro bene-fits people in Britain and we have had that endorsed in successive elections,' claimed Straw, adding that 'the issue now is on the economic arguments and that is why the Chancellor of the Exchequer has set out the five tests which are essentially whether our economy in the UK can converge with the euro.'[20]

This was untrue. Neither the 1997 nor the 2001 general elections were about the euro. On the contrary, in both elections Labour deliberately parked the issue by committing itself to a referendum on the single currency. As Joe Haines, the former Downing Street press secretary who assisted in the 1997 campaign wrote: 'In the 1997 General Election the Labour manifesto promised a referendum on the euro. Nothing else, nothing explicit or implicit about politi-cal approval for a single currency. I know that because I largely wrote the popular summary of it which went to three million voters in marginal seats and I have a letter from Tony Blair thanking me for it.'[21] Likewise the 2001 manifesto promised the British people the 'final say' in a referendum, and Jack Straw himself stated during the campaign that 'You, the British people, will have the decision in your hands in a referendum.'[22] Tony Blair was equally explicit, expressly denying that the 2001 election was about the euro. On 29 May 2001, the Press Association reported that, asked again about the euro, Mr Blair insisted: 'We are saying that this is not the issue for this election but what is the issue for this election on the question of Europe are the Conservative policies they would pursue if elected.' It was extremely disingenuous and deceitful of the British Foreign

Secretary to try and pass off a manifesto commitment to a referendum as an 'endorsement' of the single currency by the British people.

Jack Straw's deputy, Denis MacShane, has also been guilty of the same sort of attempt to adjust the past. MacShane gave an interview to the *New Statesman* in which he made the startling announcement that entering the single currency was 'economically irrelevant'. When the *New Statesman* suggested that the government had missed an opportunity to move ahead on the euro, the minister replied: 'For fuck's sake, the euro . . . this really drives me mad . . . I represent a steel constituency. Under no circumstances would I have voted in the first four or five years of the Labour government, at the rate the pound was against the euro, to go into the currency. I kept saying to people: "Stop going on about the euro".'[23]

MacShane's suggestion that he had urged people to keep quiet on the single currency over the early years of the Labour government was, however, profoundly misleading. Far from keeping quiet, he had returned to the subject time and again. In February 2001, when steelmaker Corus announced 6,000 job losses, MacShane joined sides with pro-European campaigners who claimed that Britain's exclusion from the single currency had helped cause the problem. Speaking as chairman of the steel group of MPs, MacShane declared that 'the folly of pretending the relationship of our currency with the rest of the EU does not matter is now exposed in terms of thousands of lost steel jobs.'[24] In November 1999 he moaned that 'the endless zigzag of sterling has been the most damaging thing to manufacturing industry.'[25] In 1998 he even allowed his Rotherham constituency to be used as the centrepiece of a stunt to promote the euro. Dummy euro notes were handed out to shoppers in an attempt to get people talking about the currency.

MacShane declared: 'Rotherham has got a higher level of exporting companies than people imagine. For them the euro is a stark reality.' Far from urging people to stop going on about the euro, as he later claimed, he declared: 'Where there's euros there's brass is not yet a south Yorkshire dictum but it will be one day.'[26]

At the 1999 Labour conference Tony Blair rewrote history in an even more brazen way when he informed delegates: 'To us today, it almost defies belief that people had to die to win the fight for the vote for women. But they did. That battle was a massive, heroic struggle. But why did it need such a fight? Because Tory MPs stood up in the House of Commons and said: "voting is a man's business".'

Tony Blair either did not know, or chose to ignore, the fact that it was the Conservative Party and not the Labour Party which gave women full equality at the ballot box.

The Lie Direct

The examples above show ministers inventing the truth and rewriting the past. Just as often they are prepared to tell untruths to get themselves out of a hole or for some other reason. The former cabinet minister Peter Mandelson, now Britain's trade commissioner in Brussels, was especially notorious for this. Mandelson's record dates back to well before the 1997 election.

A comical example took place in the summer of 1996. Peter Mandelson became involved in a bracing argument at a party with the *Guardian* journalist Richard Norton-Taylor about how many promises New Labour would keep in government. At the end of the conversation Mandelson strode away, taunting Norton-Taylor with the playground exclamation 'nurgh, nurgh, nuh nur-rrrrghh nuh.' An account of this contretemps, dwelling on Mandelson's childish debating tactics, appeared in Matthew Norman's *Guardian* diary. Mandelson was livid. He denied ever having uttered the phrase 'nurgh, nurgh, nuh nur-rrrrghh nuh', demanded an apology and contacted the newspaper's editor Alan Rusbridger. But Mandelson's demands for a correction were rejected.[27]

A more serious case of Mandelson's mendacity involved the *Evening Standard* two years later. In 1998 two *Standard* journalists, James Hanning and Mark Honigsbaum, launched an examination of the financing of his new home in Notting Hill. Mandelson took umbrage, pulled rank and intervened through the then *Evening Standard* editor Max Hastings. This is how Hastings describes what follows: 'Mandelson rang me up. He said, "There's no story. I'm buying my house with family money and that's where it begins and ends."'

Hastings says that 'I've always had a naïve view that if politicians make private calls to editors they are entitled to be believed until shown to be lying. So I went out of my office and told the features desk, "There's no story – Mandelson flatly denies it." They said, "You're crazy. Mandelson's a chronic liar." I said: "He says there's no truth in it – drop the piece." Everybody looked at me disbelievingly. James Hanning said I was mad to accept Mandelson's word. And one thing the political editors of the *Daily Telegraph* and *Evening Standard* had in common was that both used to tell me Mandelson was incapable of telling the truth about whether it was Monday or Tuesday. I was foolish enough to give him the benefit of the doubt.'

Several months later, front pages blazoned the story that the Mandelson house had been purchased with a loan from Geoffrey Robinson, by now Paymaster General. 'At the *Standard*'s morning conference that day, a lot of faces were looking reproachfully at me,' recalls Hastings. 'I was called out of the meeting to take another call from Mandelson himself. His opening gambit was: "What do I have to do to convince you that I'm not a crook?" I replied: "Your problem, Peter, is to convince me you are not a liar." After a measurable pause, he responded: "I always *intended* to buy the house with family money."' Hastings says that thereafter he never paid much attention to Mandelson's assertions on any subject, on or off the record.[28] Mandelson did not just lie to the *Evening Standard* about the Notting Hill home. When the *Daily Mail* asked him how he had paid for it, he said that it had come from legacies from his mother. He told the *Mail*: 'Your enquiries are entirely unwarranted and unjustified. You are trying to engineer aspersion and innuendo.'[29]

A further instance of Peter Mandelson's back-tracking came in the wake of the row over the Geoffrey Robinson home loan. The *Daily Mirror* reported that Mandelson felt that he was the victim of a 'deliberate and very ferocious hatchet job.' It quoted Mandelson saying that 'there is more of a hint of homophobia about some of the reporting.'[29] A furious Mandelson denied having made the remarks, causing surprise among the *Daily Mirror* executives to whom he had uttered them. The then *Mirror* editor Piers Morgan said, 'I'm a little surprised to see Peter Mandelson claiming that our story did not represent his views since they were the same views he represented to me on the phone yesterday.' Morgan went on: 'He volunteered these views. I would be fascinated to know which ones he thinks we misrepresented because in my view we didn't misrepresent any.'[31]

Many journalists have concluded that Peter Mandelson lies on principle or just for the sheer hell of it. Some agree with Trevor Kavanagh, political editor of the *Sun*, who wrote: 'The Rt Hon Peter

Mandelson, minister of the crown, member of the Privy Council, is a natural born liar. Deceit is second nature to him – a tried and tested weapon in his political armoury.'[32] Some reporters grew so accustomed to Mandelson's lies and equivocations that they became quite fond of them.

A full list of Mandelson's deceptions would take up a disproportionate amount of space in this book, but here are just two more. On the night Peter Mandelson was 'outed' on *Newsnight* by the broadcaster Matthew Parris, Mandelson's aides repeatedly told journalists that at no stage did he ring up Sir John Birt to complain. But according to his sympathetic biographer Donald Macintyre, Mandelson telephoned Sir Christopher Bland, the chairman of the BBC governors, and suggested that he acquaint himself with the facts. He also – contrary to subsequent denials – telephoned Birt, to protest.[33]

Paul Eastham, deputy political editor of the *Daily Mail*, was lied to by Mandelson He recalls: 'It came my way that the Prince of Wales and Peter Mandelson had formed a friendship. I checked this with Mandelson and he denied it so I left the story alone. It subsequently emerged that the story was true and that Mandelson was helping the Prince in some way with presentation.'[34]

These stories illustrate the facility with which Peter Mandelson lied. But he did it for a purpose. Mandelson seems to have regarded dishonesty and lying as a core part of his job as a British politician. As his career in British politics ended, and he embarked on a new life at the European Commission, he made a most revealing remark in a television interview. 'If I am being honest, which I will be,' mused Mandelson, 'I don't think I've got anything to lose by being honest at this stage in my political career . . .'[35] Mandelson was talking like an ageing boxer preparing to hang up his gloves. The

Guardian commentator Simon Hoggart put it like this:'It was a fascinating insight. He talked about being honest as if it was something you might take up at a certain age, like angling or DIY, an optional extra tacked on to your life.'[36]

Denis MacShane is in the same category. Late in 2004 MacShane made a trip to Durham University, where he told a group of students that Gordon Brown's five economic tests for joining the single European currency were a 'giant red herring.' Adding fuel to the fire, he said that the European Union constitution'won't be the last word'in European integration'.[37] These were inflammatory remarks which flatly contradicted government policy.

Rung up by the *Scotsman* newspaper, MacShane flatly denied ever saying such a thing.'Jesus Christ no,'he said.'I mean,"red herring"is not one of my favourite metaphors.'To drive home the point that he could not possibly have said the words he added: "If you think any Labour MP saying the Prime Minister's most important policy is a red herring, then they would not last long in the job.'He added that he would not contradict'my beloved Prime Minister and my adored Chancellor.'

According to the *Scotsman* political editor Fraser Nelson who spoke to MacShane: 'Throughout this conversation MacShane feigned complete ignorance and said that he only vaguely remembered the occasion. He added that he would have had a Foreign Office official with him and that he would not have said such a thing. He made great play of how the right-wing press was out to get him.'

Later there was a second conversation in which the *Scotsman* informed MacShane that his words were on tape. At this stage MacShane conceded that he had uttered the phrase 'red herring', but claimed that he had used it to describe not the Chancellor's five tests, but the arguments used by Eurosceptics. However, careful examination of the audio transcript carries no suggestion that MacShane was doing anything apart from referring to the government policy of five economic tests. During this second conversation, according to Fraser Nelson, MacShane's memory became crystal clear.'He suddenly remembered that the *Daily Mail* and the *Sun* had been on to him, chasing the same story. The implication of this change of tack was quite clear: it was to try and tell me that if the *Sun* and the *Mail* hadn't managed to make the story stick there couldn't be anything in it and the *Scotsman* was being sold a pup.'[38]

The trouble about a political culture that tolerates and promotes figures like Mandelson and MacShane is it sends out a message that lying is acceptable. Civil servants and others take their lead from ministers and do the same. Here are two examples of deception, one from the present head of the Foreign Office news department, the other from Stephen Byers' former spin-doctor Jo Moore. The first concerns the failed coup in Equatorial Guinea in March 2004.

The *Observer* newspaper, long famed for its African coverage, picked up a tip from a valued source. The paper was told that the British government had known of the coup plot well in advance. It checked out the story as best it could. Then, on the day before publication, the *Observer* put it to the Foreign Office, which issued a direct rebuttal. Not content with merely telling the reporter that the story was wholly untrue, the head of the Foreign Office news department took the step of ringing Roger Alton, the editor of the *Observer*. Speaking on behalf of Foreign Secretary Jack Straw, he issued an assurance that Britain had no 'prior knowledge of the alleged plot.'

Privately the official went much further. He stressed to the *Observer* that the claims being made were extremely grave. If they were true, insisted the official, then the British government would have been indirectly complicit in the plot itself, and individual diplomats guilty of a conspiracy to bring down an internationally recognised government. Since it was utterly unthinkable that HMG would ever conduct itself in such a fashion, the official stated, the *Observer* should think very carefully indeed before running such a damaging story. In these circumstances the *Observer* very naturally felt it had no choice but to change the story. A second newspaper, the *Sunday Times*, also received a robust denial that the government had known anything of the coup in advance.[39]

But the Foreign Office spokesman was misleading the *Observer*, and in due course Jack Straw was obliged to admit that the FO had known about the coup since late January 2004.

In October 2001 Jo Moore, spin doctor to the cabinet minister Stephen Byers, misled a *Sunday Times* reporter, David Parsley, who rang to check a story that Railtrack was to be taken back into government control. According to the *Sunday Times* account of the deception:

The newspaper had learnt exclusively that Railtrack was on the brink of insolvency and that Byers was in discussions with its chairman. An abusive Moore at first refused to answer Parsley's questions. He then told her: 'We are running a story tomorrow that will say Railtrack is bankrupt and that the government is taking control, renationalizing it.' Moore replied: 'If you run that

you'll look like a f***ing idiot.' But within 48 hours Stephen Byers
had appointed an administrator to run the rail company.[40]

There is no evidence that Moore's mendacity damaged her standing
with her most senior colleagues. On the contrary Stephen Byers
and, even more to the point, Tony Blair, fought for her to stay for
months after this and other episodes had damaged her reputation
irretrievably. Likewise the head of the Foreign Office news department remains in his job, with no suggestion that he has been
censured or punished. The only conclusion must be that the Foreign
Secretary Jack Straw tolerates deception by his subordinates.

Defending Lying Ministers

For some time after winning power Tony Blair continued to make
plain his abhorrence of lying, his commitment to telling the truth,
and the special depth of his own personal integrity. On 27 February
2002 he told the House of Commons that he would sack any minister who lied. And yet his reaction when ministers or aides actually
were caught out hardly reflected these solemn pledges. Rather than
express anger or disgust at the dishonesty of colleagues, he tended
to stand by them. On occasion the prime minister, in his eagerness
to stand by beleaguered colleagues, has got into battle and actually
told further lies on their behalf.

This prime ministerial readiness to tell untruths on behalf of colleagues first manifested itself in the case of Keith Vaz, who served as
Minister for Europe before the 2001 general election. Vaz found
himself in all kinds of trouble, and Tony Blair came to his defence.

The prime minister resisted all calls for Vaz to quit, claiming instead that Vaz was the victim of a 'completely extraordinary' campaign. Tackled on the *Today* programme about the charges made against Vaz, Blair insisted that 'each time one of these allegations is made, they are looked into very carefully. There turns out to be nothing in them and people simply move on to the next allegation . . . I find it very odd if you say that he should be dismissed from government when the allegation made against him was inquired into and then found there was nothing in it.'[41]

But Tony Blair was wrong, and was badly misrepresenting the findings of the Commons Committee for Standards and Privileges. This committee had found that Vaz had received a cash payment from one Sarosh Zaiwalla, a solicitor who he recommended for an honour in 1997. Vaz told Mrs Elizabeth Filkin, however, the Parliamentary Commissioner for Standards, that he had 'never requested, nor received, cash payments of any kind from Mr Zaiwalla', yet Zaiwalla's cash book revealed that such payments had indeed taken place.[42] The prime minister was telling a lie. His claim that allegations had been looked into 'very carefully. There turns out to be nothing in them' was a blatant falsehood. In fact – as the prime minister was in a position to know – eight of the allegations against Vaz had been left hanging in the air because he had refused to cooperate with Mrs Filkin. He was also in a position to know that the committee had found a cash payment from Zaiwalla to Vaz. There was plenty of other evidence of Vaz's lack of candour around. In January 2001, as the Hinduja passport controversy rumbled on, Vaz had made the claim that it was 'not unusual' for citizenship to be granted rapidly, only to be sharply contradicted by the chief executive of the Immigration Advisory Service: Keith Best said that, on the contrary, it was unusual for naturalisation to be expedited except in 'compassionate or compelling' circumstances such as the need for a passport to visit sick relatives abroad.[43] In the end Vaz was allowed to quietly bow out of the government in the post-election reshuffle.

The most flagrant example of Tony Blair throwing his weight behind a minister who had grievous difficulty telling the truth concerned the Transport Secretary Stephen Byers. Byers was caught red-handed deceiving the presenter Jonathan Dimbleby and TV viewers in February 2002. He falsely claimed that he had not got involved in the sacking of his press officer Martin Sixsmith. Dimbleby repeatedly tackled Byers on this point, who insisted that 'I do not get involved in personnel matters.'[44]

This interview with Dimbleby came at the end of a torrid week that had seen the government issue a long series of misleading and false statements about events in Stephen Byers's Transport Department. These events reached a climax with the joint departures of both press chief Martin Sixsmith and special adviser Jo Moore. But Byers's claim to Dimbleby that he had nothing to do with the Sixsmith departure from government promptly started to unravel. Martin Sixsmith stated that 'I know for a fact that Byers has been involved.'[45] Two days later Byers came to the Commons to confess that he had misled Dimbleby. 'If my answers on the programme gave the impression that I did not put forward a view or make clear my views to others inside and outside the Department, that is obviously something I regret and I welcome this opportunity in the House to clarify matters.'

Byers most certainly lied to TV viewers. It is inconceivable, as the minister sat in the studio with Jonathan Dimbleby, that he could not remember the events of the previous few days with luminous accuracy. Even his cabinet colleagues, sent out into the television studios to defend him, could see it was a lie. They went into various agonies of self-mortification as they desperately tried to defend the indefensible. The most remarkable of these verbal pirouettes came from poor Estelle Morris, the Education Secretary. She claimed that Mr Byers's lie was not really a lie, because anyone could see that what he was saying was not true. This is how she went about it:

> There's no way that anyone who knows about how government departments work would not have known that Sir Richard Mottram [permanent secretary at the Department of Transport] and Stephen Byers would have had a conversation about what happened . . . It wasn't an attempt to deceive – he couldn't possibly have thought that people wouldn't have known that they would have had that conversation . . . What I call a lie is when you say something to somebody and hope to get away with it because they won't find you out.[46]

A prime minister who really cared for the truth, as Tony Blair had claimed to do, might have used the opportunity to make it plain that it was repellent to have a lying politician in his cabinet. He could have sacked Byers, however tenderly, as an example to others. But Tony Blair took the opposite course of action. He ordered the Labour Party to rally round the minister as he came to the Commons to make his mealy-mouthed statement of 'clarification'. I was at my seat in the press gallery of the Commons chamber as Stephen Byers came in to defend himself, and watched the Labour benches, marshaled by the government whips, fill behind him to give their support. The government majority was used to roar on the lying minister. It was hard to feel anything except despair and disgust. Byers did not lie just once, but four times on the *Jonathan Dimbleby* show. But this did not disturb the Labour backbenchers, or the ministers arrayed beside him. As I watched all this from the press gallery, I reflected that a new doctrine had taken hold in British public life: that ministers can lie, be exposed as liars, and keep their jobs.

After Stephen Byers had survived in the Commons Tony Blair summoned him for tea in Downing Street. Meanwhile the Number 10 spokesman put out a statement that 'the Prime Minister is pleased that Stephen Byers has performed so well in the House this afternoon.'

This Byers appearance in the Commons was a turning point. Downing Street was forced to choose in an explicit way between power and truth. In the minds of the New Labour hierarchy, discarding Byers would have meant a humiliating political defeat. The fact that Byers had lied was deemed merely contingent. The occupants of Downing Street were hard men and women. Winning mattered to them, and loyalty to their own. So they chose to endorse falsehood, rather than give in to their political enemies. That's what was important, even if it meant turning black into white and truth into lies. Now is the time to turn our attention to the most vivid manifestation of this deceitful culture – Prime Minister Tony Blair.

4

THE LIES, FALSEHOODS, DECEITS, EVASIONS AND ARTFULNESS OF TONY BLAIR

'I am the Prime Minister and I don't lie.' – Tony Blair to *Daily Mirror* editor Piers Morgan, 29 November 2001.[1]

Reinventing the past

Tony Blair's first public act of deception was very small beer. It is to be found in the hastily typed curriculum vitae he filled out during his successful bid to become Labour candidate for Sedgefield in the 1983 general election. This flimsy document made two misleading claims, neither of them venal. It asserted that he had 'written for' the *Guardian*. But the future prime minister's sympathetic and meticulous biographer John Rentoul asserts that 'no published article can be found'.[2]

Tony Blair's assertion that 'Cherie Blair's work, unlike mine, could transfer to the north' may have been strictly speaking accurate. But its implication that Cherie might move to employment in the distant North East, while her husband remained in London as an MP, was vastly improbable.

Just as striking as the assertions contained in the CV were its omissions. Tony Blair's education at a British public school was omitted from the section on background while, as Rentoul drily notes, 'nor would you get the impression from his description of his work as a barrister that he ever engaged in corporate litigation, or represented employers.' Millions of job applicants of all kinds have engaged in this kind of pruning over the years.

As Tony Blair's career flourished, his sleights of hand grew more confident. In September 1996, as the nation prepared for the general election, Blair gave an interview to *Country Life* magazine in which he set out his pitch to rural seats. 'I wouldn't live in a big city if I could help it. I would live in the country,' he informed readers. 'I was brought up there, really.' Rentoul comments: 'This was not true, "really" or even at all. His main childhood home was an estate of private houses on the outskirts of Durham City.'[3]

A more spectacular example of Blair's ability to invent his past came when he told the entertainer Des O'Connor that he had once tried to stow away in a plane to the Bahamas in order to escape from Fettes public school. Blair told O'Connor how he 'snuck on to the plane, and we were literally about to take off when the stewardess came up to me and said: "I don't think I actually saw your boarding pass."' This account was disputed by his father Leo who responded when asked about the story: 'The Bahamas? Who said that? Tony? Never. It's news to me.' Leo Blair went on: 'He only got as far as the airport. He never got on the plane. It was not possible.' Just as embarrassing for the prime minister was the response of a spokeswoman for Newcastle Airport who said: 'In our 61-year history we never had any flights to the Bahamas from here.'[4] John Rentoul puts the best gloss on this for the prime minister, pointing out that he entered into a public debate with his father about the events at Newcastle Airport, insisting: 'I did actually get on the plane. I was taken off by the stewardess. I think Dad was trying to help because he thought I had done something terrible.' Rentoul also claims that 'the younger Blair's account was accepted by the school at the time', speculating that Blair may have been trying to get to the Bahamas via London.[5]

Another embarrassing episode concerned the future of Tony Blair's membership of the Campaign for Nuclear Disarmament. Tony Blair joined CND, which lobbied for the unilateral surrender of Britain's nuclear weapons capacity, at some stage in the early 1980s. It was a useful move for any young man in search of a political career inside the Labour Party. His membership of CND appeared prominently, for instance, in the hastily typed Sedgefield CV.

Fifteen years later, as Tony Blair sought to present himself as strong on defence in the run up to the 1997 general election, this membership of CND had become a liability. In September 1994 the Tory cabinet minister Michael Heseltine launched an attack on Tony Blair on the *Today* programme in which he scorned the new leader of the opposition for his membership of CND.[6]

Tony Blair's reaction was striking. The Labour Party simply denied that he had ever been a member and, when that deceit was rumbled, retreated to an equally false fallback position that he had never been a member of mainstream CND.[7] This is how Tony Blair's first biographer Jon Sopel describes the reaction to the Heseltine allegation:

Later that day senior Labour Party sources went out of their way to dismiss what they said was a lie. David Hill, the Party's Director of Communications, fulminated against smears from

Conservative Central Office and told Westminster lobby journalists that Blair had never been a member of CND. This denial was faithfully reproduced in the following day's newspapers and a successful damage limitation operation had been carried out. But then the Tories produced evidence which showed that as late as 1986 Blair had been a member of parliamentary CND. Hill then pointed out that it was a quantum difference to join parliamentary CND, which most Labour MPs had joined, and CND itself, which the Labour Party still maintains Blair had never been a member of. But in his hastily cobbled together CV dating from May 1983, under the heading 'membership of other organizations' Blair quite clearly lists that he was a member of CND.[8]

This kind of invention or sleight of hand repeats itself many times in Tony Blair's political career.

Direct Lies

The prime minister has consistently resorted to contemptuous falsehood when dealing both with MPs and, just as pertinently, members of the British public. These falsehoods often become lies when he is on difficult ground or faced with messy choices. The long drawn out fox-hunting saga produced several interesting examples. On two occasions he claimed that he voted to ban the sport, when in fact he had not.

Asked about hunting on BBC's *Question Time* in the summer of 1999 the prime minister declared that 'We had one try at it last session – people like myself voted in favour of banning fox hunting. I voted for it.'[9] This was false. When the Labour backbencher Michael Foster brought forward a private member's bill to ban hunting in the 1997/8 session of parliament, the prime minister did not vote. Tony Blair went on repeating the lie. Back on *Question Time* on 30 May 2001, just days ahead of the general election, Blair insisted that 'we had a free vote on hunting' adding that 'I happened to vote in favour of a ban.'

This again was not true. Tony Blair was right to assert that there had been a free vote on fox-hunting – on the government's multi-option Hunting Bill during the Committee of the Whole House consideration of 17 January 2001. But he did not vote for any of the options – for hunting, against or even the middle way.

The prime minister lied about hunting in a second significant way. On three separate occasions he falsely blamed the failure of the Michael Foster bill to ban hunting on the House of Lords, when actually it was his own responsibility. He told Radio 4 in 1999 that 'We have to find time for the vote in the House of Commons and last time it was blocked in the House of Lords,' adding that MPs 'had a go' at banning fox-hunting 'before it was blocked in the Lords'.[10] The same claim was made on breakfast TV in July 1999, with the prime minister claiming that 'the reason why this bill was blocked, it was blocked because of the Conservatives in the House of Commons who talked the private member's bill out, and then blocked it in the House of Lords.'[11] He was at it again on *Question Time* in 1999, saying that 'it was blocked by Conservatives in the House of Commons and the House of Lords' and going on to make the political point that 'the people holding it up aren't actually on my side and one of the reasons I think it's quite important in the end we get some reform in the House of Lords so that a whole lot of hereditary peers can't be brought out of the woodwork to defend what amounts (*sic*) that many people will support.' He added that 'with the fox-hunting we gave it one chance but it was blocked in the House of Lords'.[12]

These attempts to blame the 'Conservatives' and the 'Lords' were completely untrue. The failure of the Michael Foster bill had nothing to do with the Lords. Had the bill found its way to the House of Lords, it is indeed likely that it would have been blocked by a cross-party alliance of Tory and Labour peers, as happened with the Hunting Act of 2004. But it never got there. Michael Foster's bill was blocked simply because government managers did not allocate it parliamentary time. In other words, it was Tony Blair himself who bore the responsibility for stopping Michael Foster's bill, and it was discreditable of the prime minister to try and evade this responsibility by blaming an innocent third party.

Another example of deceit followed the heart scare in October 2003, when Tony Blair was admitted to hospital for tests, which established that he suffered from an irregular heartbeat. Perhaps anxious to play down the seriousness of the episode, the prime minister's official spokesman (PMOS) stressed that Tony Blair had never suffered from the problem before. The PMOS is a civil servant who acts as the public voice of the prime minister in his dealings with the media and others, and speaks with his full authority.[13] The PMOS was quite emphatic on this point. The claim was undermined, however, one week later when former US President Clinton expressed sympathy for the prime minister. Speaking while on a trip to Barcelona he said: 'I've known about this for a long time. He told me about it quite a few years ago.'[14] Clinton revealed that he had spoken to Tony Blair about the problem, saying, 'He told me it was no big deal but I knew the moment I heard what must have happened.'

When these remarks were put to the Downing Street official spokesman at a lobby briefing, the PMOS declared, 'We were slightly mystified by this story, as this was the first time that the Prime Minister had suffered from such a condition.' Indeed the PMOS was emphatic that Tony Blair had never suffered a heart problem of any kind: 'The Prime Minister,' said the PMOS, 'did not have, and had never had, a heart condition. Nor had he ever had this complaint before.'[15] The PMOS came close in this briefing to accusing Bill Clinton of lying, and Tony Blair flatly contradicted the former president later when he was asked on Jeremy Vine's BBC Radio 2 lunchtime programme if he had told Bill Clinton he had a heart condition 'No, this is the first time this has ever happened to me,' he replied.[16]

There matters might have rested but for a singular piece of ill luck. It emerged that the Queen, too, had enjoyed foreknowledge of the Blair heart problem. This detail emerged in a way that neither the prime minister nor his official spokesman could possibly have foreseen. A *Daily Mirror* reporter named Ryan Parry gained a job as a footman at Buckingham Palace, ostensibly to expose 'lax security'. In practice Parry busied himself picking up interesting royal gossip. Parry happened to be in the palace around the time of the heart scare, and was made privy to the Queen's reaction when she heard about it. Steve Niger, a page to the Queen, reportedly told Parry: 'She's very concerned about Blair. She told me, I do hope it's not too serious. He told me he's had similar complications in the past.'[17] The afternoon the Ryan Parry story broke, Downing Street was obliged to respond to difficult questions, but stuck to its original story. 'This is the first time this has happened. The Prime Minister does not have, and never has had, a heart condition.'[18]

Tony Blair often deceives for tactical advantage. An example of this kind of episode came when he was interviewed by Jeremy Paxman on 16 May 2002. The Labour Party was in the middle of an embarrassing row over accepting a donation from Richard Desmond, a former publisher of pornography who had purchased Express Newspapers eighteen months earlier. The revelation of the Desmond donation had caused special upset among women Labour MPs. The prime minister was defending the donation, pointing out that Desmond's group owned Express Newspapers. Paxman responded: 'They also own *Horny Housewives*, *Mega Boobs*, *Posh Wives*, *Skinny & Wriggly*. Do you know what these magazines are like?' Blair replied: 'No, I don't.'[19]

Unfortunately for the prime minister, five days later it emerged that he had indeed seen some of the magazines in question. *The Times* columnist Anthony Howard recalled a story told him by the late Tony Bevins, who was political editor of the *Daily Express* when Desmond bought the paper. Bevins, a man of high principle, at once resigned in protest. He happened to be with the prime minister when the news of his departure emerged. 'Blair asked him why he was going,' reported Howard. 'Bevins told me that, by way of reply, he simply took out from his briefcase some of the more lurid of the Desmond titles and threw them down in front of the Prime Minister – who, to be fair, shuddered and averted his gaze.'[20]

Tony Blair displayed the same gift for what the author Robert

Harris calls 'retailoring himself and his history to suit the moment' after he was criticised for manipulating the Labour Party selection process to choose its candidate for London mayor.'All this central-ising stuff is rubbish,' he told the *Observer* in 1999.'Labour is going to make its selection through an electoral college in exactly the same way as it elected me, John Prescott, Donald Dewar and Alun Michael.'[21] This was untrue.*

It was indeed the case that Tony Blair was elected by an electoral college, but it was emphatically not the same as the electoral college used in the election of the London mayor. The system that elected Tony Blair was the one forced through Labour conference by John Smith in 1993. It forced the unions and the constituency parties to ballot individual members within their section of the college.

The system used in the London mayoral contest, like the one adopted to fix Labour's leader in Wales a few months previously, was very different. The same percentages were used, but the New Labour leadership – acting strongly against its principles – did not force the unions to ballot their members. The crucial decision was allowing the giant AEEU union not to ballot, a decision which handed a significant advantage to Livingstone's rival Frank Dobson. As the BBC reported at the time: 'The former health secretary [Dobson] also benefited from the block vote of the AEEU engineer-ing union, which did not ballot its members.'[22]

---

* The same formulation was recited by other government loyalists. Loyal Blairite minister Barbara Roche was still repeating it on BBC Radio 5 as late as 21 February 2000. She told listeners that 'the electoral college isn't a new thing,' adding, 'We used this electoral college for the election of Tony Blair and John Prescott.' Quoted by Francis Wheen,'A Great Feat of Ballot-Rigging', *Guardian*, 23 February 2000.

John Rentoul describes the London mayoral arrangement very clearly in his biography of the prime minister:

> It had been widely assumed, not least by Blair, that the Labour candidate would be chosen in a one member, one vote ballot of party members in London. But that was just after the election. Since then, he had wanted to fix the selection of Labour's leader in Wales, and so Margaret McDonagh, the General Secretary of the party, had devised a three-section electoral college. Superficially it looked like the system under which Blair had been elected leader but there was one critical difference, in that it retained trade union block votes rather than balloting trade unionists as individuals. This was now adapted to London, with the added device of including, in the section for Labour candidates for the new Greater London Assembly, all the MPs and Euro MPs representing London constituencies. This was the section of the electoral college which delivered the nomination to Dobson . . . the result was overwhelmingly seen as a fix.[23]

Tony Blair must have known this when he falsely claimed that Livingstone had been elected by the same system he had. The most reforming Labour leader in history, he had been a potent critic of the electoral college system and champion of the far more democratic one member, one vote. He used a speech to the Fabian Society in July 1995 to express his views on the block vote system used to elect Livingstone: 'The party lost contact with the electorate, and in the name of internal party democracy gave away its ultimate source of accountability: the people at large. That is why the change to one member, one vote and the changes in the organisation of party conference are so important.'[24]

It is extraordinary how cavalier the prime minister is with facts. Coming under fire over the decision to put Railtrack into administration, Tony Blair asserted that 'the longer the administrator's work has gone on, the more financial difficulties he has uncovered.'[25] This was a powerful claim. Had it been true it would have gone far towards justifying the hugely controversial decision taken by Transport Secretary Stephen Byers to take action against Railtrack. The trouble is that, as Alan Bloom, the administrator of Railtrack, told the transport select committee, Blair's words were false.* Chris Hill, the joint administrator, said to the select committee that Railtrack was 'operating roughly in line with the budgets'. Asked if there had been any 'hidden nasties', Hill said 'No'.[26]

Different Truths for Different People

The prime minister continues to insist that he is a regular bloke. He has sought to distinguish himself from the duplicity and moral

---

* See Select Committee on Transport, Local Government and the Regions Minutes of Evidence, Examination of Witnesses (Questions 260–279) Wednesday 6 February 2002, Mr John Armitt, Mr John Smith, Mr Alan Bloom and Mr Chris Hill: 'Mr Bloom, it has been said that since you took over as administrator of Railtrack you have, as the work has gone by, uncovered more and more financial difficulties within the company. Is that true?' Mr Bloom: 'When we arrived at Railtrack on 7 October we had had no access to Railtrack before that date. Any information that we had about Railtrack was from a desktop from a distance, so we had no prior expectations as to what it was that we would see and the numbers that would be required, etc. We produced, with the help of the Railtrack management team, a forecast for funding initially for the first six months of the administration to 31 March of £2.9 billion. It is our full expectation that in the period to 31st March we will come inside that figure.' See the remainder of the Select Committee evidence taken that afternoon for a fuller picture.

squalour of Westminster, maintaining that he possesses a different and more attractive set of values. Right from the start it was an essential part of the Tony Blair proposition that he is just an ordinary person, not to be confused with other politicians. Many friendly commentators swallow this claim in full. To Julian Glover, for example, 'Nothing known about him gives us any good reason to doubt that he is what he claims to be: a Christian lawyer who lived in Islington, who probably ironed his jeans at university and really didn't smoke pot.'[27]

Tony Blair has never hesitated to make these kind of claims on his own behalf. When accused of corruption during the Ecclestone Affair he assumed a look of innocence and said he was 'a pretty straight kind of guy'. This is by no means the case. The prime minister possesses a remarkable ability to give opposing groups or individuals the impression that he is on both their sides. This chameleon quality has been a large driver of his prodigious early success, and it involves an overwhelming element of camouflage, sleight of hand and other forms of deception.

One characteristic case of this form of prime ministerial mendacity involves the *Guardian* columnist and writer Jonathan Freedland. In the summer of 1999, a group of *Guardian* journalists travelled to Chequers to visit the prime minister. Conspicuously displayed, covers spread across the table as if it was being read, was Freedland's fashionable and justly praised book *Bring Home the Revolution*, a republican tract urging the abolition of the British monarchy. The *Guardian* team gained the impression – they could hardly reach any other conclusion – that Tony Blair was reading the book. On return to London, the reporters passed this information on to their colleague Freedland. Understandably braced by this news that his work was being read in high places, Freedland told friends. Word swiftly spread through Fleet Street about the prime minister's latest reading material, in due course reaching the *Mail on Sunday* political journalist Simon Walters.

As matters turned out, Walters was offered an interview with Tony Blair as he and his accompanying press party flew to the Commonwealth Conference in South Africa. He asked the prime minister, who was with Cherie, whether he was reading Freedland's book. This is how Walters described what happened next: 'Mr Blair rolled his eyes in amazement. He'd never heard of the book or Freedland. "I can assure you I don't take it to bed with me."'"I can certainly vouch for that," chipped in Cherie.'[28] Several months later, however, when Blair went to lunch at the *Guardian*, he was happy to confirm that he had examined Freedland's book, claiming that it had been given to him by David Yelland, editor of the *Sun*.

It is easy to surmise what was going on. The prime minister is more than happy to flatter *Guardian* journalists with the notion that he is one of them, a radical thinker who reads their books and entertains republican ideas. But the *Mail on Sunday* was a very different kettle of fish. Its readers, mainly from the heart of middle England, are predominantly supporters of the monarchy. It would have been unfortunate had Simon Walters been able to inform them that the prime minister was reading a book that argued the case for the monarchy to be abolished. Tony Blair addressed this dilemma by presenting what one might delicately term an alternative version of the truth to both papers.

This little episode shows how the prime minister and his political strategists were determined to pay any price in order to put across the appropriate image to the press, including the giant loss of personal integrity. There are numerous other cases that illustrate Tony Blair's readiness to deliver conflicting messages to different audiences. Often Blair and his strategists have gone to extraordinary lengths to ensure that the correct message went out to one target audience, and a different message elsewhere.

An exquisite example of the syndrome concerns a TUC dinner, addressed by the prime minister, on 9 September 2003. Twenty minutes ahead of his speech an aide issued two pages of quotes to the press. These created the impression that the prime minister was to attack the Labour left and the unions, in a move that would win friends on the right-wing media. In particular the press release indicated that he would call the belief that there could be a left-wing alternative to the Blair government 'the abiding delusion of 100 years of our party.' It had the prime minister asserting that opposition to public service reform would be 'as big a mistake as when the 1970s Labour government rejected council house sales' and calling for the 'far left' to be defeated.

But when Tony Blair made his speech privately to trade union leaders, he pulled his punches. There are varying reports of what took place in the room – journalists were left hanging around outside – but most present maintained there was no reference to either council house sales, or to an 'abiding delusion', or even to the 'far left.' Afterwards Derek Simpson, general secretary of the giant Amicus trade union, was quoted saying: 'It's confusing that the press was told one thing and we were told another. It's not just the words that were altered but the tone. There was no inflammatory language or rhetoric as there was in the transcript. If that was deliberate it is a wicked game.' Mark Serwotka, general secretary of the civil service union PCS, said: 'It's quite clear they are spinning a certain message that was never delivered.'[29] (The sleight of hand displayed by the prime minister at the TUC dinner was an echo of a row earlier that year when he had appeared to call trade union opponents of public service reform 'wreckers'. Allies of Tony Blair were soon insisting the comments had been aimed at the Conservatives.[30]) Later, cabinet minister Baroness Amos was drawn into a deception of her own in the House of Lords when trying to defend Tony Blair's speech. Asked by Tory peer Norman Tebbit 'Whether the Prime Minister's speech made at the Trade Union Congress dinner on 9 September was accurately represented by the text of that speech issued by his spokesman', she gallantly answered 'Yes'.[31] Amos was forced to mislead parliament in order to defend the reputation of the prime minister.

There are innumerable examples of Tony Blair sending out these kinds of contradictory messages to different audiences. In 1988 he was quoted in *The Times* saying, 'Without an active, interventionist industrial policy . . . Britain faces the future of having to compete on dangerously unequal terms.' But in 1996 he told the Nottingham Chamber of Commerce that 'New Labour does not believe that it is the job of government to interfere in the running of business.'[32] At the Labour Party Conference of 1994, Tony Blair sent out a socialist message to his audience of left-wing activists, declaring, 'If you ever want to know which side the Tories are on, look at the tax system.' But the following year, when speaking to an audience of businessmen at CBI Conference, he said that 'penal rates of taxation do not make economic or political sense. They are gone for good.'

Tony Blair has often demonstrated this same lack of candour during private dealings with colleagues and others. One victim was Paddy Ashdown, who devoted his final years as Liberal Democrat leader to pursuing the illusion of a coalition with New Labour, and proportional representation. His published diaries display in agonising detail how Ashdown's hopes were raised again and again, only to be finally dashed. Ashdown was given a number of assurances that turned out to be worthless.[33]

This kind of sleight of hand played a decisive role in bringing about the disastrous, failed relationship between Number 10 and Number 11 Downing Street which has been one of the defining features of the Blair premiership. It is impossible to judge for certain exactly what took place between Gordon Brown and Tony Blair before Brown's decision to quit the Labour leadership race in 1994. But it does seem to be the case that Tony Blair allowed his rival to gain the impression that, in return for dropping out of the contest, Tony Blair would himself step down at a later date. Downing Street allies of the prime minster now deny that any deal was entered into, though Gordon Brown himself has never been so emphatic. The political journalist James Naughtie, in his well-informed and sensitive account, later wrote: 'Brown left the [Granita] restaurant believing that Blair had committed himself to supporting his own succession to the premiership, if he was able to pass on the torch. No one in Brown's most intimate circle believes anything else.' But he added: 'Blair insists that nothing so clear could have been offered, and wasn't.'[34]

A second version of this so-called 'Granita deal' seems to have taken place in late 2003, at a dinner hosted by John Prescott, the deputy prime minister. Here again authoritative details are hard to come by. Once again, however, it is clear that Gordon Brown came away with the impression that Tony Blair would step down at some point the following year. And once again it is clear that Gordon

Brown came to believe that the prime minister had come to renege on the bargain. Robert Peston, City Editor of the *Sunday Telegraph*, is the author of the most impressive and best-informed guide to these problematic events.[35] Peston states that, when Brown realised that Tony Blair planned to go back on this second commitment, he uttered the deadly phrase: 'There is nothing that you could say to me now that I could ever believe.' After Robert Peston's book was published in early 2005 the chancellor was given abundant opportunity to deny that he had ever uttered these astonishing words. He declined to do so.[36]

It is probably impossible for an outsider to get to the bottom of the poisonous feud between Blair and Brown. But many of those who have trusted the word of the prime minister have enjoyed a similiar kind of experience, or worse. One victim was Derek Foster, who was Labour chief whip when Tony Blair became party leader in 1994. The two men represented adjoining constituencies in the North East, but Blair felt no loyalty to Foster. Approximately one year after becoming Labour leader, Blair approached Foster with an unusual request. He asked whether he would consider standing down from his job as chief whip if he guaranteed him a place in the cabinet. Foster, with some nervousness, accepted the suggestion. However, in early 1997 reports started to appear in the press that Tony Blair wanted Foster to accept a peerage and become chief whip in the Lords. After a while Foster challenged Tony Blair on these reports. But Blair brushed them aside, saying that there was no truth in them, and that the deal still stood. So Foster informed the general management committee at his Bishop Auckland constituency that no less a figure than the leader of the Labour Party had reassured him that there was no truth in these stories, and was unanimously endorsed to stand in the general election. However, two weeks into the election proper he received a telephone call from Tony Blair who told Foster that he did, after all, want him to stand down and go into the Lords as chief whip. Foster told him that it was too late, and that he couldn't break his word to his constituency, least of all in the middle of an election campaign. Blair reluctantly accepted this, ending the conversation with a renewed assurance that the deal to put Foster in the cabinet after the election still stood.

But Blair was lying. The day after the election Foster was offered a job in the government, but not in the cabinet. Foster accepted it, but a day later he changed his mind and resigned. According to the *Guardian* columnist Polly Toynbee, Tony Blair did not merely mislead poor Derek Foster during this wretched saga, but journalists as well. Writing some three years later, she recorded how 'Tony Blair has sometimes been guilty of the gratuitous lie.' Toynbee cited as evidence that 'a colleague recalls with some anger his categorical lie in 1996 in Scotland that he would not appoint Donald Dewar as chief whip. Later Blair joked about how he had "fooled" the journos.'[37]

The Labour MP Tom Clarke was even more shabbily treated than Foster. In 1995 Tom Clarke was elected to the shadow cabinet. Tony Blair asked him to remain as spokesman on disability, a portfolio that did not carry shadow cabinet status. However Tony Blair promised him: 'Next year if you still want international development, it will be vacant. You will get it Tom, it will be yours.' Twelve months later, however, the coveted post was given to Clare Short. A furious Clarke demanded a meeting with Tony Blair. 'I am very unhappy,' he told him. Blair replied: 'I still want you to do disabilility, but don't worry. Tom, you will be in my cabinet.' Clarke replied: 'But I must question you, Tony. You have promised cabinet posts to at least twenty-six people and there are only twenty-one places.' Blair promised that he would 'get in before four or five others.' In the course of the conversation Blair gave him no less than five separate assurances that he would get a cabinet job. But once again Tony Blair was lying, and when the day came Clarke was offered a more junior ministerial job.

As so often, it is Peter Mandelson who expressed the keenest insight into Tony Blair's manipulative skills. Tony Blair, he once wrote, 'manages to combine firmness and clarity with the political skills that make such diverse individuals as John Prescott and Robin Cook *believe they are valued.*'[38] Mandelson understood that sleight of hand was a critical element of Tony Blair's armoury. This was not surprising, because Mandelson taught him much of what he knew.

The reporter Andy McSmith, formerly a Labour Party press officer reporting to Peter Mandelson, asked Blair about newspaper reports that Mandelson was trying to secure a nomination at the Hartlepool constituency. Blair denied all knowledge and, when pressed, 'looked as bland and bland as ever he could and repeated that he knew nothing'.[39] At the time he was actively aiding and abetting the Mandelson bid for the Hartlepool seat. Peter Mandelson even stayed at the Blair home in Trimdon as he successfully pursued his interest.[40]

Tony Blair, having studied at the feet of Peter Mandelson, felt certain that candour and honesty were impossible in the modern British political culture. He felt that deception was inevitable – and even virtuous if practised for benign ends. We have explored in the past three chapters how this belief shaped the behaviour of New Labour in opposition and later in power. It is now time to take a large step back, and examine the philosophical, historical and theological justifications for lying, and ask if it can ever be justified.

PART TWO

5

WHY POLITICIANS LIE

'Two thirds of what we do is reprehensible. This isn't the way
a normal human being acts. We smile, we listen – you could
grow calluses out of your ears from all the listening we do. We
do our pathetic little favours. We fudge when we can't. We tell
them what they want to hear – and when we tell them something they *don't* want to hear, it's usually because we've
calculated that's what they really want. We live in an eternity of
false smiles – and why? Because it's the price you pay to
lead. You don't think Abraham Lincoln was a whore before he
was a president? He had to tell his little stories and smile his
shit-eating, backcountry grin. He did it all just so he'd get the
opportunity, one day, to stand in front of the nation and
appeal to "the better angels in our nature." That's when the
bullshit stops. And that's what this is all about.' – Governor
Stanton, *Primary Colors*[1]

The Lies of Power

There have been many defences of political lying, but few more eloquent than Governor Stanton's self-vindication at the end of the
anonymous novel *Primary Colors*: Stanton, said to be modelled on

President Bill Clinton, had used shocking and deceitful methods to pursue the US presidency. He exonerated himself from conventional moral judgment by asserting that virtuous intentions and noble motives justified his corruption and his lies: the bad guys will tell them too, so the good guys have no choice but to tell them better.

Politicians have often used versions of this kind of defence. It dates backs at least as far as Plato, writing in the fourth century BC. Plato's 'noble lie', explained in *The Republic*, is part of a proposition that lying was not merely forgiveable but actually admirable so long as it is carried out for moral ends. Plato, a member of the Athenian governing class, was making a profound argument for rule by an elite, a wise and disinterested class of philosopher 'guardians' who alone are capable of insight into the truth. Indeed Plato made plain that only the ruling class were allowed to lie:

> It will be for the rulers of the city, then, if anyone, to use falsehood in dealing with citizen or enemy for the good of the state; no one else must do so. And if any citizen lies to our rulers, we shall regard it as a still graver offence than it is for a patient to lie to his doctor, or for an athlete to lie to his trainer about his physical condition, or for a sailor to misrepresent to his captain any matter concerning the ship or crew, or the state of himself or his fellow sailors . . . and so if anyone else is found in our state telling lies, 'whether he be craftsman, prophet, physician or shipwright', he will be punished for introducing a practice likely to capsize and wreck the ship of state.[2]

Plato's 'noble lie' was a kind of parable. It was false, and indeed wholly deceitful. But it was nonetheless benign in its consequences because it assured social harmony and made the population 'more inclined to care for the state and one another.'

Political thinkers have made the same sorts of argument ever since. Machiavelli wrote amidst the turmoil of fifteenth-century Italy, whose little city states lived in constant fear of invasion, either by hostile neighbours or foreign powers. The rulers of these Italian towns enjoyed a precarious life, in constant peril of death through treachery or in battle. Machiavelli provided them with a rule-book for survival. He recommended violence, tempered by deception. 'A prudent ruler', wrote Machiavelli in *The Prince*, 'ought not to keep faith when by doing so it would be against his interest, and when the reasons which made him bind himself no longer exist. If men were all good, this precept would not be a good one; but as they are bad, and would not observe their faith with you, so you are not bound to keep faith with them.'

Machiavelli warned the Prince to hide this part of his nature, and therefore to act 'a great feigner and dissembler.' If Plato sees a higher morality in the act of deception, Machiavelli sees merely an urgent necessity for survival. In the late twentieth century the philosopher Leo Strauss, now viewed as the grandfather of the so-called neo-conservative movement which is now in the ascendancy in the United States, was to become a champion of Plato and Machiavelli.

Strauss was a philosopher who fled Germany to escape the Nazi Party in 1938, and after World War Two taught at the University of Chicago. Horrified by what he had seen and experienced in pre-war Germany, he rejected the enlightenment dogma that the universal spread of truth was the great liberator of mankind. On the contrary, he feared that its hard light dissolved the bonds of society and placed too great a burden on ordinary people. 'Not all truths,' wrote Strauss, 'are always harmless.' In the words of his student Irving Kristol, 'Strauss was an intellectual aristocrat who thought that the truth could make some minds free, but he was convinced that there was an inherent conflict between philosophic truth and political order, and that the popularisation of these truths might import unease, turmoil and the release of popular passions hitherto held in check by tradition and religion with utterly unpredictable, but mostly negative, consequences.'[3] This doctrine has enjoyed enormous influence and application among the tiny group of senior advisers in the George W. Bush White House.[4]

How the Powerless Lie

Plato, Machiavelli, Leo Strauss and his neo-conservative followers all offered elaborate justifications of deception on behalf of the governing class. There is a parallel literature, just as rich and perhaps more complex, which makes the equivalent case for lying from the perspective of the persecuted and of the oppressed. Lying is certainly a method of exerting power. It is also a means of self-defence. The earliest examples of this second type of lying are to be found not among political philosophers, but among religious thinkers.

All religions have from time to time wrestled with the debilitating choice between martyrdom and feigned conformity to a hateful orthodoxy. This has been the recurrent fate of the Jews. The thousands of Spanish Jews who converted to Christianity at the end of the Middle Ages are one example. A minority of these converted Jews – no one knows how many – went to church, baptised their children and even displayed holy images in their homes in an attempt to convince their neighbours they were devout Catholics, yet continued to practise their faith in secret. These so-called Marranos sought doctrinal legitimacy for this dual existence, citing for instance the passage from Deuteronomy 5.33: 'You shall walk in all the ways which the Lord your God hath commanded you, that you may live.' This passage helped the Marranos to argue that it was the over-riding duty of devout followers of the law to stay alive, even if that meant outwardly sacrificing their faith.

A similar doctrine is also professed in the Islamic faith. The idea of *takiya*, which permits Islamic victims of persecution to dissemble their real beliefs, is identified with Shi-ite resistance to Sunni persecution. According to one mediaeval Koranic commentary: 'If anyone is compelled and professes unbelief with his tongue, while his heart contradicts him, to escape his enemies, no blame falls on him, because God takes his servants as their hearts believe.'

This kind of false conformity is always open to criticism, partly because it readily dissolves into an unprincipled excuse for taking the line of least resistance, partly on the grounds that lying is always wrong. Dissimulation was the subject of a testy exchange between St Augustine and St Jerome. St Jerome, by no means always such a worldly figure, argued that both St Peter and St Paul feigned observance of religious laws so as not to antagonise the Jews. St Augustine took a stricter line. He denied that lying or dissimulation could ever be right. To quote the historian Perez Zagorin: 'He particularly refused to countenance dissimulation for religious reasons. One of the arguments he attacked that was to be widely invoked by later defenders of dissimulation was the doctrine distinguishing between heart and tongue. According to this doctrine, the tongue could say what was false if one kept the truth in one's heart. In refuting it, Augustine observed that it dishonoured the martyrs who died for the truth and made holy martyrdom impossible.'[5]

This argument between St Jerome and St Augustine was to be echoed again and again throughout the history of the Christian church. All religious sects or minorities faced with the problem of survival in the face of a dominant orthodoxy were forced to confront the problem of deception. During the Middle Ages the Waldensians, a popular sect that anticipated Protestantism, attended the Catholic mass, but enjoyed their own clandestine worship as well. Despite all their efforts they frequently came to the attention of the papal Inquisition, and were obliged to adopt elaborate methods of deceit under questioning. The Lollards, a fourteenth-century English movement, encountered the same kind of difficulty, and developed the same kind of solutions. The Protestant reformation of the sixteenth century in northern Europe turned the tables. Now it was mainstream Catholics who suddenly became a persecuted minority. In the majority of cases they too conformed outwardly with the new state religion, attending church and passing themselves off as Protestants. In due course the English Jesuits developed new methodologies of lying and casuistry that have passed into folklore. A key doctrine was mental reservation, propounded by the Catholic theologian Dr Navarrus in his notable work 'On the Truth of an Answer Expressed Partly in Speech and Partly in the Mind and Concerning the Good and Bad Art of Dissimulation.'[6] The techniques advocated by Dr Navarrus, though denounced by literal-minded Protestants as straight mendacity, permitted his followers to say one thing but mean another.

So long as they held what they really intended in their mind, they could tell more or less anything to their inquisitors. For instance a Jesuit priest could, if apprehended and under interrogation, declare that 'I am no priest', so long as he privately added to himself, 'so as I am bound to utter it to you.' This doctrine, and the horror it inspired in Protestants, still has its echo in the oath which must be taken by those assuming public office in the United States: 'I take this obligation freely, without any mental reservation or purpose of evasion.'

The gradual dawn of the Western enlightenment from the end of the seventeenth century gradually brought an end to the necessity for this sort of religious equivocation and deceit. It was not until the rise of totalitarian movements in the twentieth century that the techniques of deception employed by persecuted religious groups came back into widespread use. When they did, those who sought to live under communist or Nazi regimes found themselves resorting to the old methods employed by victims of religious persecution. Czeslaw Milosz's great work *The Captive Mind*, which describes the predicament of intellectuals in post-war Poland, explicitly looks back to the Islamic doctrine of *takiya*, and the sanction it gave to deny with the heart what you say with the lips.

Lying in Wartime

In a properly functioning liberal democracy there should be no call for the mendacity advocated by Plato or Machiavelli, nor the dissimulation recommended by religious thinkers anxious to fend off persecution. Plato's assumptions about the virtues of good breeding, and the moral and intellectual superiority of a tiny aristocratic elite over those who were being deceived, have been repudiated under liberal capitalism. Machiavelli was writing about a particular time and place: his advice was aimed at rulers of precarious city states in a near permanent state of war. Political dissidents behind the Iron Curtain, or religious minorities in the early modern era, had been stripped of all moral and political rights. Telling the truth often led to disgrace, torture and death.

In a modern democracy none of this applies, not even remotely. The right to vote implies a liberty that extends far beyond the entitlement to mark a piece of paper in a voting booth once every four or five years. Citizens have a right to form a fair and balanced judgment, and are therefore entitled to be informed about their political choices. This includes a right not to be deceived. Lying in a democracy has long been regarded as an especially disreputable act: Members of Parliament are still forbidden to call their political opponents liars in the Commons Chamber. Deception, even when practised for the best of motives, is the worst kind of bad faith. Lying disempowers, and therefore dehumanises, those who are lied to. Politicians who lie to voters deprive them of the ability to come to a reasonable and well-informed decision how to cast their vote. In so doing, they convert them into dupes.

It is nevertheless accepted that there are extraordinary circumstances when politicians may lie to voters. There are critical moments in a nation's history when the threat to security is so great that ministers are surely entitled to lie. The clearest case involved the D-Day landings in 1944. The British government masterminded an elaborate deception operation to fool the German high command about where and when the expected invasion of continental Europe would take place. The scale of the deception was so audacious that it was impossible to confuse the Germans without deliberately confusing the British people as well.[7]

However even deception in wartime should never be ventured upon except with extreme reluctance. Such is the fallibility of human nature, and the proneness of even the most upright of individuals to self-deceit, that lying even for what may seem excellent motives can lead to unforeseen and terrible results. One of the worst examples of post-war mendacity was the secret collusion between France, Israel and Anthony Eden's Conservative government to find a pretext for the invasion of Egypt. Eden was under intense pressure from the right wing of the Conservative Party to punish Egyptian president Colonel Nasser for his decision to nationalise the Suez Canal in the summer of 1956. But the refusal of the United States secretly to countenance a retaliatory invasion left Eden powerless. In the end Eden seized at a plan colluded with by France and Israel ahead of the invasion of Egypt in 1956, then lied to the House of Commons about it after that war, telling MPs that 'there were no plans got together [with Israel] to attack Egypt.'[8] Eden was eager to find an excuse for war, partly for personal reasons. He was under pressure from the right wing of the Conservative Party, which accused him of vacillation and made hurtful comparisons between his dithering and the supposed decisiveness and courage of his predecessor, Winston Churchill.

In any case lies in wartime all too easily extend beyond the narrow end of deceiving the enemy into wider ends of propaganda aimed against one's own population. There were attempts to deceive the enemy during the wars of the last century, but they were far outweighed in number, scale and audacity by deceptions aimed at the British people. Bonar Law, Tory leader during the First World War, spoke of the need to have British patriotism 'properly stirred by German frightfulness.' The British authorities flung themselves into this task with huge enthusiasm. Arthur Ponsonby, author of a classic work about the use of propaganda during the First World War, described how 'Facts must be distorted, relevant circumstances concealed, and a picture painted which by its crude colouring will persuade the ignorant people that their government is blameless, their cause is righteous, and that the indisputable wickedness of the enemy has been proved beyond question.' Ponsonby warned that this kind of thing often ended up sapping, rather than strengthening the popular will. 'When the people at its conclusion find they have gained nothing but only observed widespread calamity around them, they are inclined to become more sceptical and desire to investigate the foundations of the arguments which inspired their patriotism, inflamed their passions, and prepared them to offer the supreme sacrifice. They are curious to know why the ostensible objects for which they fought have none of them been attained, more especially if they are the victors.'[9]

The Temptation to Deceive in a Modern Democratic State

Theoretically politicians should have very little need to deceive either the voters or even political opponents in a modern democracy. Yet we have already seen that lying, deception, manipulation and fabrication of the truth have become routine and to a large extent systemic inside the political system. The arts of political manipulation and deception have rarely been as in demand as they are in Britain today.

None of the conventional justifications for lying – war, the entrenchment of a governing elite – now apply. The substantive arguments that mitigate in favour of lying are simply not there. But there has been a massive change in British political culture in the past few decades. It is this change in culture, rather than internal or external pressures, which has produced the conditions for the catastrophic contemporary decline in standards of political truth-telling. It is impossible to understand this new culture without trying to grasp how the relationship between politicians and voters has changed, partly as a result of the emergence of new technologies of mass communication.

Colin Crouch, in his brilliant pamphlet, 'Coping with Post Democracy', explains the new set of circumstances as follows:

> If one looks back to the different forms of political discussion in the inter- and post-war decades one is surprised at the relative similiarity of language and style in government documents, serious journalism, popular journalism, party manifestos and politicians' public speeches. There were certainly differences of vocabulary and complexity between a serious official report designed for the policy-making community and a tabloid newspaper, but compared with today the gap was small. Today the language of serious documents remains more or less similar to what it was then. But tabloid newspaper discussion and party manifestos are totally different. They rarely aspire to any complexity of language or argument. Someone accustomed to such a style suddenly requiring to access a document of serious debate

would be at a loss as to how to understand it. Television news presentations, hovering uneasily between the two worlds, probably thereby provide a major service in helping people make such links.

Politicians' election broadcasts from the early post-war years seem comical when we view them now; but they are comical because these are people talking in the normal language of serious conversation, and with the mannerisms and quaintnesses that we all possess. This seems odd because we have become accustomed to hear politicians, not speaking like ordinary people, but presenting glib and finely honed statements which have a character all of their own. We call these 'sound bites', and having dismissed them think no more about what is going on. Like the language of tabloid newspapers and party literature, this form of communication resembles neither the ordinary speech of the person in the street, nor the language of true political discussion. It is designed to be beyond the reach of scrutiny by either of these two main modes of democratic discourse.[10]

Crouch attributes this impoverishment of our common political language to the emergence of techniques of mass communication, drawn mainly from the advertising industry. Dictators like Hitler, Mussolini and Stalin were first to understand the brilliant use to which these techniques of mass persuasion could be put. In the post-war epoch Western democracies gradually caught up, putting to use methods from the advertising and marketing professions, and selling political parties as 'product.'

Western democracies have rejected alternative traditions of large-scale communication, which were inherited from religious preachers, schoolteachers and serious popular journalism. Instead they have tended to adopt a model of addressing the electorate very similar to and to a very large extent drawn from advertising copy: brief, simplistic, and often deceitful. Political debate is no longer, as it aspired to be fifty years ago, an informed discussion among equals. Instead it is the hard sell, the stark assertion and the shock image. Humanity, complexity and truth are all being driven out of this kind of discourse.

A number of consequences have flowed from this degradation. The most important of these is that political debate is no longer qualified to address the deep and profound issues about what kind of society we should seek to be, or how underlying problems such as terrorism or immigration should be addressed. Instead argument centres around isolated, hastily constructed episodes such as 'Jennifer's Ear' in the 1992 election or the NHS treatment of Rose Addis after 2001. These angry disputes are almost incomprehensible even to those most closely involved, defined by a mixture of mendacious claim and counter-claim, judged according to a set of rules imposed in part by the deadlines and imperatives of a media audience. Episodes like these are quite incapable of shedding light on great issues such as the management of the NHS.

In parallel a cult of personality has grown up in British politics. This is an alien phenomenon, only emerging as a structural feature over the past quarter of a century. The appearance, clothing, attitudes, private life and so forth of political leaders have always been important in dictatorships, with their prevalent cult of personality. But attempts to impose this kind of style in Britain, whether by Randolph Churchill in the nineteenth century or Oswald Mosley in the 1930s, invariably failed. (Winston Churchill, the triumphant war leader in his post-1945 apotheosis, is an exception.) Baldwin, Attlee, Wilson and Callaghan were all quietly spoken political leaders. These were men who emerged during a period when political parties were strong, and political discourse serious.

Margaret Thatcher, whose image was in part created for her by professional advertising men, was the first peacetime British political leader to deliberately develop a personality cult. Her successor John Major, who never sought to do so, was a reversion to an earlier type of leader, in the mould of a Baldwin or Attlee. It may be that Major's inability or unwillingness to engage with celebrity culture was a reason for his political failure. Tony Blair, by contrast, applied the insights of the Thatcher premiership, imported many other techniques and attitudes from the US presidential system – first Bill Clinton and later George W Bush – and developed into a new kind of prime minister sitting at the top of a largely novel kind of political system.

Colin Crouch has christened the contemporary system 'post-democracy', a stunningly telling and accurate phrase. He argues with great plausibility that the British system of democracy as we enter the twenty-first century has more in common with the eighteenth than the twentieth century. This is because the new era of politics has brought back the ancient distinction between a tiny governing elite and an apathetic and largely disenfranchised electorate. Political parties have almost ceased to engage in any direct sense with voters. Instead they use technical devices, either sophisticated polling techniques or focus groups in which they seek the opinions of a carefully chosen 'cross-section' of the voting public. This process, observes Crouch, has 'all the advantages of discovering the public's views without the latter being able to take control of the process for itself.'[11] Meanwhile the new elite talks a private language of its own and has private interests of its own.

It alone can harness the specialised skills that can make post-democracy work. A modern political leader, whether a Blair or a Bush, must surround themselves with members of this new elite – Karl Rove in the case of Bush, Alastair Campbell or Peter Mandelson for Tony Blair. One aspect of their job is to mislead and cheat on behalf of the leader in order to manufacture his image for public consumption. Another is to cut private deals, right away from the public eye, with important corporate and media interest groups. One account of events is given privately to the business interests that fund political parties, another to lobby groups, another to foreign leaders, yet another to the voters through means of the mass media. Thus readers of the *Sun* were told before the 1997 general election of Tony Blair's patriotic affection for sterling, but pro-EU business leaders were left in no doubt of his support for the euro. Ahead of the Iraq War, as we shall see in Chapter 8, the Bush White House was told from an early stage that Britain supported regime change, but the British people were told that 'weapons of mass destruction' were the main issue and that regime change was not a reason for war. There are many comparable examples, a large number cited in this book, of this kind of deceit. In each of these cases the prime minister had a clear objective of his own, but his predicament as a post-democratic leader prevented or discouraged him from revealing what it was to the voters. So he preferred to deceive them, and advance through subterfuge.

This is why it is so easy for advisers like Karl Rove or Alastair Campbell to treat the whole of perceived reality as one enormous fabrication to bolster and support the image of the leader they serve.[12] This approach can often bring short-term advantages. But it means that the population at large ceases to participate in the political process. It has been reduced to the role of dupe or victim, to be manipulated by the expert media and communications manipulators, who have emerged as the new Platonic guardians.

This is a complex new world, where fact and fiction merge. It is important to point out that the abolition of the truth does not merely manifest itself in politics. It is also a phenomenon in other spheres. Public reporting of show business, pop music, football, even the arts is about the creation and display of elaborate fictions. These largely lie outside the scope of this book, but the rise of political lying cannot be understood without a glance at the manipulation and deceit that has come to dominate almost all of British mainstream culture. Romances between pop stars seem to be manufactured in order to sell newly released singles. Access to top celebrities is controlled by PR people and agents who demand rights of copy approval, forcing journalists to produce hopelessly distorted or false copy.[13] Max Clifford, one of the most powerful celebrity PR agents in London, the originator of hundreds of tabloid stories, cheerfully admits to deceit and fabrication. He told the *Observer* newspaper:

'Course I would, 'course I would lie, to you, to the rest of the press, to whoever, whenever . . . If the public are deceived because they believe Rock Hudson or whoever loved the women, and like him for it, and I know the truth, then which is more important? To me, the fact that the public is deceived is no problem, I have no problems at all with that.[14]

Politicians have now become part of this amorphous and corrupted culture. Those who resist assimilation, like the short-lived Tory leader Iain Duncan Smith, are mocked and ridiculed. Those who join the game as a whole flourish and prosper. Tony Blair is the acknowledged expert. Much of his premiership has been based on contrivance and artifice stolen from showbiz. It began on his first day in power, when television viewers witnessed cheering crowds, young children very much to the fore, waving union jacks and greeting the new prime minister as he entered Downing Street. It looked spontaneous, but had all been choreographed well in advance.

Not long before he died the philosopher Bernard Williams, once married to the former cabinet minister Shirley Williams, observed how politicians were being assimilated into showbiz culture, and noted the consequences for political truth. He observed:

Political leaders and aspirants certainly appear before the public and make claims about the world and each other. However, the way in which these people are presented, particularly if they are prominent, creates to a remarkable degree an impression that they are in fact characters in a soap opera being played by people of the same name. They are called by their first names or have the same kind of jokey nicknames as soap opera characters, the same broadly sketched personalities, the same dispositions to triumphs and humiliations which are schematically related to the doings of the other characters. When they reappear, they give off the same impression of remembering only just in time to carry on from where they left off, and they equally disappear into the script of the past after something else more interesting has come up. It would not be right to say that when one takes the view of these people that is offered in the media one does not believe in them. One believes in them as one believes in characters in a soap: one accepts the invitation to half believe in them.[15]

There are many consequences of this kind of emptying out and trivialisation of traditional political culture. The most devastating, as noted by Williams, is that 'the status of politics as represented in the media is ambiguous between entertainment and the transmission of discoverable truth.' There are no rules in this new and unfamiliar world. There is no longer any yardstick against which statements can be judged. Truth-telling boils down to bold assertion and the exercise of power.

This is the environment in which British politicians are now obliged to operate. It is tempting to label it postmodern, it is just as accurate to call it barbaric. Political success falls to the party that can most successfully create and sustain its own version of the truth in the age of mass communication. In the 1980s the winners were the Tory Party, whose electoral success was in part founded on the advice of the advertising agency Saatchi & Saatchi and the endorsement of the media magnate Rupert Murdoch. In the second half of the 1990s New Labour emerged with a far more advanced political technology and even more striking readiness to adapt to the new media brutalism. The next chapter will explain why New Labour was so precisely adapted to a world where truth and falsehood blurred.

6

CONSTRUCTION OF THE TRUTH

'I only know what I believe' – Tony Blair, Labour Party
Conference, 2004

The Divine Right to Lie

It is more than simply the strategic imperative to make headway
within what it regards as a corrupt public culture that gives New
Labour the confidence to deceive. It also feels that another course of
action would be little short of immoral, so much is at stake for the
good of the British people and the nation. Like many movements
from the Left, New Labour cherishes a special sense of its own
virtue. Its politicians and activists genuinely believe that they are
working for the greater good. Lies, frauds and deceit are purely
altruistic.

This means that the Left's attitude towards dissimulation is very
different to the traditional Right. Classical Tories take a gloomy view
of human nature, and interpret it as hopelessly flawed and limited.
They believe that only traditions, rules, institutions, morality and the
other social contrivances can prevent humanity from doing acts of
great harm. The Right believes that no individual or group can break

these rules without paying a great cost, however well intentioned the motive. It is equally suspicious of grand schemes to change humanity or alter society. It feels sure that no group of human beings, however virtuous, can manage change without falling prey to unforeseen consequences. The Left takes a wider and more generous view. It believes in the noble possibilities of human nature and has always looked with a friendly eye on tremendous schemes for the rearrangement of society, regarded with a jaundiced eye by Tories. It feels impatient with institutions, conventions and moral codes that stand in the way of virtuous change. Both Left and Right believe in achieving what they see as the general good: they simply have contradictory ways of going about it.

The profound contrast of visions has all kinds of manifestations, none less significant than attitudes to truth and falsehood. The Left places much greater stress on sincerity. It can excuse falsehood if it thinks that the motive is pure and the ambition is splendid. The Right, sceptical of the ability of mankind to engineer outcomes, looks for scrupulous behaviour in smaller things: duty, obeying the law, telling the truth.

Perhaps this is why, for New Labour, deception and mendacity are more readily excused if they can be placed in a wider context. Why does the small sin of telling a lie in an election campaign matter when set beside the benefits in terms of better hospitals, better schools and the more generous society that will naturally follow if New Labour wins the election? Lies are easily forgiven if they are told for the right reasons and in good faith, especially if your opponent is bent on the destruction of everything that is good and decent, and is a liar to boot. The late trade union leader Alan Fisher, General Secretary of the National Union of Public Employees, is reported to have been in the habit of asking would-be press officers at their final interview: 'Are you prepared to lie on behalf of the union?'[1] Fisher would have considered his question quite legitimate, since the over-riding cause was the betterment of conditions for his union's members.

This helps explain one of the paradoxes about the relationship between New Labour and the truth. Though there is incontrovertible evidence that Tony Blair and his colleagues regularly distort, manipulate, mislead and even invent the truth on a massive scale, they regard any attack on their personal integrity as an outrageous calumny. During the Hutton Inquiry the prime minister declared that the allegations made against him by the BBC 'went in a sense to the credibility, I felt, of the country'.[2] Blair himself has consistently referred to his own integrity in terms which, coming from anyone else, might well be criticised as boastful or vainglorious (see Chapter 1). Even when he or colleagues are caught red-handed telling fibs, New Labour tends to respond that all concerned acted 'in good faith', a key phrase frequently uttered in defence of mendacious ministers. In New Labour's view, the truthfulness of a statement matters much less than whether it was inspired by a virtuous motive.

Sometimes a higher purpose is cited as a justification for falsehood. A revealing example concerns the unsubstantiated claim repeatedly made by the British government that Saddam Hussein's son Udai liked to terrorise the members of the Iraqi football team in order to make them play better. This allegation was given great prominence in December 2002, some four months before the invasion of Iraq, when the Foreign Office issued a dossier of atrocities allegedly committed by Saddam Hussein. The document cited 'one infamous incident of mass torture' when Udai Hussein 'ordered the national football team to be caned on the soles of their feet after losing a World Cup qualifying match.'[3] This was basically a regurgitation of the assertion made four years earlier by Foreign Secretary Robin Cook that, 'A speciality of his [Saddam's] torture is the beating of the soles of the feet, indeed last year his son Udai ordered this punishment for the entire Iraqi football team after they lost a match to qualify for the World Cup.'[4] Unfortunately for the British government, it soon emerged that FIFA, the international football federation, had looked into these allegations some years before and exonerated Iraq.

The revealing aspect was Tony Blair's response when the FIFA investigation was put to him in the House of Commons on 4 December by Labour MP Tam Dalyell. The prime minister showed surprisingly little alarm or distress that the truth of a government assertion, which had been given a prominent role in a document issued only the day before, was being called into question. Instead he indicated that it did not matter whether or not the claim was accurate, because of the over-riding point that Saddam Hussein had committed many other human rights abuses. The Commons exchange was illuminating. Tam Dalyell asked: 'As FIFA investigated this matter and on November 4th 1997 made a statement that there was no truth in it whatever, do the Government have better information on a footballing matter than FIFA?' The prime minister replied: 'No, I would not say that we had better information than FIFA. But leaving aside that incident . . . I ask my hon friend to focus on the human rights abuses in Iraq that are beyond doubt . . . The Iraqi football team may be one matter, but these human rights abuses are self-evident.'[5] In other words the details of what the government said were of little significance, and only an abstract or more general truth mattered.

Tony Blair produced the same category of response when questioned about the failure to find weapons of mass destruction in Iraq. He insisted that the failure to find them was relatively inconsequential, because Saddam Hussein had been toppled. The fact that the British government had cited the existence of WMD as *casus belli* was neither here nor there: the greater good had been achieved. This carelessness about detail is characteristic of a strand of the liberal Left, to which Tony Blair is a broad adherent. As the economist Joseph Schumpeter remarked, 'the first thing a man will do for his ideals is lie'.[6]

It is not unreasonable to speculate that the prime minister has a strong tendency to fall victim to a common conceptual muddle: the failure to understand the distinction between truth versus *falsehood* and truth versus *error*. Tony Blair, and many of his colleagues, consistently seem to feel that they are lucky enough to have been granted a privileged access to the *moral* truth. This state of grace produces two marvellous consequences. It means that whatever New Labour ministers say or write, however misleading or inaccurate, is in a larger sense true. Likewise whatever their opponents say or write, whether or not strictly speaking accurate, is in the most profound sense false. The philosopher Sissela Bok outlines the nature of this confusion: 'Many religious documents or revelations claim to convey what is true. Those who do not accept such a belief are thought to live in error, in ignorance, even in blindness. At times the refusal of nonbelievers to accept the dogma or truth revealed to the faithful is called, not merely an error, but a lie. The battle is seen as one between upholders of the faith and the forces of deception and guile.'[7]

This analysis should not only be brought to bear on religious groups. It can often apply to political parties, as well as individuals within them. As his premiership has persisted, many of Tony Blair's statements have ceased to be grounded in ordinary, practical, testable fact. It is as if he has departed on an epistemological adventure of his own. Towards the end of his life the great Liberal Democrat statesman Roy Jenkins was asked whether he and Paddy Ashdown had been deceived by Blair during their discussions about a Lib/Lab merger. 'I don't think for a moment he deliberately took us for a ride,' said Jenkins. 'A significant remark Paddy made to me was when he friendlily said of Blair: "He always meant it when he said it."'[8] The implications of Paddy Ashdown's insight bear investigation. It suggests that truth for Tony Blair boils down to little more than what he believes or says at a particular moment. On the eve of the Iraq War he told Jeremy Paxman on *Newsnight*: 'I may be wrong about this but it's what I believe.'[9] The appeal here was ultimately not to evidence, or fact, or to documentation and empirical proof. It was a simple statement of strength of conviction and purity of motive. The prime minister produced an even more remarkable comment twelve months later when attempting to explain the failure to find weapons of mass destruction in Iraq: 'I only know what I believe.'

In the summer of 2002 the *New York Times* writer Ron Suskind met a senior adviser at the Bush White House. He was surprised to find that the aide dismissed his remarks:

> The aide said that guys like me were 'in what we call the reality-based community,' which he defined as people who 'believe that solutions emerge from your judicious study of discernible reality.'
> I nodded and murmured something about enlightenment

principles and empiricism. He cut me off. 'That's not the way the world really works any more,' he continued. 'We're an empire now, and when we act, we create our own reality. And while you're studying that reality – judiciously as you will – we'll act again, creating other new realities, which you can study too, and that's how things will sort out.[10]

The logical consequences of this doctrine, as set out by the anonymous Bush aide or the British prime minister speaking to his party conference, are startling. It gives Bush or Blair total freedom to make whatever statement they like about Iraq, about weapons of mass destruction, or for that matter to attest that the moon is made of green cheese. Perhaps this is what allows George Bush to announce, as he did in May 2003, that 'we have found the weapons of mass destruction.'[11] Perhaps it enables the prime minister unblushingly to contradict himself as much as he likes. Thus he told the 2002 party conference: 'The test is to listen, adapt and move forward,' but informed delegates twelve months later that 'I've not got a reverse gear.' Sometimes it helps him talk the sheerest nonsense as when, at the 1999 party conference, he told his audience: 'Everyone within the next two years will be able to see an NHS dentist just by phoning NHS Direct.' The political commentator Matthew Parris caught the flavour of this bogus remark when he wrote four years later: 'I don't mind that he said it without quite knowing how he would deliver it. Politicians do that kind of thing. I mind that he did say it; did not make any serious attempt to deliver it; has never bothered to explain when he might or why he can't; and presumably just thinks we'll all put it from our minds, as he has.'[12]

Postmodernism and Political Lying

This hostility to a 'reality-based' analysis of events in the outside world, such a driving force in the Bush administration and marked feature in Tony Blair's personal rhetoric, marks a prodigious episte-mological leap among the governing class on both sides of the Atlantic. It is far too soon to make an authoritative sketch of the origins, let alone outline the consequences, of this spectacular change in outlook and procedure inside the White House and 10 Downing Street. It can, however, be traced back tentatively to two doctrines, one exceptionally ancient and the other strikingly con-temporary.

The first is the religious tradition, powerfully appropriated by the religious right in the United States, which rejects the modern scien-tific method and prefers to base its understanding of the external world on close study of long-established texts. It is relatively easy to discern the impact of this methodology on the Republican Party and the Bush White House, somewhat less so on Tony Blair's Downing Street. A number of friendly and well-informed com-mentators have, however, placed great stress on the importance of Blair's personal relationship with God as the decisive factor in key decisions, above all the 2003 invasion of Iraq.[13]

The second doctrine is postmodernism, which has become a fashionable orthodoxy among teachers of philosophy, and indeed other academic disciplines, in universities on both sides of the Atlantic. Postmodernism is one modern manifestation of extreme philosophical scepticism, a tradition which can be traced right back to the beginnings of thought and the ancient Greek school of Pyrrho. This school despaired of the notion that truth was accessible and deduced that no ultimately stable distinction could be drawn between truth and falsehood.

At first sight there seems all the world of difference between a knowing, ironic, secular doctrine like postmodernism and the roaring fundamentalism of the religious Right in the United States. The one denies that the truth can ever be known, while the other makes emphatic truth claims that permit no rival nor rebuttal. Yet they converge around one crucial point of agreement: words like falsehood, accuracy and deception, at any rate as used in ordinary speech, have no validity. Both doctrines are obsessed with the truth in the largest sense. But neither is much concerned with its narrow dictionary meaning. The religious Right is preoccupied with fighting the eternal battle between truth and error, while postmodernism concerns itself with the competing claims of rival truths. The idea of verifiable reality, so important to the Anglo-American school of empirical philosophy, is dismissed as an absurdity.

Postmodern thinking grew up in the astonishingly influential school of French philosophy which flourished in the 1970s and 1980s and is perhaps associated in particular with the historian and philosopher Michel Foucault and the philosopher Jacques Derrida. Foucault ridiculed the notion that truth could be independently available, asserting that it only made sense as part of a wider system of politics or society. 'Truth is to be understood,' he argued in one of his typically unfathomable remarks, 'as a system of ordered procedures for the production, regulation, distribution, circulation and operation of statements. Truth is linked in a circular relation with systems of power which produce and sustain it, and to effects of power which it induces and which extend it.'[14] Truth was, for Foucault, no more than an effect of the rules of discourse, itself a highly problematic concept, and for Foucault all discourses were equally valid. Perception and truth were there to be created. Though he was famous for historical studies of sex, madness and prisons, Foucault declared that 'I am well aware that I have not written anything but fictions.' Foucault sometimes argued that truth was the effect of power relations, the expression of dominance, whether political, economic or sexual. This idea was used, for instance, by Edward Said to demonstrate how 'orientalism' created the mental boundaries for Western understanding of the Middle East in the nineteenth century.

The influential American philosopher Richard Rorty helped take the work of Foucault and Derrida across the Atlantic. Rorty shared the view of the French school that truth claims could never be incontestably grounded, and argued that an alternative way of giving weight to words was to 'construct' what he called a 'narrative'. This has the effect of shifting the emphasis of argument from truths which can be verified to 'narratives' that can be manufactured.[15]

Right from the start of the Blair period, these twin phrases – 'narrative' and 'discourse' – fascinated New Labour intellectuals. Agonisingly aware how the British Left had become associated with degradation and failure, New Labour thinkers were fascinated by the way the Conservative Party, through Margaret Thatcher, had created what they saw as a benign myth which carried great power in the public mind. The Left resolved to create an alternative. The historian Tristram Hunt, a protégé of Peter Mandelson who at one stage worked as a neophyte inside New Labour's Millbank machine but nevertheless retained an independence of intellect by no means guaranteed among the elite graduates of that seminary, has given an interesting glimpse into the political utility of the postmodernist concept of narrative. Writing some time after the 1997 general election victory, Hunt wrote:

> It is this use of power to close down alternative visions of the past that makes the idea of narrative so irresistible to politicians. Once the New Right had established the idea of British postwar decline as the dominant discourse, Thatcher's narrative of neoliberal renewal seemed all the more convincing. The self-imposed challenge for New Labour appears to be to establish the 1980s as a valueless time when there was no such thing as society, and boom and bust stalked the land.[16]

The passage above could not have been written either by a Tory or by an Old Labour writer. What makes it quite unmistakably New Labour is the assumption that political reality was not something that exists 'out there', checkable and subject to independent verification. On the contrary, it has suddenly become something that can be shaped and used as part of the battle for power. Tory Party propagandists certainly used advertising and other techniques to make the most of Mrs Thatcher's various triumphs and play down her mistakes and failures. But they never departed from the common sense assumption that her national reputation was firmly based on what they continued to think of as real achievements like the Falklands War and the defeat of the miners' strike. Old Labour was no more imaginative. It stolidly continued to present what it saw as the truth.

New Labour has always felt liberated from this boring reliance on mere facts. From the very beginning it believed that reality was capable of being created afresh. It imported the postmodernist notion of 'narrative', and the associated proposition that the truth is something that can artfully be 'constructed', into the British political system. It is quite easy to show that this is the case through the use of traditional empirical methods, thankfully without recourse either to the language or the methods of the French philosophical school. It can be done through study of use of the word 'narrative' in British political debate, and ordinary language, over the past two decades.

This is an elementary exercise to carry out, greatly helped by the search engine on the Hansard website and the easy availability of newspaper databases. According to the *Oxford English Dictionary*, the word narrative has no less than three meanings. There is a strict legal usage, dating back centuries: 'that part of a deed or document which contains a statement of the relevant or essential facts'. There is a literary usage: 'an account or narration; a history, a tale, story, recital (of facts etc)'. It can also be used to describe 'the practice or act of narrating; something to narrate'.

Nowhere does the *OED* refer to the kind of use made of the word 'narrative' by postmodern theorists. That is not surprising. This usage, while prevalent in philosophical schools and university English faculties for two decades, did not start to enter more general circulation until the early 1990s. The evidence suggests that this was a direct result of the emergence of New Labour.

The first case I have found of the word being given its novel meaning, but used outside its academic birthplace, comes in spring 1994. The agent of this act of liberation was none other than the New Labour intellectual Geoff Mulgan, founder of the Demos think tank from which Tony Blair pillaged so many of his ideas, and later to hold powerful jobs in Downing Street and Whitehall. He was writing shortly before the death of John Smith. 'But now under John

Smith,' complained Mulgan, 'all sense of narrative seems to drown in a morass of platitudes about social justice and economic efficiency.'[17] The Mulgan article appeared at the very end of the two-year period between the resignation of Neil Kinnock and the death of John Smith when the New Labour clique – Peter Mandelson, Philip Gould, Alastair Campbell, Tony Blair – were out of sympathy with the leadership and played the role of an internal opposition. Mulgan supported this faction and frequently articulated its concerns. It is highly significant that this very early New Labour use of the term 'narrative' in its postmodern mode should crop up in the context of an attack on Smith, scornful as he was of the modernisers and an old-fashioned social democratic politican.

Mulgan seems to have concluded that the word, with all the weight placed upon it by postmodern thinkers, was far too good to be wasted upon academics. The following July, the month that Tony Blair was crowned party leader, Mulgan teamed up with another New Labour intellectual, Charles Leadbeater, to write: 'Politics is essentially about communicating ideas, choices and decisions between the governed and the governors. It is about constructing narratives that make sense to people: stories that encompass their identities, aspirations and fears, and the policies that reflect them. Yet it is in these central tasks that politicians seem at times to be most deficient.'[18] (The inventive Leadbeater at this stage was an assistant editor of the *Independent* newspaper where, the same year, with the author Helen Fielding, he dreamed up the Bridget Jones's Diary column.)

Will Hutton, then a fashionable economics commentator friendly to Tony Blair, was swift to spot and make use of the neologism. He lamented in the *Guardian* on 9 July 1995 that the Labour Party's policy commissions 'have not been organised into a strong political narrative and sold hard'. Hutton soon embraced the term as if it were his own. The following year he once again scornfully blamed the traditional Left for failure to organise a 'strong political narrative'. He said that 'the Old Labour left still hankers for more traditional responses'. Once again the postmodern concept of narrative is being used to express the concerns of the New Labour faction around Tony Blair, and undermine the traditional methods of the Labour Party.

Peter Mandelson, the foremost New Labour strategist, understood the thinking, or at any rate employed the language, of postmodernism. He entertained the proposition that truth is independent from reality with an alarming enthusiasm, announcing to an interviewer in August 1997 that he pleaded guilty to the charge of trying to create the truth. 'If you're accusing me of getting the truth across about what the Government has decided to do, that I'm putting the very best face or gloss on the Government's policies, that I'm trying to avoid gaffes or setbacks and that I'm trying to create the truth – if that's news management, I plead guilty.'[19] I e-mailed Mandelson some years later to ask him exactly what he meant. He claimed he had meant something else. His full reply read as follows: 'In haste: the quote (of which I have no memory) reads a bit like a stream of Mandelson consciousness. I was not weighing every word (or so it seems to me). If I am quoted accurately – I cannot verify – it seems fine that I would have meant 'establish' rather than 'create'. You cannot create truth although you can create an understanding of truth.'[20] Purists are entitled to object that there was a Stalinist as well as postmodern undertone in this Mandelson remark – a thoroughgoing postmodernist would have said that 'I'm trying to create a truth.'

As far as I can discern, the first MP of any party to give the word 'narrative' its postmodern meaning in parliament was the modernising Labour MP Patricia Hewitt, soon to accelerate through the ranks of the Blair government, when taking evidence on the Social Security Committee in June 1998. She declared that 'for these measures to mean something they have to reflect a story, there has to be a narrative in here'. To be sure, the old uses of the word persisted. The Labour MP Joyce Quin, not a member of the Blairite vanguard, attempted to stem the tide when she used the word in its increasingly quaint dictionary sense, referring to the 'narrative report accompanying the expenditure of the Foreign and Commonwealth Office'. Lord Donoughue, a Downing Street aide during the long-lost days of the Harold Wilson governments, nostalgically informed the House of Lords that 'the Victorian County Histories include narrative and analysis and [are] a key part of our national heritage.'[21] Doubtless all this was the case. But resistance was useless. By the start of 2000, the new usage had become commonplace in parliament. Even comparatively obscure Labour MPs like Angela Eagle were thoughtlessly adopting the postmodern idiom. 'We shall be extremely interested to ascertain whether we can establish an effective narrative on rights and responsibilities.' Soon it was being let loose on the television studios. Ace Labour strategist Douglas Alexander told *Newsnight* in March 2002 that 'we face a challenge of explaining not just policy changes but the political narrative that accompanies it.'[22]

Towards the end of 2000 the word starts to crop up in lobby briefings by Alastair Campbell, the prime minister's official spokesman (PMOS). In September that year he was telling journalists that 'the Prime Minister and Chancellor were absolutely clear that we had an under-invested country and we had to take the decisions necessary to modernise it for the long term. This was the narrative of this Government for this Parliament and it was not going to change.' In December the PMOS pronounced that, 'As the Prime Minister had said on Friday there was a clear narrative to this Parliament. We believed the economic foundations that had been laid were strengthening.' The following month the PMOS declared that 'we had always recognised there would be an economic narrative to this Parliament' that 'there was a narrative for our public services which was unfolding' that 'clearly there was an overall narrative to the Government's public service reform agenda' and that 'there was a clear narrative for our public services'.[23]

Political commentators and, very shortly afterwards, modernising Tories anxious to ape Tony Blair's success, were all at it. The post-modern use of the word narrative, released from its thralldom to academia by Geoff Mulgan, had become what the grammarian H.W. Fowler deprecated as a Vogue Word. This is Fowler's definition:

> Every now and then a word emerges from obscurity, or even from nothingness, or a merely potential and not actual existence, into sudden popularity. It is often, but not necessarily, one that by no means explains itself to the average man, who has to find out its meanings as best he can. His wrestlings with it have usually some effect upon it; it does not mean quite what it ought to, but to make up for that it means some things that it ought not to, by the time he has done with it.*[24]

---

* 'Narrative' also manifests many of the qualities attached by Fowler to what he terms 'slipshod extension', which 'is especially likely to occur when some accident gives currency among the uneducated to words of learned origin . . .'

In a House of Lords debate on 31 October 2000 the political scientist Lord Dahrendorf noted the derivation, and significance, of the new usage. Talking about the so called 'Third Way', an ineffable doctrine conjured up by New Labour thinkers eager to lend coherence to the Blair government, Dahrendorf observed: 'The Third Way was never actually a programme. It was intended to be what in postmodern language – not mine really – would be called a narrative.' He went on:

> It is a narrative in the sense that it was intended to provide a big story which pulled together the necessarily varied and diverse strands of the policy of a government. Such big stories are rare. I am not talking about the very big stories of communism and fascism, I am talking about the next level – the national big stories.
>
> There were two big stories, whatever one feels about them. There was the Attlee story of extended citizenship rights for all and everything that goes with the extension of citizenship rights, not least as a response to the experience of the nation during the war.
>
> There was the big story which one might call the Thatcher story of rolling back the state, and perhaps curtailing private power within the country in the interest of a more open economy and society.
>
> If one does not have a narrative of this major kind, one is left with a list of achievements. That is fine. But it marks the difference between great governments and good governments. New Labour at a certain point hoped to have such a narrative.

Lord Dahrendorf's remarks help explain how New Labour appropriated the idea of 'narrative' to illuminate its presence in government, and create an explanatory framework that would define the political landscape in its own terms. It is noteworthy that it has its origins in a school of philosophy that holds that standards of truth and falsehood are determined by power and experience. The prime minister has often spoken of his desire to 'modernise' Britain. But it is rather more accurate to assert that he and his New Labour co-conspirators set out to postmodernise British political debate. As Tony Blair and his New Labour faction seized power in the Labour Party, they set about – to use their own own private language, purloined from French postmodern philosophical salons – the 'construction' of the truth.

7

CONSTRUCTING A CULTURE OF DECEIT

'When I joined the lobby in 1992, I would abandon a story if No 10 denied it. By the time I left I sometimes felt justified in merely recording the denial at the bottom' – Robert Shrimsley, News Editor, *Financial Times*, who left the lobby in 2002.

New Labour's desire to 'construct' the truth differentiated the party sharply both from the 'Old' Labour values of John Smith and John Major's seedy but shambolic Tories. This insight helped produce one insight into government which had never been applied in the past: that reality and presentation were identical. This was rich with practical consequences.

Like Bishop Berkeley New Labour believed that *Esse est percipi* – to be is to be perceived. Berkeley used this proposition to demonstrate the existence of God. New Labour used it to create spin-doctors. The term 'spin-doctor', like the modish use of the word 'narrative', only came into widespread use in Britain in the early 1990s. Spin-doctor, though also to become indelibly associated with New Labour, arrived first. The term, said to have derived from baseball, first became current in the United States in the 1980s before spreading to Britain. Spin-doctor was more than just a smart term to glamorise press officers: it usefully indicated a change both in role and status.

Press officers in Whitehall had been around since before the Second World War. They performed an essential, but lowly, function: the communication of facts about the activities of government departments to journalists. Though there were a few startling exceptions, they carried out their job unobtrusively. They did not seek, as a general rule, to take the initiative. Nor did they become involved with policy-making in their own departments. Instead they confined themselves to acting as a useful conduit, or just as often barrier, between ministers and the press. It was this modesty of demeanour and ambition that inspired New Labour's contempt.

Tony Blair demanded an entirely new, interventionist, activist, system of news dissemination that went out and aggressively made the government's case. He was responsible for the creation of a machine that was prepared to harass, bully, lie and smear in order to ensure that the government made its case.* This kind of work needed to be carried out by a trusted cadre of Labour loyalists, not old-style Whitehall press officers. Within two years of taking power in 1997 New Labour had sacked seventeen of the nineteen infor-

---

* The bullying, smears and harassment are strictly beyond the scope of this book. They are nevertheless well documented. Political opponents, inconvenient ministers and awkward members of the public could all be targeted. Cabinet ministers Gordon Brown, Mo Mowlam, Clare Short, David Clark and others were subject to this treatment from Labour spin-doctors and loyalists. So were the Paddington rail crash victims and other innocent bystanders. See Beckett and Hencke, Oborne and Walters, and others.

mation chiefs in Whitehall, a staggeringly high turnover. It sought spin-doctors who would go out and promote the government message using methods and on a scale that had never been used or envisaged before. New Labour told government press officers: 'We had a very successful operation in opposition and we intend to use the same techniques to ensure we get good coverage for government events and the government generally. We are going to take the initiative with the media announcing stories in a cycle determined by us.'[1] New Labour did not merely obtain power in May 1997. It set out to obtain ownership of the truth.

This doctrine led to a number of consequences. One of them was a dramatic change in the role of Downing Street press secretary. This job had always carried weight. But it could never be compared in status or power to other senior posts around the prime minister: cabinet secretary, private secretary, head of the policy unit, foreign affairs adviser. Bernard Ingham was a famously dominant press secretary under Margaret Thatcher. But even he was a less considerable figure by some distance than John Redwood, when he was policy chief, or foreign affairs expert Charles Powell.*

With New Labour this relationship changed. The new importance of presentation radically transformed the power of the Downing Street media boss. Tony Blair's press secretary Alastair Campbell, later to be given the grander title of Director of Communication and Strategy, overshadowed his policy chief David Miliband. In an unprecedented move Campbell's authority was

---

* In the last years of Margaret Thatcher, as she grew isolated and dependent on old trusties like Bernard Ingham, this situation changed to some extent. During this period, Ingham's role in a minor way anticipated the Blair arrangement, in which the spin-doctor was the dominant figure in Downing Street.

entrenched by the issue of special Orders in Council within days of the 1997 election.

This move was unsuccessfully resisted by then Cabinet Secretary Sir Robin Butler, and for a very telling reason. These Orders in Council gave Campbell, a political appointee or 'special adviser', special powers to take executive authority over civil servants. This breached the key constitutional principle, dating back to the great Gladstonian reforms of the mid-nineteenth century, that the machinery of government should be kept free from party influence. Civil servants were supposed to be disinterested servants of the state, owing their loyalty to the Crown, not to the government of the day. For the first time in 150 years this principle was smashed. Campbell's explicit loyalty lay not to the Crown but to the prime minister and to the Labour Party.

He nevertheless had the power to appropriate the resources of government. He saw his job quite clearly as to carry out a party political function from within Downing Street. Campbell fostered a cadre of New Labour apparatchiks to do the same from outlying Whitehall departments. Jo Moore, the disgraced special adviser at the Department of Transport, was one of them. Even after she had been caught abusing the truth, and faced allegations of bullying, Campbell and Tony Blair fought hard to save her. Joe McCrae, who gave the game away when he boasted that he told civil servants that 'you can't win twenty-first-century political battles with techniques and technology from 30 years ago', was another. He was based at the Department of Health and the Cabinet Office.

Just as New Labour elided reality and perception, it also trans-gressed the boundary between party and state. Information had come to be seen primarily as a political tool, to be used sparingly and for party advantage. One important and evocative example of New Labour's ownership of the truth was its approach to parliamentary questions. Civil servants were asked to investigate the background and motives of MPs before answering their queries. Officials were instructed to determine whether a question was 'friendly'. Political profiles of MPs were consulted before questions were answered. In other words facts were no longer neutral matter, the common property of all citizens and political parties. They were, in the opinion of government, loaded. Of course all previous governments had sought to prevent the issue of embarrassing information. But this became systemic under New Labour.[2]

Thanks to his new role as press secretary, and the powers that came with it, Alastair Campbell became the most powerful figure in Downing Street besides the prime minister. He was able to order most cabinet ministers – Chancellor Gordon Brown was an exception – around more or less as he liked, and exert enormous power throughout Whitehall. In due course, in a frightening abuse, he was even allowed to chair meetings with intelligence personnel present. The emergence of New Labour, with its novel emphasis on presentation, had turned traditional procedure upside down. It had converted the press secretary, hitherto a relatively humdrum role, into a figure which shaped the culture both of Downing Street and Whitehall. This was to have dramatic consequences for the integrity of British government.

Tony Blair did not make one of the party intellectuals his information chief. Instead he chose a political bruiser with a background in tabloid newspapers. Though no intellectual Alastair Campbell was highly intelligent, with an animal instinct for how power works and how to use it. He set the tone for New Labour's style in government from his appointment as press secretary in 1997 to his departure in the wake of the death of the government scientist Dr David Kelly in 2003.

Alastair Campbell's Reverence for the Truth – and Hatred of Liars

Campbell has repeatedly insisted that he never told, and would never have dreamt of telling, lies. In 1997 he told the journalist John Mulholland of the *Guardian* that he would never lie. 'There are certain things you just won't talk about,' he informed Mulholland, 'but I think lying is something completely different.' Campbell conceded that on occasions he told falsehoods or misled journalists, but these occasions were inadvertent and not his fault: 'There are occasions where I have been misinformed. But I've always tried to correct things if I do misinform people.'[3] Seven years later, and out of Downing Street, he told the same story to interviewer Robert Crampton of *The Times Magazine*, only with even greater emphasis: 'If you were in the position I was in and you tell a single lie you're out, you're finished, you're dead.'[4]

It should be stressed that Campbell was not alone in paying tribute to his own honesty. When he announced that he was standing down in the summer of 2003, the cabinet minister Tessa Jowell testified to his 'integrity'. Roy Greenslade, the *Guardian*'s media commentator, went further still, declaring that 'Campbell had never lied to me, that I had never found him out in a lie, and never been knowingly misled by him'.[5]

Alastair Campbell, both during his time in Downing Street and still more forcefully since, has always made clear that respect for truth was at the heart of everything he did. Speaking in front of a Commons committee after stepping down from office he defined his job as 'putting a case in public, founded on fact, founded on truth, founded on what the politicians have decided they are going to say in opposition or do in government'. He insisted that politicians have a 'responsibility to tell the truth'.[6]

He always maintains with real passion and vehemence that the New Labour government is straightforward and honest. But this admirable love of truth and probity is, if anything, exceeded by his special horror of falsehood. Campbell loves wearily to contrast his own palpable integrity with the mendacity, bad faith or deception of others. He is very quick off the mark to level deadly accusations of falsehood, bad faith and lying at political opponents, journalists and hostile regimes.

Journalists are a frequent target of Alastair Campbell's invective. According to him: 'They write drivel. They write rubbish. They tell lies.'[7] He complained that they do not merely tell lies on their own behalf, but on behalf of Britain's enemies. Before the invasion of Afghanistan he appealed to the media not to take note of claims by the Taliban government:

I am not asking the media to take sides with us, but the media does have a duty to take sides between truth and falsehood . . . The media have responsibilities beyond simply saying, 'One side says this, the other side says that . . . I don't think the media should suspend its own moral judgement . . . When [Zaeef] says, 'We have shot down a B-52 bomber', or 'We know the Americans have been using chemical and biological weapons', these things are proven to be untrue. I can't for the life of me understand why journalists who sat there and listened to the first pack of lies don't say to him, 'why should we believe a single word you say, when you sat there yesterday and gave us a different pack of lies?'[8]

Ahead of the Iraq War, he made a similar complaint to Australian Broadcasting about the onerous demands placed upon the British government to tell the truth. 'In democracies we are expected to explain, we cannot tell lies in the way that dictatorships tell lies all the time. It gives them an advantage in the way this thing is prosecuted.'[9]

Alastair Campbell does not merely denounce journalists for telling lies. His central proposition is that the twenty-first-century British media are a dangerously destructive force because they treat politics in an unrelentingly negative way. He frequently claims that when he was a journalist he had been different, and more generous about the political process than reporters today. 'I always respected politicians,' he told an audience at the Foreign Press Association in November 2003. Writing the previous year in the *British Journalism Review*, Campbell said: 'I also felt I had a sort of respect for the politics and the political process and I felt there was an alternative that I'd speak up for. Today there is a fostering of cynicism and disillusion about politics, and in some quarters, I think, about pretty much everything else as well.'[10]

A Closer Inspection of Campbell's Daunting Claims

These assertions by Campbell that he was less destructive or cynical than other journalists are wholly false and self-serving. Indeed there is no example of a practising political reporter on a mainstream British newspaper, tabloid or broadsheet, who would use anything like the kind of offensive or contemptuous language that were Campbell's stock in trade before working for Tony Blair. He once labelled John Major 'this piece of lettuce that passes for prime minister'. In one column he boasted that Major, shortly after becoming prime minister, had paused to chat with him on an overseas trip. Campbell boasted to his readers that he had responded as follows: 'Oh sod off, Prime Minister. I'm trying to do my expenses.' On another occasion he called Major 'simply a shallow, lying little toad of a man'.[11]

All this from a man who, when giving evidence to the Intelligence and Security Committee in his capacity of director of Communications and Strategy in Downing Street, solemnly lamented that Britain was in a 'new age' and a 'world where sadly the word of public figures is not always taken at face value. It is a world where the automatic respect, if you like, that was given to certain bodies and institutions is no longer there.'[12]

Far from being reverential towards politicians and politics, as he mendaciously claims, he abused his privileged position as a reporter to hand out vindictive abuse both in print and in person which seemed improper then and still seems improper today. Campbell boasted at the time that it was he who had put into general circulation the story that John Major tucked his shirt into his underpants. He doled out these kinds of insults far and wide. Lord Spencer was denounced as a 'hypocritical upper class little pillock', his sister Princess Diana 'vacuous, shallow, silly and egomaniacal' and Prince Charles 'an overprivileged twit'.[13]

Campbell was not merely hopelessly misrepresenting his credentials as a responsible political journalist. He had a track record of mendacity that was far more shameless than anything committed by the reporters he enjoys denouncing today. Many reporters have got stories wrong, but comparatively few have actually made one up, like the notorious *New York Times* reporter Jayson Blair who was sacked after a long history of plagiarism and fabrication was exposed. Alastair Campbell came close to a Jayson Blair moment came when he reported on the *Daily Mirror* front page that the campaigner Jill Morrell was to be asked to stand as a Labour MP. Campbell later admitted that the story about Jill Morrell, girlfriend of Beirut hostage John McCarthy, was completely untrue. After filing his copy he told a rival journalist, Jon Craig: 'It's bollocks. I wouldn't touch it if I were you.' *Mirror* colleagues speculated that he filed the story to distract attention because Neil Kinnock had been 'getting a hammering from the Tory papers'.[14]

Campbell was happy to write partial and misleading articles in order to help the *Daily Mirror* or its proprietor, the tycoon Robert Maxwell. One memorable example was a sycophantic profile of an American politician named John Tower, whose nomination by President George Bush as US Defense Secretary had been rejected after allegations of womanising, drinking and conflicts of interests thanks to links with the defence industry. The article claimed Tower had been the victim of an injustice, and blamed the 'media' for causing his downfall. It did not mention that Tower was a business crony of Maxwell who had just been given a place on the board of his £1.5 billion Macmillan Publishing group (not to be confused with the British publisher of the same name), as well as other Maxwell concerns.[15]

Campbell was often ready to carry out favours for his proprietor Robert Maxwell. He vigorously took the tycoon's side in his feud against the Tory MP Rupert Allason, a feud which eventually led to an unusual legal case in 1996, when Allason took Campbell and Mirror Group Newspapers to court on a charge of malicious false-hood. Allason claimed that Campbell had fabricated a *Daily Mirror* story in November 1992 which stated that fifty MPs had signed a Commons Early Day motion urging Allason to give a £250,000 libel pay out from the *Mirror* to Mirror Group pensioners. The *Mirror* admitted that the story was wrong (only seven MPs had signed the motion and the pay out was £200,000). The paper also admitted organising the EDM. Allason's most damaging allegation was that Campbell had organised it because he held a grudge against the MP. Campbell admitted he disliked Allason, but said that he had had nothing to do with the EDM: it was the idea of his deputy David Bradshaw. This story was backed up by Bradshaw and in the absence of proof of financial loss the case was settled.

In his summing up, however, the judge, Sir Maurice Drake, was scathing about Campbell. He said: 'I did not find Mr Campbell by any means a wholly satisfactory or convincing witness', adding that 'Mr Campbell was less than completely open and frank, he did not impress me as a witness in whom I could feel 100 per cent confident.'[16]

Campbell's very breakthrough into mainstream journalism was partly based around deception. His first appearance in a mainstream Fleet Street newspaper came in the *Sun* on Friday 9 May 1980. A photograph of Campbell appeared next to the headline 'Wanted – Men for Hire'. In this article Campbell was quoted at great length passing himself off as a professional gigolo operating in the South of France. 'The women I met were mainly between 35 and 50 and wanted a young man who would make them feel good. It was all done very discreetly,' Campbell informed the *Sun* reporter Liz Hodgkinson.[17] Today she remembers being convinced by Campbell's story: 'He told me that he had acted as a gigolo in the South of France and that all those middle-aged women down there were gagging for it and he was providing it. I had no reason to disbelieve him.' Later, however, Campbell insisted that this youthful account that he worked as a gigolo was all 'totally in the imagination'.[18]

Lying for Tony in Opposition

Alastair Campbell was appointed press secretary to Tony Blair approximately six weeks after Blair was elected Labour leader in the summer of 1994. It was not long before Campbell had started to mislead journalists. The first reporter who formed the impression that his account of events could be partial and not wholly reliable was Nicholas Jones, the BBC political correspondent. After Tony Blair dropped his Clause Four bombshell at the Labour Party Conference of 1994, Jones suggested on air that 'John Prescott was only on board a week ago and did advise against it.'

This was, for New Labour, a damaging suggestion. The proposal to drop Clause Four – the party's constitutional commitment to a continuing programme of nationalisation – could not have been more sensitive or more potentially explosive. Any notion that the Deputy Leader of the Labour Party had reservations about dropping it was inflammatory. After the broadcast, according to Jones's account, Campbell asked to see him. He told Jones that Prescott had been aware of the move for several weeks and had been 'fully on board every step of the way'.[19] Campbell used the episode to humiliate the BBC man publicly and demonstrate the muscle and firepower of his own press machine.

Campbell's assertion that Prescott was 'on board all the way' is simply wrong. Prescott's biographer, Colin Brown, provides a detailed account of his conversion to the proposal that Clause Four should be abolished. He makes plain that it was a laborious process in which Campbell himself played a prominent role. Brown records that the 'deputy leader maintained his opposition right up to seeing the first drafts of Blair's speech for the conference. Then, like a reluctant craftsman, drawn into a project to make it work, Prescott relented.'[20]

Another episode before the 1997 election showed how obstructive Campbell and New Labour were capable of being. Early the previous year the *Sunday Express* ran a story that a close and intimate political friendship had sprung up between Tony Blair and Roy Jenkins. With Blair facing dissent on the left of the party, the report highlighted the sensitive issue of New Labour collaboration with the old Social Democrats who had broken away from Michael Foot's Labour Party in the early 1980s. When the *Express* rang Campbell for confirmation the story was comprehensively rubbished. The denial was specific. It was claimed that the two men had met only once since Tony Blair had become Labour leader, at a dinner with a number of others present. The paper, confident of its sources, went ahead and ran its account anyway. The *Sunday Times* tried to follow up the *Express*. Michael Prescott, the paper's political correspondent, rang Peter Mandelson for confirmation, but he too denied it. A month later a television programme made by Michael Cockerell showed that the *Express* story was even truer than its reporters had realised. It proved that Jenkins and Blair had become personally and politically close, and showed that Blair had even been a welcome visitor at Jenkins's country home.[21]

These two episodes demonstrate Alastair Campbell's readiness to lie while Labour was in opposition. More significant by far, Campbell imported his culture of deception from opposition into 10 Downing Street, the heart of government.

Lying for Tony in Government

Tony Blair must have known about Alastair Campbell's record as a journalist, and the withering assessment of his integrity from the High Court judge Sir Maurice Drake, when he appointed him Downing Street press secretary in 1997. But there is no record that the prime minister was at all disturbed by it, any more than Peter Mandelson's well-earned reputation for dissimulation and falsity seems to have worried Tony Blair at this stage.

It is still not appreciated well enough, even by quite seasoned Whitehall observers, what a very sharp change in culture and approach Alastair Campbell represented. It is certainly the case that in opposition Labour spokespeople had been accustomed to use the phrase 'Tory lie machine' and other formulations. In reality, however, the integrity of Downing Street itself – as opposed to some individual ministers and Tory backbench MPs – never came under question.

This was in part because the post of press secretary was always given to a career civil servant of reasonably high calibre. This meant that there was a minimum of conflict of interest between the political and government machines. The civil servants had their long-term careers and reputations to consider. While they doubtless became personally attached to the politicians they served, they never owed a loyalty to the governing party. Like all civil servants, they were prepared to serve under a government of any colour.

There was never an issue surrounding the integrity of any of the press secretaries during the John Major years. Gus O'Donnell (1990–94) was widely liked and trusted by journalists. After his stint in Downing Street he returned to the Treasury, where he is now permanent secretary. Christopher Meyer (1994–6) was a career Foreign Office official who served as ambassador to Washington in the Blair government. Jonathan Haslam (1996–7) in due course left the civil service to find a job in the City of London. None of them were regarded as liars by those they dealt with.

Bernard Ingham, Margaret Thatcher's press secretary from 1979 to 1990, was attacked for allowing himself to become too political. And it is certainly the case that Ingham stayed around for a dangerously long time, and became much closer to the prime minister than either of John Major's three press secretaries. But no journalist ever successfully accused Ingham of acting in bad faith. Shortly after he stepped down in 1990 one political journalist, Anthony Bevins, attempted to accuse Ingham of manipulating the media. This produced an immediate response from other lobby journalists. Trevor Kavanagh of the *Sun*, in his formal capacity of chairman of the lobby, wrote a letter of protest, attesting that Ingham was 'straight as a gun barrel'. Before writing this letter he consulted colleagues from other papers, including Alastair Campbell who was then political editor of the *Daily Mirror*. According to Kavanagh, Campbell 'agreed without demur at all.'* Campbell himself was different. He changed the nature of 10 Downing Street so that it became permissible to lie, deceive and cheat.

---

* Conversation with Trevor Kavanagh. Kavanagh, who is often accused of being too close to Downing Street, says that he could not have written such a letter about Campbell. He insists, however, that he 'would have been happy to write the same about Gus O'Donnell, Chris Meyer or Jonathan Haslam'.

Under Campbell, the Downing Street machine continued to insist on its honesty and probity. Godric Smith, a Downing Street spokesman, told lobby journalists on 14 February 2002: 'You can say what you like about us but we don't lie.' Godric Smith himself did manage to fight his corner and salvage a reputation amid the general wreckage. But as a general rule, Smith's proposition that Downing Street did not lie was false.

The ugly habit of mendacity meant that working journalists simply ceased to believe what Number 10 spokesmen and spokeswomen say any more. The situation has become so grievous that Robert Shrimsley, news editor of the *Financial Times*, a paper typically sympathetic to the government, felt compelled to write in 2003: 'When I joined the lobby in 1992, I would abandon a story if Number 10 denied it. By the time I left I sometimes felt justified in merely recording the denial at the bottom.' Robert Peston, then the *FT*'s political editor, made the same observation: 'With previous press secretaries one always thought that if one asked the right question one would get the right answer. Not necessarily with Alastair. He was more obsessed with controlling the flow of information.'[22]

Almost every crisis faced by the prime minister – examples include the death of David Kelly, the Mittal Affair, 'Cheriegate', the Hinduja Affair, Black Rod, and the Foot and Mouth crisis – have either been accompanied or brought about by government deception and falsehood. Many of these episodes are well enough known not to need too much treatment here. The casual cynicism of the deception is often breathtaking. Campbell's record of deception, half-truth, deviousness and straight mendacity is extensive. He was on the whole a fairly cunning, sophisticated and inventive liar, so it is helpful to break down his various perversions of the truth into certain core categories or variations.

Deviousness

Campbell was fond of using a methodology of deceit which, while not necessarily resorting to falsehood, created, and was intended to create, a false impression in the mind of the questioner. A critical early example of this form of mendacity was Campbell's official denial of a report in the *Financial Times* that Tony Blair had 'intervened on behalf of Rupert Murdoch . . . by speaking to Romano Prodi, the Italian premier, about the media magnate's attempt to acquire an Italian television network'.

This was a sensitive story, with its embarrassing suggestion that Blair was ready to use his position as prime minister to do favours on behalf of the most influential pro-government press baron. Campbell blustered. He did not deny that some kind of conversation between Tony Blair and Romano Prodi had taken place, but described the *FT*'s story as a 'complete joke'. He added: 'It's balls that the Prime Minister "intervened" over some deal with Murdoch. That's C-R-A-P.' Campbell spelt out each of the four letters of the word 'crap' for extra emphasis.

Two days later the *Financial Times* revealed that Murdoch had told colleagues only the previous week 'that he would ask Tony Blair for help in ascertaining whether the Italian government would block his £4 billion acquisition of Mediaset, Italy's leading commercial television network'. Campbell was exposed.

Campbell has always insisted that he did not lie over this

episode. When he was grilled three months later by MPs on the matter he said this: 'I described that story as a joke and I happen to think it was a joke. I think it is the oddest form of intervention to sit in your office waiting for a phone call from the Italian Prime Minister.' Nevertheless, his remarks to journalists were misleading. They were calculated to give the impression that the *FT*'s story was false, when it was in large part true.[23]

Part of Campbell's tactic in the Prodi episode was to seize on a relatively insignificant mistake in the *Financial Times* story – the claim that the telephone call had been made by the prime minister, when in fact it had apparently been initiated by Romano Prodi – to give the impression that the entire story was false. One extraordinary instance of this form of deviousness involved the political journalist Matthew Parris. It is worth telling in some detail in order to demonstrate how Campbell would operate. The Parris story is particularly telling because it shows how Campbell would bully, threaten and use the might of the Downing Street machine in order to disseminate a fundamentally false version of events.

The Downing Street intimidation began after Parris told a story concerning Alastair Campbell in his autobiography *Chance Witness*. He recalled how in 1994, during the Labour leadership campaign, he and Campbell, then still a journalist on the *Today* newspaper, travelled together in a cab to BBC Millbank to interrogate Tony Blair for BBC *Breakfast News*. Parris wrote that the two reporters had discussed lines of questioning for the interview. He recalled how Campbell successfully urged him not to question Blair on why, as an opponent of opt-out schools, he had sent his son Euan to the elite London Oratory. Parris said that Campbell persuaded him that to pursue that line of enquiry would have been a cheap trick, without adding that he was actually at work on behalf of the Blair campaign, therefore an interested party rather than a fellow journalist offering a disinterested assessment.*

Campbell's response when Parris published this story was devastating. Writing on Downing Street notepaper to the editor of *The Times*, Campbell insisted that Euan still had a year's primary schooling ahead of him at that date, and could not possibly have been at the Oratory. Simultaneously a letter from Downing Street went to Parris's publishers Penguin Books: 'In accepting that he [Parris] was factually incorrect, he is accepting that I did not seek to prevent him asking Mr Blair about his choice of the Oratory for his son. At the time I did not know Euan was going to the Oratory. Nor did Mr Parris. Nor did Euan. Nor did Mr Blair.' Campbell went on to tell Penguin that he had been 'advised' that Parris's remarks were defamatory: 'You say that there can be no question of offering me redress. I ask you to re-examine that statement before I take the matter further. [Otherwise] I will need to consider what steps are open to me to ensure that the book is not published until an appropriate correction is made.'[24]

These letters prompted grave doubt, bordering on panic, in the minds of both Parris and his publishers. If the Blairs had not decided to send their son to the Oratory at this stage, how could Parris have known about it, let alone discussed the issue with Campbell in the back of the car? Parris's first reaction was that perhaps his memory had been playing tricks on him. In fact subsequent research showed he was mostly right. Though Euan had not yet started at the

---

* For instance Campbell drafted the Blair prospectus 'Principle, Purpose, Power'.

Oratory, the Blairs had already visited the school to discuss sending him there. Furthermore this was public knowledge, so there was no mystery about how Parris knew about it during the leadership campaign.[25]

Parris had, however, made a small mistake. He wrote that Euan Blair was already at the Oratory in 1994. Euan actually joined the school a year later. Campbell's art was to seize on this inaccuracy, and seek to use it to prove that the whole Parris version of events was a fiction, that the encounter in the car had never taken place, that he had never sought to dissuade Matthew Parris from asking questions about Euan Blair. On this basis he threatened steps to block the distribution of the Parris book.

The technique here is interesting, because it was used by Downing Street and by Alastair Campbell on a number of other occasions. A story might be fundamentally truthful and correct, but he would seize on one minor detail or inaccuracy to create the impression that it was utterly false.[26] The story incidentally demonstrates Campbell's deceitful use of his journalistic status to perform a political role. The veteran political columnist Anthony Howard was another who was bullied and harassed by Campbell after suggesting that he might have been playing a double role. Howard recalls how in 1990:

> I happened to write a long piece about Kinnock for a Sunday colour supplement. In the course of it I included Campbell's name on a list of those who, formally or informally, then advised the Labour leader. How did the Political Editor of the Daily Mirror react at the time?
>
> He jumped up and down and threw a wobbly. He was, he

insisted, a totally independent journalist and I had injured his professional reputation by suggesting otherwise.[27]

Another Alastair Campbell tactic was to create the impression that a story was false by denying a claim or assertion that had not actually been made. A nice example of this strategy concerns the well-known film-maker Peter Kosminsky, director of *The Project*, a BBC drama about New Labour screened not long after the 2001 general election victory. Kosminsky revealed that, while the film was being researched, Downing Street had banned all special advisers, researchers and party employees from talking to the BBC about it. Alastair Campbell promptly issued a denial in the following terms:'I have had no conversations with anyone from the BBC about Peter Kosminsky's programme,' said Campbell.'Nor have I, contrary to his claims, ever sent letters to any Labour Party worker, or indeed anyone else, about it.'[28]

The problem here was that neither Peter Kosminsky, nor anyone else, ever made the 'claims' that Campbell so angrily refuted. As Kosminsky politely remarked at the time: 'Campbell's being disingenuous. We've never claimed he sent out the memo personally – it was sent out by one of his most senior lieutenants, Lance Price, who was Campbell's deputy at the Number Ten press office before later becoming Labour's Director of Communications.'[29]

Artifice

Campbell used the power and access which the post of press secretary gave him to place in the public domain versions of events that were simply false, or in some cases had never happened at all. They were simply what New Labour wanted the world to believe at any given moment.

A minor example of this occurred during Tony Blair's trip to South Africa in January 1999. During this trip the prime minister – as he often did while abroad – used the occasion to make a 'keynote' speech mainly aimed at the domestic audience in Britain. The day before this speech Campbell briefed the lobby journalists on the trip that Tony Blair would signal 'harsh and authoritarian' measures on the welfare state.[30] This line duly appeared in the following morning's papers. But when the speech actually came to be delivered all mention of these harsh measures had disappeared. Some of the lobby journalists seem to have accepted this omission without demur but one reporter, Joy Copley of the *Scotsman*, complained, accusing Campbell of peddling a false line.

Campbell's response was interesting. He could have apologised to Copley, explained that there had been a last-minute change of plan, something of the sort. Instead he scornfully dismissed her complaint. 'The lobby all write garbage anyway,' he said. Copley refused to be bullied. 'You fed us that garbage,' she said. 'You made us write a story that wasn't true.' Campbell responded: 'I wouldn't wet your knickers about it,' he said. To his credit he later apologised for this last offensive remark. But the real interest of this otherwise fairly unimportant story is Campbell's utter lack of remorse that he had used journalists to put false information into the public domain.

A more significant example of the way Alastair Campbell misled journalists was the briefing which he gave to lobby reporters, both collectively and individually, following the resignation of Peter Mandelson just before Christmas 1998. He told them how

Mandelson had been devastated at the way news of his secret loan from Treasury minister Geoffrey Robinson had come out. So he had phoned the prime minister at 10 p.m. on the evening of 22 December and informed him that he saw no alternative to resignation. Blair listened sympathetically, told Mandelson to 'sleep on it', but felt in his heart that 'Peter's mind was made up.' This is how *The Times* reported the story: 'The Minister telephoned Mr Blair at about 10 p.m. and, in an emotional exchange, said that he was angry with himself for landing the government in trouble. He then told the Prime Minister that he intended to resign. In another conversation at around 10 a.m. he confirmed his decision and Mr Blair did not attempt to dissuade him . . .'[31]

In fact the story was entirely different, and the official Downing Street account was fanciful. Far from telling the prime minister he felt he should quit the previous night, Mandelson had actually fought to stay right up to the last moment. We know this because of the dramatic diary kept of these events by the Downing Street press officer Lance Price, which shows that Mandelson was still very hopeful of staying in office when he spoke to Tony Blair on the morning of 23 December.[32] Today Price is candid about the story 10 Downing Street issued to the public: 'It was a lie. It was to make life easier for him [Peter Mandelson]. In a sense it was to make it nearer the truth, because it was his own decision to resign. William Hague [leader of the Tory opposition] was calling on Peter to go that morning and we didn't want to give him any credit. To help Peter we invented the fact that Peter Mandelson offered to resign the night before when really he resigned in the morning.'[33]

Once Mandelson's mind had been made up for him Campbell drafted the former cabinet minister's resignation letter. 'Dear Tony,' it began, in an achingly postmodern moment, 'I can scarcely believe that I am writing this letter to you.' Since Mandelson did not in fact write it, this sense of incredulity was entirely understandable.*

It remains a matter of surmise why Campbell should have been ready to use the authority of the Downing Street machine to permit a false account of events to distributed to the British public. There were several obvious presentational advantages in the deception, however. It made Peter Mandelson look contrite, and the prime minister more compassionate and less ruthless than was really the case.

Likewise, in the affair of the second Mandelson resignation, just over two years later, Alastair Campbell fed false information to the parliamentary lobby. He misled journalists for certain once, and in all probability twice, during the course of the affair. Indeed it was he who was the source of much of the confusion that led to this particular Mandelson resignation.

The first confusion emerged at the morning lobby briefing of 22 January 2001, where Campbell was asked about Srichand Hinduja's application for a British passport. His answer implied that Peter Mandelson had had no personal involvement of any kind, something that Mandelson himself had by no means claimed.[34]

But the most blatant and upfront piece of invention from Campbell came at the following day's 11 a.m. lobby, when he contradicted the previous briefing. According to the Downing Street website, Campbell told journalists that 'yesterday, with offices back

---

* According to Mandelson's biographer Donald Macintyre, 'Mandelson changed his letter scarcely at all, pausing only to write a separate, private, handwritten note congratulating Blair for being such a decisive and strong leader. See Macintyre, p. 447.

up and running after the weekend, Mr Mandelson's office had been able to look at the records in full and discovered that he had had a very brief telephone conversation in June 1998 with Mike O'Brien [the then Immigration Minister] which had been set up by their two private offices'.[35] In fact Peter Mandelson's office has not to this day discovered any documentary evidence of a telephone call between Mandelson and Mike O'Brien. Once again it is impossible to fathom why Campbell chose to resort to fabrication at this moment, though it is possible to speculate that he was trying to conceal the real reason why Downing Street had changed its story, namely the intervention of Home Office minister Mike O'Brien.

Another episode of Downing Street invention caused Mark Bolland, a senior member of the Prince of Wales's private office, to ring up Alastair Campbell personally to complain. This came in the wake of the row following Northern Ireland Secretary Mo Mowlam's decision to invite both Prince Charles and Sinn Fein leader Gerry Adams to the annual Hillsborough Castle garden party. The Prince was irritated and upset because he felt that the decision to invite Adams had been kept from him. On the Monday after the story became public, the Prince's office was alerted that Downing Street was briefing journalists that the Prince of Wales had been made aware of the meeting some time before and had approved it. The Prince was so angry about this that Bolland rang up and informed Campbell that, unless he himself set the record straight, the Prince's office was ready to publicly contradict the Downing Street version of events.[36]

Routine Downing Street Denials

More common, however, were straight, contemptuous denials. They became routine during Campbell's years in Downing Street, though the instrument used was often a junior spokesman. One victim was the journalist Paul Waugh after he revealed that a Downing Street source had smeared the government scientist Dr David Kelly as a 'Walter Mitty' character. At first a Number 10 spokeswoman gave the impression that no one in Downing Street had made the remark. 'Nobody with either the prime minister's or anyone else in Downing Street's approval would say such a thing,' she said.[37] Later Downing Street was obliged to admit that the remark had come from within Downing Street itself.

Many lobby journalists have their personal stories of obstruction or deceit. A year after the 1997 election Joe Murphy, then of the *Mail on Sunday*, learnt that special in-flight beds were being built so that Tony Blair could sleep on long-haul journeys. It was a perfectly sensible proposal, but at first it was denied the beds had been ordered at all, then it was falsely claimed that the order had been placed by the Tories before New Labour won power. *Financial Times* reporter Liam Halligan ran a story in November 1998 saying that ministers had dropped a plan for compulsory saving for pensions. This was dismissed by press secretary Alastair Campbell as 'crap'. Two months later, when the story was confirmed as true, Campbell was asked why he rubbished the story. He denied having done so.[38]

Faced with the prospect of embarrassment in the following day's newspapers, Downing Street will often give a false impression of the truth. In January 2003 a row broke out after it emerged that President Mugabe of Zimbabwe had been invited by French

President Chirac for a summit in Paris. In that morning's press briefing the prime minister's official spokesman gave a strong impression
that news of the Mugabe visit came as a surprise. Asked whether or
not Britain would veto the plan, the Downing Street record shows
the PMOS to say he had 'only just been made aware of the reports
and could only respond in general terms at this stage. If it was the
intention of the French government to invite Mr Mugabe to such a
summit, then we would obviously expect them to share the full
details with us.'[39] The impression given could not have been clearer.
The briefing caused Charles Reiss, the scrupulous political editor of
the *Evening Standard*, to file a report that 'a new row erupted today
between Tony Blair and President Chirac' after the Mugabe invitation. 'No 10 and the Foreign Office were caught on the hop as it
became clear that Britain had been neither consulted nor
informed.'[40]

In fact the impression given by Downing Street that it knew
nothing about the trip was completely false. As French sources soon
made clear the British government had known about the Mugabe
visit weeks in advance, and actually agreed to it.[41]

In 2001 the prime minister and his family went on holiday in
Egypt. A Downing Street spokesman told reporters that the Blairs
paid for their holiday and that it was 'entirely private'.[42] In fact the
Blairs did not pay for the holiday themselves, nor was it 'entirely private', as the spokesman claimed. The luxury holiday came courtesy
of the Egyptian government, which paid for the prime minister,
Cherie and children to fly from Cairo to the Red Sea resort of
Sharm-el-Sheikh and then to stay at private villas in the grounds of
an hotel. This involvement only became public knowledge when the
prime minister was obliged to make an entry in the House of

Commons Register of Members' Interests several months later, at which point it was revealed that he made a charitable donation of an unspecified amount said to be equal to the cost of the stay in the villa and the travel to the government of Egypt. Doubtless the Blairs deserve credit for making their charitable donation, but the Downing Street account of events was heavily misleading, since the holiday was arranged and paid for by the Egyptian government and the prime minister had dinner with the Egyptian president during his stay.[43]

On 18 March 2004 the former sports minister Kate Hoey hinted to the Commons Public Administration Committee that Alastair Campbell had organised the knighthood for Manchester United manager Sir Alex Ferguson. She said: 'Clearly somebody somewhere in Downing Street thought, "Hang on, this is a good one, we will bring this in," and it was literally a few weeks afterwards that he was knighted.' But this was promptly denied by a Downing Street spokesman who insisted that Number 10 officials had no involvement in the nomination process for honours. 'This is a Cabinet Office process,' said the spokesman. 'It looks at the list and works out the nominations. There is no question of Number 10 getting involved in that.'[44] But it almost at once emerged that the Downing Street riposte was false, and that Campbell had actually offered the knighthood in person to Ferguson in the immediate aftermath of Manchester United's famous European Cup victory in Barcelona. The *Daily Mail* quoted Campbell telling a business dinner: 'I was told that if Man United won the treble then I could approach Alex and ask him if he would be prepared to accept a knighthood. I was there at the European Cup final and when United won I had to try to get to Fergie.'[45]

Another deception may have concerned the *Sun*'s revelation of the 2001 general election date. At the time Downing Street denied being the source of the story.[46] The trouble is that this account of events has been contradicted by a former Downing Street spin-doctor, Lance Price. According to the *Daily Mirror*, Price confessed at a conference in summer 2001 that Downing Street had leaked the story to the *Sun*. According to a verbatim note given to the *Mirror*, Price's admission came out as follows:

> *Question:* 'What was the question behind announcing the post-ponement exclusively in the *Sun*?'
> *Price:* 'If I could give an honest answer to that question I would. It caused us a lot of grief that it came out that way.'
> *Question:* 'The reason was surely that the *Sun* had consistently been told that it would be in May, had argued very vociferously that it should be May and had to be bought off . . . the only way to do that was to give them the story exclusively.'
> *Price:* 'That is almost entirely correct.'[47]

When the prime minister's official spokesman was asked about Price's remarks the Downing Street website records: 'Journalists had been contacting Downing Street just before an announcement had been made and we had been spelling out some of the factors in the prime minister's mind at the time. Some people had made judgements about what had been said. Others hadn't. The idea that we had been telling people the date of the election before Buckingham Palace had been told was wrong.'[48] Price has never challenged the *Mirror*'s account of this conversation. On the other hand, Price says today that he does not know for sure how the *Sun* got the story.

A much more important example of Downing Street mendacity came during the Mittal Affair in February 2002. This case involved Downing Street deception on a worrying scale, starting with the prime minister himself. The episode began with the discovery of a letter from Tony Blair to the Romanian prime minister, Adrian Nastase, concerning the sale of the Romanian Sidex steel plant to Lakshmi Mittal's LNM. The most striking thing about this letter is that it referred to LNM as a 'British company'. This was an absurd formulation. LNM Holdings was registered in the Dutch Antilles, while no more than 100 employees were employed in the UK out of a 125,000 worldwide workforce. LNM's closest relationship with Britain was perhaps in its capacity as a donor to the Labour Party, to which it had given £125,000.

At first Tony Blair and the Downing Street machine stood by the claim that LNM was 'a British company', but rapidly weakened that line, so that by 13 February the prime minister was merely express-ing his delight that 'a British-based company has succeeded', and by 14 February Downing Street was reduced to blustering, 'Look, there isn't any legal definition of what is a British company.'[49]

The claim that Mittal was British is just one of numerous false-hoods uttered by the prime minister's official spokesman (PMOS).* In an attempt to distance Tony Blair from the incriminating letter, the PMOS asserted that the letter had been drawn up within the Foreign Office and that the 'Prime Minister had signed it and sent it back unchanged'. This assertion was repeated in the afternoon's lobby meeting.[50] This, however, turned out to be false. It emerged

---

* The quotes are taken from the Downing Street website, from which it is impossible to tell whether they were actually uttered by Godric Smith or Tom Kelly.

that Downing Street staff removed a reference to Lakshmi Mittal, described in an earlier draft as a 'friend'.[51]

Downing Street also misled reporters by claiming that LNM 'had donated to other political parties as well'. When this suggestion was denied, the PMOS blamed 'reports over the weekend' for the error. Put to him that Mittal's office denied that he had given donations to other parties, the PMOS said that 'if that was so, he would bow to the wisdom of Mr Mittal's office.'[52]

Doubt also surrounds the initial Downing Street claim that the letter from the prime minister to his Romanian counterpart was simply a formality, and simply 'congratulatory', as Downing Street insisted. But on 13 February the British Embassy in Romania suggested to the BBC that the letter from Tony Blair had been a major factor in helping 'finalise' the takeover.[53] The newspaper *Bucharest Business Week* reported on 23 July 2001 (the date Tony Blair sent his letter) that even at that late stage the French company Usinor was still confident of winning the contract and that the 'issue is high on the agenda of visiting French Prime Minister Lionel Jospin who arrives today'.[54] The leading Labour Asian peer Lord Paul, himself a steel tycoon, was quoted as saying, 'The Romanian government were teetering on the edge about whether to give him [Mittal] the contract. They were not satisfied with his credentials. He needed the Blair letter to give his bid a lift.'[55] Downing Street, however, was able to deliver testimony from the Romanian prime minister that 'the Romanian Government had already taken the decision at the moment when we received the letter from Prime Minister Tony Blair.'[56] These remarks seemed to contradict remarks made by Adrian Nastase in his speech at the signing ceremony for the deal on 25 July 2001. Quoted on the Romanian government website he said, 'Some have considered our partner somewhat ineffable, dwelling somewhere in the isles and with a post office box as head-quarters.' This being the case, reassurance that LNM was a 'British' company would have been highly material information.[57]

The Mittal affair was a bizarre episode, with 10 Downing Street changing its story on a number of occasions in an attempt to make sense of why the prime minister should have personally backed a bid by LNM, a company with no significant British links, for the Sidex steel contract. Even today a number of questions remain unanswered. According to the Downing Street account, the idea that Tony Blair should intervene at head of government level to secure the Mittal contract came from the British ambassador in Bucharest. This, like many of the details in the affair, is unconvincing. One curious detail is why Tony Blair seems to have displayed no anger at his staff or upset at having his integrity called into question after signing a mendacious letter to the Romanian prime minister.

Deceit Off the Record

Off-the-record briefing, because of its secretive nature, lends itself readily indeed to mendacity. For obvious reasons, this kind of lying is normally difficult to demonstrate in a book such as this, which is wholly transparent in its sources. One amusing case where it can be proved that journalists were misled in secretive private briefing came at the height of the public furore over the measles, mumps and rubella (MMR) triple vaccination.

On Saturday 22 December 2001, Tony Blair issued a statement designed to bring the issue to an end: 'The suggestion that the

Government is advising parents to have the MMR jab whilst we are deliberately refraining from giving our child the treatment because we know it is dangerous, is offensive beyond belief,' the prime minister wrote.[58] By any reasonable interpretation of these words, baby Leo had indeed had the jab. Most newspapers interpreted those words as confirmation, even though the prime minister did not say that in so many words. However, the political editors of the *Observer*, on the morning of 23 December, went further than a mere extrapolation from Tony Blair's text. Political editor Kamal Ahmed indicated that he had received private briefing from Downing Street sources to the effect that the jab had indeed been delivered. Ahmed wrote: 'Leo Blair has been given the controversial triple vaccination for measles, mumps and rubella, the *Observer* can reveal. Sources close to Tony Blair gave the clearest indication possible last night that the 19-month-old child has had the MMR injection.' Simon Walters, political editor of the *Mail on Sunday*, received similar briefing from 'sources close to the Prime Minister'.[59]

There was always something fishy about the pre-Christmas media operation on MMR – the very carefully worded statement from the prime minister accompanied by off-the-record briefing to Sunday papers at a time when the MMR row was threatening to spiral out of control. Six weeks later Andrew Grice, the respected political editor of the *Independent* who has close links to Downing Street, wrote a story that Leo had received the jab at the end of January. 'Tony Blair's son Leo was given the MMR vaccine last week, the *Independent* learnt yesterday,' he wrote. The Grice story went on to give authoritative-looking details about the vaccination, saying that 'newspaper reports shortly before Christmas suggesting that Leo had been vaccinated were wrong. It is believed the Blairs always intended Leo to have the vaccine, but delayed it because he was unwell. The Blairs were reluctant to explain this publicly because they feared it would amount to giving a "running commentary" on their children's health.'[60]

If Grice is right, then the *Observer* (and everybody else who made the mistake of taking the prime minister's statement on MMR at face value) was deliberately deceived six weeks before. If the *Observer* was right, then someone had cruelly hoodwinked Grice. At any rate, it can be said with confidence that either the *Observer*'s Kamal Ahmed or the *Independent*'s Andrew Grice was the unwitting victim of a deliberate heist, or quite possibly both. The MMR business was in many ways a trivial affair, but it demonstrates once again the casual and cynical approach that the Blair government has towards accuracy and truthfulness, even on a trivial matter.

Conclusion

The Downing Street reputation for integrity and truth-telling collapsed during the six-year period when Alastair Campbell ran its media operation. It must be stressed, however, that personal motives were never a contributing factor towards Campbell's mendacity. Campbell is, so far as one can tell, a figure of high standards in his private life. He did not mislead journalists and the wider public for personal gain or any other venal motive. On the contrary, he was concerned at all times to promote what he understood as the interests of the prime minister and the general benefit of the New Labour government. It is this characteristic that may have given culture secretary Tessa Jowell the licence to praise Campbell as a man of 'integrity' – on the face of things an extraordinary comment – when he left Downing Street.

The commentator Anthony Barnett made this point nicely in his important article for *OpenDemocracy*, entitled 'The Campbell Code', in which he called Campbell's conduct a method of 'preserving and renewing traditional rule from above in the era of a vermin press'.[61] Campbell may have justified his cheating, deception and falsehood because he believed they served a general good. This distinguished his lies and mendacity from the lies of the Tory period in government, which in large part were driven by greed, ambition or squalid personal motives. As the philosopher Sissela Bok wrote: 'It is crucial to see the distinction between the freeloading liar and the liar whose deception is a strategy for survival in a corrupt society.'[62] This doctrine of benign mendacity led to the defining event of the Blair government: British involvement in the Iraq War.

8

IRAQ

'There are different kinds of truths for different kinds of people. There are truths appropriate for children; truths that are appropriate for students; truths that are appropriate for educated adults, and the notion that there should be one set of truths available to everyone is a modern democratic fallacy. It doesn't work' – Irving Kristol [1]

Neither the falsehoods which preceded the invasion of Iraq, nor the lies which followed it, nor the crisis of trust that has resulted, were an accident. They flowed directly from the changed structure of government that was imposed after the victory of New Labour in the general election of 1997, and its revalidation four years later in 2001.

The period between 1997 and 2002, the year the Blair government started to make its case for war, saw several developments. The most important of these was the very rapid debasement of the traditional idea of a disinterested civil service, a development which was briefly sketched out in the last chapter. Downing Street no longer expected officials to provide them above all with the facts, however inconvenient. It now expected them to concern themselves as much with the presentation as the substance of policy, and give their loyalty in a more committed way to the government of the day.

This did not simply apply to the domestic civil service. The change of approach also made itself known in the Foreign Office and, most shockingly of all, in the intelligence services. The most senior personnel in the intelligence services ceased to treat facts as neutral and value-free. Instead they enthusiastically used them as mere building blocks towards the construction of a wider 'narrative', to be discarded or rearranged to fit the requirements of the government of the day. The tradition of caution, astringency and integrity was partly maintained, but only in the more junior ranks, by analysts like Dr Brian Jones of the Defence Intelligence Staff (DIS) whose scrupulous approach could, however, be easily thrust aside.*

In addition there was another change in civil service methodology, related to but distinct from the rapid abandonment of the old ideal of a disinterested, fastidious public ethos. This saw the rapid atrophy of the cabinet system, with all that it entailed in terms of formal meetings, careful procedure, record-keeping and minute-taking. Those civil servants that accommodated themselves to this way of doing business – like the prime minister's principal private secretary Jeremy Heywood – were encouraged.† Those who did not got frozen out. Sir Robin Butler and Sir Richard Wilson, Tony Blair's first two cabinet secretaries, suffered this fate. Indeed the post of cabinet secretary, which throughout the twentieth century carried mythic status and power in Whitehall, a symbol of integrity at the heart of government,

---

* And the late Dr David Kelly, though he was not strictly in the intelligence services.
† Eventually the refusal of the wider civil service to allow Tony Blair to grant Heywood accelerated promotion to permanent secretary rank caused him to leave the civil service.

suffered very rapid degradation after 1997. Much of its power and status flowed straight into the post of spin-doctor.

The Blair government preferred to operate with small, informal, undefined but highly politicised structures. There is no reason to suppose that there was anything at all sinister in Tony Blair's motives, as he set in motion these new procedures. Doubtless the bustling young prime minister, in his tremulous eagerness to set the world to rights, quite genuinely felt that the old, formal methods were an obstruction to progress. But his decision to scrap established Whitehall practice overlooked the fact that it contained ancient wisdoms and protections.

The result has been witheringly described by the former permanent secretary Sir Michael Quinlan as an environment where 'there was a sense of all participants – ministers, civil servants, special policy advisers, public relations handlers – being treated as part of an undifferentiated resource'.[2] For instance, during the political crisis which followed the death of David Kelly, the intelligence chief John Scarlett found himself in a group clustered round a word processor in the Downing Street press office helping compose a press release.* Nine months earlier, by contrast, the press chief Alastair Campbell was allowed to chair a meeting where intelligence personnel were present

---

* John Scarlett, chairman of the Joint Intelligence Committee during the Iraq War, was later appointed head of the Secret Intelligence Service. He became a friend of Campbell but I have been unable to find evidence from transcripts that Campbell ever referred to John Scarlett as his 'mate' as has been widely alleged. The nearest equivalent seems to have come when Campbell told the Foreign Affairs Committee on 25 June 2003 (Q1002) that 'I phoned up and said to John [Scarlett], who is a friend of mine and who I work with closely and regularly . . .' The earliest claim that Campbell called Scarlett a 'mate' comes in the *Observer* on 3 August 2003. It is possible that Campbell's 'friend' became Campbell's 'mate' in the intervening period through a process of Chinese Whispers.

and intelligence was discussed. However, when Campbell is described as having chaired 'intelligence meetings', this is probably stretching the meaning of the phrase. He chaired the Iraq Communications Group, which had intelligence officers on it. It is clear that, despite Campbell's attempts to pretend otherwise, he effectively had intelligence officers doing his bidding. Campbell told Lord Hutton on 22 September that he chaired meetings with both SIS and DIS officials present but asserted 'they were not meetings about intelligence'. He also spoke of how he chaired a dossier meeting on 9 September at which John Scarlett was present, but then marvellously explained how Scarlett was 'if you like superior to me' with regard to the content of the dossier while his role was limited to presentation points. The meeting took place, it should be borne in mind, under Alastair Campbell's chairmanship, and in his room.

This transmutation of roles of intelligence chief and press chief suddenly made the truth malleable. A greatly empowered spin-doctor was liberated to present the facts not in a way that conformed to the truth, but instead helped to build the picture the government wished to present to the outside world. The particular skills, knowledge and responsibilities of each individual were no longer brought to bear. Instead they merged their personalities and their disciplines into a conspiracy to achieve the common goal. This meant that the checks and balances entrenched in the Whitehall system, which usually served to head off egregious cases of error and misrepresentation, were cast aside. According to the commentator Anthony Barnett:

> In the days of the old constitution – the constitution in which ministers are accountable to parliament and served by disinterested

professionals, imbued with a public service ethic – Campbell's role in the preparation of the notorious intelligence dossier [on Iraq] would have been an outrage. In the age of manipulative populism, in which 'spin' and policy making are a seamless web, Campbell, or Campbell surrogates, are inescapably part of the landscape.[3]

It should be stressed that the doctrine which led Tony Blair and his henchman Alastair Campbell to set aside the traditional rules, regulations and restraints of Whitehall had exactly the same origins as the doctrine which led them to take such a dismissive attitude towards conventional measures of truth and falsehood (see Chapter 6). For them it was mainly the bigger picture or – to use the language that by the turn of the century had become accepted around Whitehall – 'narrative' which mattered. In an exquisite manifestation of this new method, Campbell even created a Whitehall post called 'Head of Story Development'. This was filled by one Paul Hamill, who played a role in the production of the shambolic February 2003 dossier on Iraq's so-called Weapons of Mass Destruction. In due course MPs questioned Alastair Campbell about this curious new public office, its title as characteristic of the postmodern period as Gentleman of the Bedchamber was of the seventeenth century. Campbell explained: 'what that means is somebody who takes a brief, an issue – as I say, we are talking about different themes that we are trying to pursue – and then turns them into products that might be of interest to the media. That is what they do.'[4]

This new environment meant that anything that got in the way of Downing Street, whether an inconvenient statistic or annoying piece of Whitehall convention, was bypassed or suppressed. Alastair Campbell and Tony Blair were justified and sanctioned by their privileged access to a higher vision. They felt free to treat the facts in a contingent manner, use them as instruments to an end, make misleading statements, and to recount false and sometimes laboriously elaborated accounts of events because they were so utterly confident in the virtuousness of their motives.

The facts became what they said they were, and the rules were the ones which suited them. By the start of the twenty-first century the destruction of Whitehall procedures had created near perfect laboratory conditions for the radical New Labour epistemology to flourish.* For the time being nothing could stand in its way. Decisions became unaccountable, structures inchoate and facts could be polished, embroidered, redeployed and in certain cases invented. In 2003 this startling state of affairs made it possible for Britain to invade another country on the basis of a lie.

Lies, Deceptions and Half-Truths on the Road to War

Possibly convinced that the destruction of Saddam Hussein's murderous government was much the best outcome for the Iraqi people and the world, Tony Blair and Alastair Campbell set about making the case for confrontation. They were unscrupulous about how they set about it.

---

* The arrival of a new cabinet secretary in 2002, Sir Andrew Turnbull, perhaps marked the final turning point. Turnbull's predecessor Sir Richard Wilson had fought a battle for the old barriers between party and state to be reinforced and strengthened through a Civil Service Act. This was one important reason why Sir Richard ended up partially estranged from the prime minister. One of Sir Andrew Turnbull's first acts as cabinet secretary was to make it known that he did not believe that the Civil Service Act, and thus the protections it would have entrenched, were necessary.

From early 2002 onwards Tony Blair uttered a series of false and misleading statements about the existence of weapons of mass destruction in Iraq, and their threat to the wider world. However perverse these statements subsequently turned out to be, they would have been to some extent forgivable if they had reflected accurately what British intelligence assessments were telling the British prime minister at the time.

But it is now easy to show they did not. It is now possible to compare the statements made by Tony Blair about the menace of Saddam ahead of the war with the contemporaneous judgements made by the intelligence services. This is thanks in main part to the work carried out by Lord Butler's inquiry into the faulty claims made about the existence of weapons of mass destruction ahead of the war, and also due to the investigation carried out by the Intelligence and Security Committee.*

1. In the spring of 2002 Tony Blair made a series of statements about Iraqi 'weapons of mass destruction' which were stronger than what was merited by what British intelligence knew at the time.

The British prime minister told Australia's Channel Nine on 3 March that 'we know they [Iraq] are trying to accumulate weapons

---

* This section is partly drawn from the outstanding analysis carried out by Glen Rangwala, lecturer in politics at Cambridge University, and the writer and campaigner Dan Plesch. It can most easily be accessed by reading *A Case to Answer, A First Report on the Potential Impeachment of the Prime Minister for High Crimes and Misdemeanours in Relation to the Invasion of Iraq.* Spokesman Books, August 2004, pp. 11–45. It cries out to be read in full. An earlier achievement by Rangwala was the discovery that Downing Street's second 'dodgy' dossier was based in part on the contents of an article, taken without attribution. A second invaluable guide to the deceptions during the run-up to war is David Morrison, *Iraq.*

of mass destruction.'[5] On 3 April Tony Blair told NBC news that 'we know that he [Saddam Hussein] has stockpiles of major amounts of chemical and biological weapons, we know that he is trying to acquire nuclear capability, we know that he is trying to develop ballistic missile capability of a greater range.'[6] On 10 April the prime minister told the House of Commons that Saddam Hussein's regime 'is despicable, he is developing weapons of mass destruction, and we cannot leave him doing so unchecked. He is a threat to his own people and to the region and, if allowed to develop these weapons, a threat to us also.' The trouble is that these statements were in direct contrast to the intelligence assessments of the Joint Intelligence Committee (JIC) at the time. The JIC assessment of 15 March warned: 'Intelligence on Iraq's weapons of mass destruction (WMD) and ballistic missile programmes is sporadic and patchy.' It went on: 'From the evidence available to us, we believe Iraq retains some production equipment, and some small stocks of CW agent precursors, and may have hidden small quantities of agents and weapons.'[7] As Glen Rangwala points out: 'The latest JIC assessment available to the prime minister in March and April 2002 emphasised how little was known about Iraqi NBC [nuclear, biological and chemical] programmes and stopped short of any definitive claims either way on the existence of stockpiles of weapons, or the development of them.'

The contrast between the prime minister's Commons statement and the JIC assessment is baffling. The JIC speculated on 15 March that Iraq 'may have hidden small quantities of [chemical] agents and weapons'. The prime minister stated as a matter of fact on 3 April that 'we know that he has stockpiles of major amounts of chemical and biological weapons.'

2. The prime minister made repeated claims that the intelligence services were telling him that Iraq posed a threat to the wider world and to UK interests. On 10 April 2002, for instance, Tony Blair told MPs that 'there is no doubt at all that the development of weapons of mass destruction by Saddam Hussein poses a severe threat not just to the region, but to the wider world.' This claim put him at variance with the Joint Intelligence Committee, which stated that 'Saddam has not succeeded in seriously threatening his neighbours,' adding that 'Saddam has used WMD in the past and could do so again if his regime was threatened.'[8] The prime minister issued numerous bloodcurdling warnings that Iraq posed – to quote from just one example – 'a unique threat to the security of the region and the rest of the world'. However, intelligence assessments made, so far as we can tell, no reference to any intention by Iraq to use WMD outside its borders, unless it came under attack itself. Indeed this view was so firm that the JIC-approved drafts of the dossier on Iraqi WMD, published in September 2002, referred to only two scenarios in which Saddam Hussein might use chemical and biological weapons. The first related to an internal uprising, while the other related to circumstances that might arise if Saddam 'believes his regime was under threat'. This last proviso was omitted from the published dossier after an intervention by Jonathan Powell, the Downing Street chief of staff.

3. Though he embellished and stretched some information from the intelligence services regarding WMD, Tony Blair played down or ignored other information which weakened the case for war. Above all he never mentioned a JIC warning that attacking Iraq could increase the risk to Britain of terrorist attack. According to the

Intelligence and Security Committee (ISC) Report of September 2003,'the JIC assessed that al-Qaeda and associated groups continued to represent by far the greatest terrorist threat to Western interests, and that threat would be heightened by military action against Iraq . . . The JIC assessed that any collapse of the Iraqi regime would increase the risk of chemical and biological warfare technology or agents finding their way into the hands of terrorists, not necessarily al-Qaeda.'[9] The prime minister's failure to draw attention to this warning that the invasion of Iraq might increase the risk of terrorism is all the more extraordinary since he repeatedly claimed that one major reason for the war was to confront international terrorism. For instance he declared on 5 March 2004 that 'the risk of this new global terrorism and its interaction with states or organisations or individuals proliferating WMD, is one that I simply am not prepared to run.'[10] But this greater risk of terrorism was not necessarily a telling argument against war. On the contrary, the government was entitled to take the honourable position that the long-term gain of ousting Saddam Hussein was worth the short-term pain of more terrorist attacks. The point here is simply that this relevant information was obscured from the British public.

4. The prime minister presented the intelligence sources available to him as overwhelming and decisive, for instance informing the House of Commons that the intelligence picture contained in the September dossier was 'extensive, detailed and authoritative'.[11] In his foreword to the September dossier, the prime minister said: 'What I believe the assessed intelligence has established beyond doubt is that Saddam has continued to produce chemical and biological weapons . . .'

In fact, the intelligence had not established this 'beyond doubt'. There were uncertainties in the intelligence assessments Blair saw, but he never referred to these. One JIC assessment issued shortly before the dossier was published has as its second sentence: 'Intelligence remains limited and Saddam's own unpredictability complicates judgements . . .'[12] The Intelligence and Security Committee, which had access to the JIC assessments, makes clear that the JIC did not know what had been produced and in what quantities, and concludes: 'We believe that this uncertainty should have been highlighted to give a balanced view of Saddam's chemical and biological capacity.'[13] Tony Blair, by excluding such uncertainties, was misleading the British people.

5. Tony Blair misrepresented the danger of civilian casualties in the run-up to the war. This is what he told the House of Commons on 19 March 2003, the eve of the invasion:

> Of course, I understand that, if there is a conflict, there will be civilian casualties. That, I am afraid, is in the nature of any conflict, but we will do our best to minimise them. However, I point out to my hon. friend that civilian casualties in Iraq are occurring every day as a result of the rule of Saddam Hussein. He will be responsible for many, many more deaths even in one year than we will be in any conflict.

The prime minister was telling MPs that, however many Iraqis would be killed in a conflict, Saddam would kill far more in a single year. This comment was pure nonsense, and wholly false and misleading. According to Amnesty International, by no means an admirer of the Iraqi regime, Saddam Hussein was responsible for the execution of 'scores' of people in 2001 and 2002, the two calendar years immediately preceding the invasion, and 'hundreds' in the year 2000. No one could ever condone or admire this kind of brutality, but it was less bloody by far than the state of affairs brought about by the coalition invasion. According to a controversial article in the *Lancet* on 29 October 2004, the extra Iraqi deaths from all causes since the invasion of Iraq stood at around 100,000. Even assuming this figure to be four times too high, it would still have taken Saddam Hussein more than one hundred years at the rate he was going to match the carnage resulting from the coalition invasion. Tony Blair's parliamentary answer seems to have rested on the assumption that the invasion would kill no more than a few hundred innocent Iraqis at most. This was a recklessly unjustified assumption to make.

6. The prime minister was also ready to mislead the House of Commons about the position of other world leaders. On 25 February 2003 Tony Blair told the House of Commons that 'not a single member of the international community seriously believes' Saddam Hussein's denial that he held any WMD. But the prime minister had actually been standing alongside Russian President Putin the previous October when he declared: 'Russia does not have in its possession any trustworthy data which would support the existence of nuclear weapons or any weapons of mass destruction in Iraq, and we have not received from our partners such information as yet.'[14]

Lies, Deceptions and Half-Truths After the War

The failure to discover WMD in Iraq after the war was deeply embarrassing for George Bush and Tony Blair. A perhaps desperate Blair announced, on 2 June 2003, that 'we already have, according to our experts, two mobile biological weapons facilities that were almost certainly part, according to our intelligence, of a whole set of those facilities.'[15]

In fact the prime minister, as so often when discussing intelligence matters, was talking pure nonsense, and the trailers turned out to have nothing whatsoever to do with biological weapons – they were probably devices to fill hydrogen observation balloons. It may well be that optimistic intelligence sources were telling him that they did have something to do with WMD. But British experts (not the same thing as intelligence sources, although Blair appears to think they are) did not start examining the trailers until several days after Blair had made his claim. It was not until 5 June that a group of experts, including Dr David Kelly, arrived in Iraq and had a chance to examine the trailers. According to Kelly's boss at the MoD, Dr Bryan Wells, there was a 'spectrum of opinions' about the trailers within the group, but Kelly himself decided that 'these were not biological weapons facilities'.[16]

Some of the most obvious and most reckless lies uttered by the British government, however, followed the report by the BBC reporter Andrew Gilligan that the September dossier had been 'sexed up' following pressure by Downing Street. Ninety minutes after Gilligan's broadcast, at 6.07 a.m. on 29 May 2003, Downing Street issued a defiant rejoinder: 'Not one word of the dossier was not entirely the work of the intelligence agencies.'[17] This assertion was wholly false. While the Joint Intelligence Committee had had what was called 'ownership' of the document, Downing Street had been closely involved in the preparation of the dossier, and had suggested various changes. Under normal circumstances this Downing Street input would not have come to light for thirty years at least. It was only the Hutton Inquiry, prompted by the death of Dr David Kelly, which made clear the extent of the Downing Street involvement in the preparation of the dossier. It was wholly impossible to foresee on 29 May, however, that the Downing Street statement would be disproved so soon. The assertion from Alastair Campbell that the Gilligan story was '100 per cent wrong'[18] was also a lie. Though there were indeed serious errors in his report, a great deal of what he had to say later turned out to be true.

Likewise the government statement claiming that 'any suggestion that there was pressure or intervention from Downing Street is entirely false' was nonsense.[19] The bald assertion perhaps failed to give full weight to the last-minute intervention by the Downing Street chief of staff Jonathan Powell, a political appointee. In an e-mail dated 19 September 2002, after the deadline for submissions to change the dossier, Jonathan Powell e-mailed John Scarlett: 'I think the statement on page 19 that "Saddam is able to use chemical and biological weapons if he believes his regime is under threat" is a bit of a problem.' Powell expressed alarm that the statement could give credibility to the 'argument that there is no chemical and biological weapons threat and we will only create one if we attack him. I think you should redraft the para.' The sentence had already been passed by members of the JIC in a number of drafts, with no objections. But John Scarlett looked at the issue again, and took the offending statement out of the document. The effect of this action was to change the whole meaning of the dossier, removing what amounted to a caveat that Saddam Hussein would only use his alleged deadly WMD in the event that he himself came under attack. Blair's own claim, speaking to MPs on 4 June 2003, that 'there was no attempt, at any time, by any official, or minister, or member of No. 10 Downing Street staff, to override the intelligence judgements of the Joint Intelligence Committee', is a marvellous example of his facility with the non-denial denial. 'Override' is not the same as 'intervene in'. In strict terms, it is true that he and his officials did not override intelligence judgements – why should they when they could get exactly the same result by simply intervening?

The prime minister uttered a clear falsehood during the Commons exchange on 4 June 2003. He told MPs: 'The allegation that the 45-minute claim provoked disquiet among the intelligence community, which disagreed with its inclusion in the dossier – I have discussed it, as I said, with the chairman of the Joint Intelligence Committee – is also completely and totally untrue.' In fact, as later emerged during the Hutton Inquiry, there was widespread scepticism, alarm and consternation among the intelligence community about the claim. Indeed on 19 September 2002, just five days before the publication of the dossier, Dr Brian Jones, the head of the nuclear, biological, chemical, technical intelligence branch of the DIS Staff, took the unusual step of recording his disquiet in a minute to management: 'We have a number of questions in our minds relating to the intelligence on the military plans for the use of chemical and biological weapons, particularly about the times mentioned and the failure to differentiate between the two types of weapons.'[20]

There is no reason to suppose that Tony Blair was not speaking in good faith. But, as emerged later during the Hutton Inquiry, his assurance to the House of Commons was grievously misleading. The most disturbing thing is not that the prime minister uttered these words in the first place, but that he never came back to the House of Commons to correct the misleading impression that he had created.

A fresh series of lies and misrepresentations started to emerge from the British government after the suicide of the weapons expert Dr David Kelly on 17 July 2003. The first came from Geoff Hoon, the Defence Secretary, who told the BBC on 19 July that 'we made great efforts to ensure Dr Kelly's anonymity.' This was a contemptible lie. In fact the government went to remarkable lengths to facilitate the release of Kelly's name to the public, including an extraordinary instruction to MoD press officers to confirm Dr Kelly's name if it was put to them. Nor was it just the press who were misinformed about circumstances surrounding the release of Dr Kelly's name. Much more significant, so was Kelly himself. As the Kelly family's QC told the Hutton Inquiry in his closing remarks, 'Dr Kelly was left with the impression that a statement might be issued that would not identify him, and would not lead to his identity being revealed.'[21] Furthermore, in an attempt to play down the significance of Dr Kelly as the BBC source, government ministers and officials produced a series of false and misleading statements about Dr Kelly's real status. Press officers were advised to describe him as a 'middle-ranking official' in the briefing notes which accompanied the government press release announcing that he had come forward.[22] Shortly afterwards this description appeared to be contradicted when it emerged that Kelly had on one occasion appeared alongside Foreign Secretary Jack Straw at a Commons committee. But then the Foreign Secretary let it be known that he had been upset to be accompanied by so junior a figure, to which Kelly reacted with a 'hysterical laugh', according to his widow. 'He was deeply, deeply hurt.'[23] In fact, as emerged in due course, Dr David Kelly was a very distinguished individual indeed, one of Britain's leading experts in his field, possibly the leading expert. He was already the holder of a very high diplomatic honour, the CMG, colloquially known within the Foreign Office as 'Call Me God'. According to the order's website it is awarded to 'men and women who have held, or will hold, high office, or who render extraordinary or important non-military service in a foreign country.'[24] He was apparently being considered for a knighthood.

The Downing Street press office produced a fresh lie three days later, on 22 July, when the prime minister's official spokesman claimed that the case of David Kelly had been 'handled in accordance with MoD procedures and had been overseen by those at the top of the MoD in view of the fact that it had been the lead department'. In fact Downing Street, not the MoD, took the key decisions in the handling of the Kelly story. Even the idea that it was 'handled in accordance with MoD procedures', whatever they may have been, seems to have been nonsense. When the prime minister was asked during the course of the Hutton Inquiry whether procedures existed for cases such as Kelly, he replied: 'No. Obviously, you know, this was, as I say, a very unusual set of circumstances.'[25]

Furthermore, Tony Blair seriously misled the House of Commons about the extent of British government awareness of the abuse of prisoners by American soldiers in Abu Ghraib.

On 12 May 2004, as the shocking pictures of prisoner abuse went round the world, Tony Blair informed MPs that no member of his government knew of the scandal. This is what he said to Tory leader Michael Howard at Prime Minister's Questions: 'It is not correct that ministers or I were aware of these allegations in respect of American troops. The ICRC report was not passed to us.'

These protestations of ignorance from Tony Blair were not soundly based. Bill Rammell, a junior minister at the Foreign Office, had indeed been informed about the abuse allegations. He had been told by Dr Kellenberger, the President of the International Committee of the Red Cross, almost two months earlier. We now know this because of a parliamentary answer given by Foreign Secretary Jack Straw some time later.* According to the official account of events, Bill Rammell then failed to tell any other minister. He apparently kept the information to himself despite the devastating nature of the scandal, which when it broke did catastrophic damage to the moral authority of the coalition not just in Iraq but around the world. According to the official account contained in Jack Straw's written answer of 16 June 2004 he simply discussed the matter with his officials, and then forgot about it.

There is every reason to suppose that Tony Blair was acting in good faith when he falsely told MPs that ministers had been ignorant of the Abu Ghraib abuse allegations. But he did not go back to

---

*This is what Straw said in his reply: 'The President of the ICRC, Dr Kellenberger, did mention briefly to my honourable friend the Parliamentary Under-Secretary of State at the Foreign and Commonwealth Office [Mr Rammell] in their meeting on 18 March that the February ICRC report contained allegations concerning treatment of detainees by forces other than UK forces, though naturally the part of their discussion which covered detainees in Iraq focused on specific allegations against UK forces. The Minister discussed the concerns raised by Dr Kellenberger with officials on his return to London. Officials had already received assurances that US investigations were under way into allegations of abuse of detainees at Abu Ghraib prison.' *Hansard* Written Answer, 16 June 2004.

the Commons, as the ministerial code demands, to correct his mistake 'at the first opportunity'. Instead the junior Foreign Office minister Bill Rammell shuffled out information that there had been ministerial knowledge of the abuses some five weeks later in a written parliamentary answer.

How Alastair Campbell Misled the Foreign Affairs Committee

We have seen how government ministers and officials produced a long series of direct lies, falsehoods, as well as various statements with some intermediate grade of mendacity, in the aftermath of the Iraq War. But nothing illustrates the prevalent culture of deceit inside Downing Street so well as the misleading remarks made by Alastair Campbell, the Downing Street director of communications and strategy, in front of the House of Commons Foreign Affairs Committee (FAC).

Campbell was at first very reluctant to appear before the FAC to give evidence on the background to the war with Iraq. He cited constitutional precedent, but his true nervousness may have related to an unwillingness to face questioning over his role in the second so-called 'dodgy' dossier published in February 2003. This was a document which made much of the fact that it contained secret intelligence, and was issued to journalists and put before parliament on that basis. This is how it was presented to MPs by Tony Blair during a parliamentary statement on 3 February:

We issued further information over the weekend about the infrastructure of concealment. It is obviously difficult when we publish

intelligence reports, but I hope some people have some sense of the integrity of our security services. They are not publishing this, or giving us this information and making it up. It is the intelligence that they are receiving, and we are passing on to people.

The prime minister was quite right to state that some fresh intelligence material was contained in the February dossier. However, his remarks failed to give anything like the full flavour of the material, which turned out to have been based in part on an article pirated from the internet, which was then embellished to intensify its anti-Saddam message. Furthermore, the material was not 'published' in any sense by the security services: indeed they were not even consulted before the material was placed in the public domain. The Intelligence and Security Committee indicated as much when it concluded that 'it was a mistake not to consult the agencies before their material was put in the public domain.'[26] This means that the security services cannot be regarded in any important way as publishers of the February dossier, as Tony Blair told MPs that they were. They were simply acting as providers of some of the raw material, a very different matter.

This meant that the prime minister's statement to the House was at best a very partial, and extremely misleading, representation of the February dossier, which was prepared by a team controlled by Alastair Campbell. The FAC report, published the following July, deemed as much when it concluded that 'by referring to the document on the floor of the House as "further intelligence" the Prime Minister – who had not been informed of its provenance, doubts about which only came to light several days later – misrepresented its status and thus inadvertently made a bad situation worse.' To be fair to Tony Blair, there is no evidence that he was aware of this at the time. But he has never come back to the House of Commons to set the matter straight, as both Commons prece-dent and the Ministerial Code demanded that he should.

The main culprit was Alastair Campbell, and not Tony Blair. Campbell's fear that he was bound to find himself at the receiving end of criticism for his role in the shambles may have played some part in his reluctance to appear before the FAC. However, by the time that Campbell appeared in front of the committee another rather more serious row was going on. This related to the first dossier, published the previous September, a much more substantial document which had been published with the full imprimatur of the Joint Intelligence Committee.

Alastair Campbell misled the Foreign Affairs Committee over two issues. The first, and less important, concerned the nature of his apology to intelligence chiefs for the shambles of the second dossier and will be dealt with in the section below. The most important case of deception concerned Campbell's role in compiling the September dossier.

When Campbell appeared before the FAC on 25 June MPs questi-oned him closely about what changes to the dossier he had suggested to John Scarlett, the JIC chairman. In reply to a request from the Labour MP Andrew Mackinlay, Campbell agreed to supply further details. He duly did so. Alastair Campbell's Supplementary Memorandum to the FAC[27] gave what had every appearance of being a very full and comprehensive response to the FAC request. In fact it was a partial and therefore misleading list which omitted some crucial information.

We know this because, during the Hutton Inquiry, the memo sent by Campbell to Scarlett was published in full. The first thing to note here is that such a memo existed. In his evidence to the FAC, which was prepared with Scarlett's assistance, Campbell gave no indication that any written record had been made. On the contrary, the tone of his Supplentary Memorandum suggests a chat between two colleagues, doing their best to remember the details as best they could after several months had elapsed. The phraseology is inexact. At one point Campbell writes: 'The JIC chairman and I believe that the following is an accurate reflection of my requests for changes to the text of the WMD dossier.' At another he writes: 'as far as we recall, our discussions on the text took place over 17 and 18 September. The following are the changes I requested, and the responses of the JIC chairman.'

But these laborious protestations of vagueness were disingenuous. Campbell submitted to the committee a carefully worded partial précis of two written minutes which must have been in front of him at the time. The memo from Campbell to Scarlett, and Scarlett's reply, were both still on file, and it is clear that Alastair Campbell examined them before he provided the FAC with his 'accurate reflection' of the changes requested. This can be demonstrated by comparing the list of changes cited in Campbell's Supplementary Memorandum with the list that appears on Campbell's original memo to Scarlett. The version of the list in the Supplementary Memorandum, though incomplete, follows the order of the Scarlett memo with a precision that can only mean that the original document was consulted.*

---

* Only the first point in Campbell's memorandum to the committee, concerning the use of the phrase 'vivid and horrifying', did not follow the strict order of points raised in Alastair Campbell's memo to John Scarlett of 17 September 2002. It was placed at the top of the list, which was natural enough as it was the point which had been raised in Campbell's oral discussion with the FAC.

This is what makes it so peculiar that only eleven of the original sixteen points were included in Campbell's so called 'accurate reflection'. It is true that some of the missing points were trivial. Point 13, for example, refers to a typographical error, while point 16 was concerned with the number of bullet points in the executive summary. But one of the points was emphatically not trivial, and indeed went to the heart of the allegation that Campbell had 'sexed up' the document. This was point 10: 'On page 17, 2 lines from the bottom, "may" is weaker than in the summary.'

The sentence referred to in the 17 September draft read:

The Iraqi military may be able to deploy chemical or biological weapons within forty five minutes of an order to do so.

In the next draft, produced on 19 September, John Scarlett changed the language and meaning as follows:

The Iraqi military are able to deploy chemical or biological weapons within forty five minutes of an order to do so.

It cannot be claimed that Alastair Campbell was unaware of what he was doing. During his oral evidence to the FAC he was heavily pressed on the forty-five-minute claim, and insisted justifiably that he had played no part in the decision to include the claim in the dossier. But he then went on to make the false statement that the wording had not changed from the first draft, as the following exchange shows:

Q987 Richard Ottaway: You use some rather interesting wording in your memorandum that to suggest it was inserted against the wishes of the intelligence agencies was false. Was it put in at your suggestion?

Mr Campbell: No, otherwise – it existed in the very first draft and, as far as I am aware, that part of the paper stayed like that.

This claim from Campbell that the wording of the forty-five-minute claim never changed must be regarded as knowingly mendacious because he was instrumental in getting the wording changed. His assertion that the claim existed 'in the very first draft' of the dossier also turned out to be problematic. A drafting process had been going on for months, run by the Foreign Office. When Tony Blair pressed the button for the September dossier, these FCO documents, which did not include the forty-five-minute claim, were circulated, but rejected as inadequate. A Cabinet Office team led by John Scarlett then produced the draft of 10 September. It did contain the forty-five-minute claim, and was substantially a new document. So it is possible to justify Campbell's statement that the forty-five-minute claim existed in the 'very first draft' of the dossier, even though it is not quite the whole truth. For instance the ISC report, para. 73, describes the 10 September draft as 'the first draft of the dossier'.

It is important to stress that in the normal course of events it would have been impossible to check these documents, or Campbell's oral testimony, against other official sources until thirty years had passed. But the death of Dr David Kelly, and the resulting inquiry by Lord Hutton – events that Campbell could not conceivably have foreseen when he was giving evidence to the FAC – caused these official documents to be brought to light.

When giving evidence later in front of Lord Hutton, Alastair Campbell sought to explain away the failure to include his remark on the relative weakness of the forty-five-minute claim as a mere 'comment.' He said that he was 'not making the request for a change.'[28] This was an unconvincing explanation in any case. And if this really was the approach being adopted to the memorandum, point 2 in Campbell's minute to Scarlett of 17 September – 'In the summary you are clear that Saddam's sons have authority to authorise CW/BW [chemical/biological weapons] use. In the text (Page 23) it is weaker "may have"' – was equally just a 'comment' on inconsistent language. Yet while point 2 was happily included in the memorandum sent by Campbell to the FAC, point 10 was left out.

If the Downing Street director of communications and strategy withheld key material from the Foreign Affairs Committee, he misled parliament. There was indeed some talk within the FAC that Campbell ought to be recalled and give an explanation of the inconsistencies in his evidence.[29] On 9 March 2004 Richard Ottaway, a Tory member of the committee, proposed that not merely Alastair Campbell, but also the journalist Andrew Gilligan and Foreign Secretary Jack Straw, should be asked to 'comment upon any discrepancies between the evidence given to the Committee in its inquiry into the decision to go to war in Iraq and that given to Lord Hutton as part of his inquiry into the circumstances surrounding the death of Dr David Kelly CMG'. But Ottaway was heavily outvoted on the Labour-dominated committee, which thereby made the extraordinary decision that it would not even seriously investigate evidence that parliament might have been misled by the prime minister's closest adviser in Downing Street.

Evasions and Deceptions Connected to Campbell's Apology to Intelligence Chiefs

There was a final matter upon which Alastair Campbell misled the Foreign Affairs Committee. It concerned the episode of the 'dodgy dossier' in February 2003, and whether or not he had apologised to intelligence chiefs. Once again, Campbell misled parliament. Furthermore, it is a case that vividly illustrates a classic Campbell defensive strategy when confronted with a potentially damaging story. Even if the story is fundamentally true, Campbell will cast around to identify a deniable detail. He will then focus in on that detail and, by denying that for long enough, hope to cast doubt on the truth of the larger accusation. We have already examined this strategy as used by Campbell in connection with his attempt to deny Matthew Parris's story about his role in the Blair leadership campaign, and on other occasions.

The episode began on 8 June 2003, when the *Sunday Telegraph* revealed that Campbell had apologised to Sir Richard Dearlove, then chief of the Secret Intelligence Service, for the discredit brought on the service by the so-called 'dodgy dossier'. Almost everything about this story was true, with the exception of the fact that Campbell had not actually sent a letter.

It was natural for MPs to question Campbell about this claim when he appeared before the FAC two weeks later. Campbell promptly went into denial mode:

Q906 Chairman: Why did you then send a letter of apology to Sir Richard Dearlove, because he had nothing to do with that?

Mr Campbell: I did not send a letter of apology to Sir Richard Dearlove.

Q907 Chairman: Have you sent letters of apology to anyone?

Mr Campbell: I have not sent a letter of apology to Sir Richard Dearlove.

Q908 Chairman: Have you sent letters of apology to anyone?

Mr Campbell: Not in relation to this. I do not think we have actually got to the impact of that mistake . . .

Q910 Chairman: Back to my question. Have you, as a result of that document, apologised to anyone?

Mr Campbell: On the day that the mistake was revealed, first on Channel 4 and then on BBC *Newsnight*, and Mr al-Marashi went on to the media, the following day – this indicates how seriously we took it – I spoke to the security intelligence co-ordinator, I spoke to the Permanent Secretary of the Foreign and Commonwealth Office, I spoke to the head of the Secret Intelligence Service, I spoke to the Chairman of the Joint Intelligence Committee to explain that something had gone wrong. Equally, the other thing that we did was the Prime Minister's spokesman on behalf of the Prime Minister at a briefing that day acknowledged that mistakes had been made and we said that this should not have happened, and obviously subsequent to that we sought to establish what had happened.

Q911 Chairman: What you did in those conversations could not be construed as an apology?

Mr Campbell: What it was, was saying to the intelligence services that the care that should have been taken in the production of a document which contained some of their material was not sufficient. I have a sufficiently good relationship with these intelligence officials not for them or me to present that as an apology but as a discussion about how this had happened and how we stop it happening again.

Anyone watching this exchange could have been left in no doubt that Campbell had made no apology. However, Campbell also gave evidence to another committee, the Intelligence and Security Committee, and told them a different story. Their report says: 'Alastair Campbell confirmed that, once he became aware that the provenance of the document was being questioned . . . he telephoned both the Chief of the SIS and the JIC Chairman to apologise.'[30] In other words, it seems that there was an apology, but not a written apology. This Intelligence and Security Committee statement that Campbell apologised to intelligence chiefs is completely authoritative, even though on the face of it it conflicts with the evidence that Campbell himself gave to the Foreign Affairs Committee. The Committee is composed only of extremely senior MPs, all of them privy counsellors. All evidence is taken in private, giving an extra dimension of trust and confidence. Unlike other parliamentary committees, ISC reports are published by the prime minister, along with a government response. When that response came it did not challenge the ISC statement that Campbell had apologised both to the Chief of the Secret Intelligence Service and the Chairman of the Joint Intelligence Committee.[31]

Alastair Campbell did not merely mislead the FAC about his apology to intelligence chiefs. He also misrepresented it to Lord Hutton. When Campbell appeared before the Hutton Inquiry on 19 August 2003 the following exchange took place:

Q. On 8th June what was your reaction to the continuing press coverage?

A. The story of the so-called apology was leading the news, leading the BBC News.

Q. This so-called apology related to?

A. It related to the fact that on the February briefing paper, which I covered in my evidence to the Foreign Affairs Committee, we had acknowledged mistakes were made, and we had put new procedures in place and this would not happen again. Then, at the same time, and with an illusion it was actually about the WMD dossier, the *Sunday Telegraph* led on a story that I had sent a written apology to Sir Richard Dearlove about that, which is not true. That led the BBC News through the Sunday.[32]

These remarks by Campbell to the Hutton Inquiry were misleading in at least two respects. According to the Intelligence and Security Committee, Campbell had indeed apologised to intelligence chiefs. It had not been a 'so-called apology', as Campbell claimed to Hutton, it had been the real thing. Secondly, the *Telegraph* story had been wholly clear about the fact that Campbell's apology had related to the 'dodgy dossier' and not to the September dossier. Nor was it even true, as he also told

Hutton, that the apology story 'led the news through the Sunday', though it did make the lead in some bulletins for the early part of the morning.

How Campbell Lied to Jon Snow

Two days after Alastair Campbell's evidence to the Foreign Affairs Committee, he made the memorable live, finger-wagging appearance on Channel Four News in which he denounced the BBC for, among other things, lying. 'I do believe that anyone with an interest in good, decent journalism,' declared Campbell, 'should understand that when allegations are made, when lies are broadcast, when there is not a shred of evidence to substantiate the allegation they should apologise and then we can move on.' Be that as it may, Campbell misled Jon Snow twice.

The first episode concerned the circumstances which led to Campbell's appearance on this show. Alastair Campbell claimed that Channel Four were given ample warning that he would appear. He insisted as much to presenter Jon Snow personally, and made similar claims to the press. According to *Sunday Telegraph* political editor Colin Brown, 'Mr Campbell last night denied storming on to the programme . . . He said the programme had asked his office whether he would appear. When he heard about the offer, he cleared it with the Prime Minister and Donald Anderson, the chairman of the Foreign Affairs Committee.'[33] (Campbell also pooh-poohed the story when giving evidence to the ISC, saying that he had 'allegedly' stormed Channel Four studios.) However, Campbell's arrival in the Channel Four studios came as a total surprise to Jon Snow and to Channel Four Television producers.

The true story of what happened demonstrates once again Campbell's readiness to twist the facts. Channel Four did indeed invite Campbell on to the programme, but Jon Snow says Downing Street gave an extremely 'dismissive' response. At some stage in the afternoon, which he spent watching the Wimbledon tennis championships, Campbell seems to have changed his mind. Even though his journey back into central London by car could have taken up to an hour, he did not use that time to inform Channel Four he was on the way.

The only warning he gave was a message he left on the voicemail on Jon Snow's office desk. 'He put it down on the recording voice-mail on my phone at 6.49 p.m. I had long gone into the studio,' recalls Snow. 'So there was no prospect of anyone getting it till the programme was over. He claimed that he had warned me in advance. There was a message but not one that I could pick up.

'He said: "Oh yes I did, I left a message."'

'Look, he was in a taxi for forty-five minutes coming from Wimbledon, and only chose to ring in at the last minute. He had plenty of opportunity to tell us early and also sensibly. If he had really wanted to tell us he would have rung the news desk.

'Hell, if we had known he was coming in we would have put it at the top of the news list, but we didn't. We really did not know that he was coming in.' Snow speculates that 'I think he did not want preparations made for it. It was a very neat way of making sure we didn't know he was coming in.'

This was a classically duplicitous Campbell strategy. He, of all people, knows how if you ring a presenter at his desk eleven minutes before a programme goes out, he won't be there. He knew that, in any case, the key call to make would have been to the Channel Four news desk, which is responsible for ensuring the necessary logistical arrangements are in place to handle interviewees. As so often with Campbell, he wasn't quite lying – he had made a call of sorts. But he was manipulating the facts to create an entirely false impression.

He did lie to Jon Snow on that Channel Four programme, however, once again on a trivial matter. This lie came when Jon Snow, in an aside, noted that Campbell had misspelt the word 'weasel' in the angry statement he had put out denouncing Richard Sambrook, BBC head of news. 'If I may say so,' replied Campbell, 'the statement that you are reading from was read to the Press Association, so that I wouldn't get hung up on a spelling mistake by somebody who's typed it.' This attempt by Campbell to blame the Press Association for sloppy spelling was disingenuous. The paragraph in question was not read out to a PA reporter, but faxed or e-mailed to the PA. It was a very minor deceit, about a very unimportant matter, but demonstrates yet again how Alastair Campbell was habitually untruthful.

Conclusion

When New Labour was in its gestation stage in the early 1990s, it lied because it felt powerless. As I argued in Chapters 6 and 7, Labour's deceits bore comparison to those of a religious sect or revolutionary movement that felt threatened by enemies in the midst of a corrupt public culture. Its private doctrine affirmed the legitimacy of false conformity to prevailing orthodoxy as a means of gaining power, and thus changing the world for the better. The practice of dissimulation, and outright lying, was tolerated and sometimes encouraged because New Labour believed that the penalties for truth-telling were so great.

But in the years after 1997 New Labour swiftly established itself as the ruling party. As time passed by, and it entrenched itself in power, the springs of its falsehood have to some extent changed. Its dissimulations gradually ceased to be the desperate contrivances of the oppressed. They became instead the useful lies of the governing class.

As Downing Street prepared for the confrontation with Iraq, there were two types of truth. There were the speculative and uncertain judgements within the intelligence community about the doubtful threat posed by Saddam Hussein. These were based on the long-standing intelligence gathering precepts: empirical, cautious, sober, down to earth. And there were the false certainties about the threat posed by WMD projected to the British people through the prime minister's speeches and public documents.

It is too early to say – and in any case such speculation is well outside the scope of this book – but there are numerous indications that the real motive behind the invasion was not the one told to the British people: namely the eradication of Saddam Hussein's non-existent weapons of mass destruction. There is a crucial piece of evidence which proves that Tony Blair's public and private objectives were wholly divergent. This is the leaked memo sent by the Downing Street foreign policy adviser Sir David Manning to Blair on 14 March 2002, reporting back on a conversation with Condoleezza Rice: 'I said that you would not budge in your support for regime change but you had to manage a press, a Parliament and a public opinion that was very different than anything in the States.'[34]

In other words, by March 2002 Tony Blair had given the US administration an assurance that his objective was regime change, and not merely disarmament as prescribed by Security Council resolutions and Tony Blair's public position at the time. This was confirmed a few days later in a memo from the British ambassador in Washington, Sir Christopher Meyer, to Sir David Manning. In it, he reported on a conversation with Paul Wolfowitz on 17 March 2002 in the following terms: 'I opened by sticking very closely to the script that you used with Condi Rice. We backed regime change, but the plan had to be clever and failure was not an option.'[35]

These private assurances that Britain backed regime change were never made public. On the contrary, Tony Blair went out of his way to tell parliament on 24 September 2002 that regime change was not his purpose. When asked in the Commons debate on the September dossier whether regime change was his objective, the prime minister replied: 'Regime change in Iraq would be a wonderful thing. That is not the purpose of our action; our purpose is to disarm Iraq of weapons of mass destruction.'

These many lies on Iraq marked a climacteric moment in the trajectory of New Labour deceit. New Labour lies were no longer the lies of the powerless. They had become the lies of the ruling elite. Domestically, the dissimulations on Iraq required the active and enthusiastic connivance of the British government machine and the intelligence bureaucracy. Abroad, they merged into the wider strategy and ambition of the George W. Bush administration. The neo-conservative faction which dominated the agenda in the Bush White House, and drove the forward policy on Iraq, had no compunction about deceit. On the contrary, the neo-conservatives, following the doctrines of the philosopher Leo Strauss, believed that democracy was a flawed political system precisely because the wider public could never be trusted with more than partial glimpses of the truth.

This view that democracy and truth are irreconcilable was well expressed in an essay on Strauss written in 1999 jointly by Abram M. Shulsky and Gary Schmitt. Both men were key instruments of the neo-conservative conspiracy, Shulsky a former head of the Pentagon's Office of Special Forces and Schmitt head of the Project for a New American Century, the think tank where the Iraq War strategy was originally conceived. The two men argued that Strauss's thought 'alerts one to the possibility that political life may be closely linked to deception. Indeed, it suggests that deception is the norm in political life, and the hope, to say nothing of the expectation, of establishing a politics that can dispense with it is the exception.'[35]

Another disciple of Strauss, Paul Wolfowitz, the US Deputy Defense Secretary, was following in this line of thought when he remarked to *Vanity Fair* magazine: 'For bureaucratic reasons, we settled on one issue, weapons of mass destruction, because it was the one reason everyone could agree on.' New Labour and the American neo-conservatives did not simply share a common foreign policy analysis. They shared a common understanding that truth was contingent, at best a useful tool. It is an irony that New Labour epistemology should have found a lasting resting place as an instrument of US foreign policy.

PART THREE

9

POLITICAL LYING AND THE THREAT TO TRUST

'Trust takes years and years to build up and it can be destroyed overnight – Evidence to the Anderson Inquiry into Foot and Mouth

Arguments for Deception

According to the academic Dr Glen Newey, Reader in Politics at the University of Strathclyde, political lying is the price Britain pays for being a democracy. In a paper for the Economic and Social Research Council published in 2003, Newey argues that truthfulness and democracy may be mutually inimical, most obviously because truth-telling will sometimes conflict with other things which the electorate wants from its politicians, such as efficiency, effectiveness and security, as well as with politicians' professional self-interest.[1]

Newey blames the electorate for the lies of politicians. 'The more the electorate expects from the politicians they elect, the more likely it is that politicians will be economical with the truth.' He argues that contemporary calls for political transparency have led to more deceit:

> Demands for openness and accountability create a culture of sus-
> picion which makes it even more likely that politicians will resort
> to evasion and misrepresentation. These demands often arise
> because of increasing alienation by voters from the political
> process that they democratically control. Yet the greater the
> demands for truthfulness, the less autonomy we give to our dem-
> ocratic institutions and the harder it is for our democracy to
> function effectively.[2]

Newey reached his conclusions after a study of archive material concerning the Arms to Iraq affair – which took place under the last Tory
government – and a study of certain episodes in modern American
history, including the attempted impeachment of President Bill
Clinton, Watergate, and the Iran-Contra affair. His argument does
not take account of the experience of the last seven years. It stops
some way short of the thoroughgoing justifications for political
deception or concealment put forward by the American neo-conservatives, or by supporters of the New Labour government such as
the *Guardian* columnist Polly Toynbee.[3] Newey is nevertheless argu-
ing a modern variant of an ancient thesis; that governments have a
duty or perhaps an obligation to conceal and to mislead. His intelligent defence of government lying is one that will be accepted by
many busy, pragmatic politicians from all political persuasions. They
would argue – like Governor Stanton at the end of *Primary Colors*
(see Chapter 5) – that little lies have to be told all the time. Politicians
use them to flatter their constituents, fend off lobbyists, protect their
families, deal with journalists. They make deals among themselves
that would perplex and disturb a generally unsophisticated
electorate, and be used to stir up trouble by political enemies. They

enter into negotiations whose smooth course would be imperilled if revealed at an inconvenient moment. As the Tory minister William Waldegrave remarked to a Commons committee in 1994, government 'is much more like playing poker than playing chess. One cannot always have all the cards face up.' According to this plausible, worldly and pragmatic argument, no government, and no politician, could survive without its necessary little deceits.[4]

Dangers of Mendacity

There is a nevertheless a heavy price to pay for dissimulation and lying, even when it is well-intentioned. Though lies almost invariably make excellent sense to those who utter them, they rarely seem so satisfactory from the point of view of those at the receiving end.[5] Lying has many of the characteristics of an assault, which is why Machiavelli urged it as an alternative to war. It strips the victims of the ability to make a soundly based judgement, treats them as children, converts them into instruments, removes their humanity and turns them into dupes.

This is why the philosopher Immanuel Kant was hard on lying. He argued that all human beings possessed an intrinsic moral worth, which derived from the fact that they possessed the ability to make moral choices, and reach rational decisions. For Kant lying corrupted that essential humanity because it deprived human beings of that precious ability to make rational choices.[6] This was the tragedy about the debate that preceded the invasion of Iraq. The British government converted speculative evidence about the threat of WMD into hard fact, while concealing a great deal of information, including a warning from the intelligence services that the war would increase the risk of terrorism. Meanwhile the main reason for war – which seems to have been, though it is too early to say with certainty, a decision reached quietly between the US and Britain to remove Saddam Hussein from power – was suppressed and denied. The British electorate was therefore never given the ability to make an intelligent choice, and therefore grant an informed consent. Nor were the direct recipients of this mendacity, the British voters, the only victims. The indirect victims of the lies told by the British and American governments were the tens of thousands of Iraqis who have been killed or maimed as a result.

As the Iraq tragedy demonstrates, when politicians lie they change their relationship with the electorate from one of equals to one of master and servant. This applies even from the point of view of lies made from virtuous motives. A politician who deceives in order to obtain a higher good is expanding his role beyond its normal and proper sphere. He is stealing the moral autonomy, and the right to choose, of the voter. He is deciding on his own, without a wider consultation, what voters may or may not be told. This means that he is making exceptional demands not merely on others but also on himself. In the long run this can cause as much damage to the lying politician as to those he lies to. The philosopher Sissela Bok writes:

Some come to believe that any lie can be told so long as they can convince themselves that people will be better off in the long run. From there, it is a short step to the conclusion that, even if people will not be better off from a particular lie, they will benefit by all maneuvers to keep the right people in office. Once public servants lose their bearings in this way, all the shabby deceits of Watergate – the fake telegrams, the erased tapes, the elaborate cover-ups, the bribing of witnesses to make them lie, the televised pleas for trust- become possible.[7]

In the short term lying is of immense help to the politician who lies. It stops his being exposed in scandal, averts a public row, secures good newspaper coverage. But the dangers are overwhelming. The habit of lying becomes compulsive. Having got away with a lie once, he tends to think that he can do it again. One lie often tends to generate another. The knowledge that he has lied puts him on his guard, makes him suspicious of the electorate.

Politicians rely on moral authority: the ability to mobilise public opinion and take voters with them. But lying destroys that ability. This is where Governor Stanton's self-vindication at the end of *Primary Colors* is faulty. It may well be the case, as he claims, that lying can help a politician attain power. But it hampers him from exercising it. For once the victims of lies realise they have been duped, they feel let down and betrayed. They become cynical, impervious to fresh assurances. They lose faith in what politicians say. The Iraq War is an example of this. Had Tony Blair been open with the British people about the fact that his objective was regime change, he might well have taken voters with him. Little of the bitterness and crisis of trust that has followed the war would have followed. The consequence of British government deceit ahead of Iraq is profound and long lasting. It will be far more difficult for a British leader to be believed again if they try to take Britain into a pre-emptive war.

The bitter aftermath of mendacity does not just apply to war. In his report on the 'lessons to be learned' from the Foot and Mouth crisis in early 2001, Iain Anderson reported the consequences that flowed from government minister Nick Brown's early erroneous comments that the disease was 'under control': 'The Minister's comments contributed to the loss of trust on the part of rural communities. Many people, including some of those directly involved in managing the outbreak, still find it difficult to reconcile their experiences during this period with the notion of the disease being under control.' Anderson then went on to quote from a devastating transcript from one of the public meetings held by his inquiry:

Night after night on television news we had Jim Scudamore [the government's Chief Veterinary Officer], or Mr Brown, sometimes the Prime Minister, [or] Professor King [Sir David King, British Government Chief Scientific Advisor] [stating that] it is under control, it is completely under control, it is definitely under control and we felt absolutely insulted and patronised by these lies that we were told. And furthermore it did a great deal of lasting damage because it meant that we are all now so completely cynical about anything the government says. It has destroyed trust, trust takes years and years to build up and it can be destroyed overnight, and that is one thing that happened.[8]

Iain Anderson's report further suggests that the lies told by the government had a more practical effect than loss of public trust. It led to the wrong policy prescription. As Anderson put it: 'The Minister's comments also sent a message to Government as a whole that the outbreak was being comprehensively managed by MAFF

[Ministry of Agriculture, Fisheries and Food]. It was another 11 days before COBR was opened.'[9]

COBR was the Cabinet Office Briefing Room meeting, chaired by the prime minister, which finally brought the full weight of a central government emergency response. In other words the mis-statements of the position by Nick Brown and others delayed an effective resolution to the Foot and Mouth tragedy. Likewise in the case of the Iraq War, it is reasonable to speculate that the pre-war focus on WMD distorted the policy aims of the British and American governments. Had Tony Blair and George W. Bush been open and honest that their real objective was regime change, there would have been a fuller debate, inside and outside government, about the consequences of deposing Saddam. Many of the problems that followed the war arose because the occupying powers had not given nearly enough thought in advance to the massive internal dislocation caused by Saddam's removal.

Once mendacity forms a normal part of government statements, public discourse becomes meaningless. It ceases to be about seeking a common solution to the problems that affect us all, and instead becomes an exercise in manipulation, intrigue and brutal power. This is why lying is an attack on civil society. There are endless cases in the recent past of these betrayals: the voters who supported John Major on the basis that he would cut taxes, or those who were swayed by Tony Blair's claim that there would be no tax rises 'at all'; the voters who believed the manifesto pledge that Labour would never bring in tuition fees. All of these cases – and the many others cited in this book and elsewhere – lead to the disempowerment of the electorate.

In the end voters despair, and lose the appetite to vote. This is starting to manifest itself in British politics, with lower turn-outs in general elections, and a dismaying collapse in faith in politicians themselves. All poll surveys show a steady weakening of trust. Some politicians are beginning to understand the problem. A pamphlet published in early 2005 by Neal Lawson, chairman of the Labour Party pressure group Compass, gave a glimpse into the mood of the electorate, as tested by focus groups. The people interviewed were genuinely nostalgic for the political prospects they recalled in 1997. Tony Blair held out real hope of 'a bright new future' – 'things could only get better'. But these hopes were buried under personal emotions of loss and betrayal. Maureen from north London said she 'feels so conned'. The view from one man from Birmingham was that 'they had proved us wrong.' Across all the groups New Labour politicians were 'just a bunch of liars.'[10]

The New Labour government is now chronically conscious of this crisis of public trust in contemporary British democracy. It has become very important for New Labour and its supporters to argue that the problem is the creation of the 'media'. In the next chapter I will examine more carefully the frequently repeated claim that a mendacious media is the principal cause of the collapse of public trust in contemporary Britain.

Today's politicians still hold to the doctrine, taught by Machiavelli 500 years ago, that lying is a legitimate tool for rulers. It may well have been in fifteenth-century Italy, stuck in an endemic state of war where men's loyalty could only be obtained by bribery or by force. But it is a wretched state of affairs in a twenty-first-century democracy.

10
THE ROLE OF THE MEDIA

'Only if we build a public culture – and above all a media
culture in which we can rely on others not to deceive us – will
we be able to judge whom and what we reasonably trust' –
Onora O'Neill, Reith Lectures

The angry charge that the British newspaper press and, to a lesser
but nevertheless marked extent, broadcasters, systematically lie and
distort is a common reflex of almost all government ministers.
Charles Clarke, the Home Secretary, gave eloquent expression to
this thesis when he claimed that much criticism of the government
'is pious and hypocritical, sometimes entirely manufactured, coming
from parts of the media which themselves have done their best to
bring democratic politics into disrepute'. His predecessor David
Blunkett dismissed the media as being 'almost on the verge of
insanity'.[1]

The government has important allies in the academic world in its
crusade to demonstrate that the media destroy public trust. The
most eloquent support has come from the philosopher Onora
O'Neill, Principal of Newnham College Cambridge, and a student of
the work of Immanuel Kant. O'Neill is censorious of the British

media. 'In this curious world,' she writes, 'commitments to trust-worthy reporting are erratic: there is no shame in writing on matters beyond a reporter's competence, in coining misleading headlines, in omitting matters of public interest or importance, or in recirculating others' speculation as news. Above all there is no requirement to make evidence accessible to the readers.' O'Neill argues that con-frontation with a corrupt media culture is the primary issue for those looking for a solution to the collapse of public trust: 'Only if we build a public culture – and above all a media culture in which we can rely on others not to deceive us – will we be able to judge whom and what we can reasonably trust.'[2]

There are plenty who make the same argument within the media themselves. The most powerful of these is the journalist John Lloyd, whose important work *What the Media are Doing to Our Politics* has led to a welcome, and long overdue, debate on the role of news-papers and broadcasters. In his book, and a series of polemical articles, he alleges that the media produce a systematically false picture of British politics. Other commentators who have projected more or less the same view include Roy Greenslade, Polly Toynbee, David Aaronovitch and Jackie Ashley in the *Guardian*, Alice Miles in *The Times*, Steve Richards and Johann Hari on the *Independent* and numerous others.

These criticisms of the growth of media power have considerable legitimacy and strength. The press has constructed an architecture of public debate which obliges politicians to lie or pay a heavy conse-quence in terms of adverse newspaper publicity. Michael Howard's career as leader of the Tory Party provides two neatly contrasting, though relatively minor, examples of this phenomenon. This first moment came before Howard actually became Tory leader. Howard was asked during the final months of Iain Duncan Smith's period as Tory leader whether he would ever stand for the leadership. His answer was an emphatic 'No'. Michael Howard insisted that he could envisage no circumstances of any kind in which he would stand for leader. When asked if he would stand 'even if Duncan Smith stood down', he still replied, 'No.'[3]

It is very easy to understand why Michael Howard would give such an answer. Had he answered that, yes, he would like to be Tory leader, his response would have given rise to a crop of stories to the effect that he was ready to mount a challenge to Duncan Smith. Whatever angle Howard was coming from, this would have been unfortunate. If he really was the Duncan Smith loyalist he claimed to be at the time, giving rein to leadership ambitions would have destabilised his ally. If – as seems rather more probable – Howard was already entertaining thoughts of succeeding a doomed Duncan Smith, the effect of his remarks would have been just as unfortunate. It would have alerted rivals to his ambition and enabled them to take steps to pre-empt his bid. So it was simpler to utter what seems to have been a lie. When Michael Howard did indeed launch his bid for the Tory leadership later, there was no price to be paid for this falsehood. The press made nothing of it: probably his denial was generally accepted as a ruse in the political game. This is no defence of Howard. It would have been far better if he had found some form of words that defused the question without resorting to deception. Michael Heseltine perhaps succeeded in finding such a formula rather more elegantly during Margaret Thatcher's final months, when he would claim that he could 'envisage no circumstances' when he would challenge her leadership.

The second example concerns Michael Howard's honesty rather

than deceitfulness. In January 2005 he was asked on Radio 4's *Today* programme whether he would stay on as leader of the Conservative Party in the event of a defeat in the forthcoming general election. Howard answered: 'If my party want me to do that and I think I can continue to make a contribution, then yes I will.' This unequivocal answer was almost universally hailed in the newspapers and broadcasting media as a 'gaffe'. Howard's crime was to break the longstanding political convention that no party leader, however desperate his plight, should ever publicly entertain the prospect of electoral defeat.

The comparatively staid *Independent* newspaper told the story under the headline 'Tory leader admits he may lose next election', while the more demotic *Daily Mirror* announced: 'Dracula Stakes Himself'.[4] The significant point here is that when Howard acknowledged something that everybody knew to be true – that the Conservative Party was not certain to win the looming general election – he was torn to shreds. But when he said something which everybody suspected to be false – that he had no wish to be Tory Party leader – his mendacity was universally accepted as conforming to the rules of the Westminster game. In the one case the media rewarded Michael Howard for falsehood, while in the other it punished him for telling the truth.

This is evidence that newspapers create a harsh and unforgiving environment where mendacity is the safest refuge for any public figure. But the stronger claim, which is often made by critics of the press, that the newspapers systematically lie and invent the truth, needs to be treated with caution. This assertion has never been properly substantiated. John Lloyd's influential book, which argues so passionately that our domestic press has a unique charter to distort, contains scarcely a single example of a lie published by a British newspaper. (It places immense weight on Andrew Gilligan's famous 6.07 a.m. BBC broadcast on 29 May 2003, with a few examples taken from foreign media.) Likewise Onora O'Neill makes a number of eye-catching claims about the British press:

> If powerful institutions are allowed to publish, circulate and pro-mote material without indicating what is known and what is rumour, what is derived from a reputable source and what is invented, what is standard analysis and what is speculation, which sources may be knowledgeable and which are probably not, they damage our public culture and all our lives.[5]

Regrettably Dame Onora fails to provide any evidence that the British press conducts itself in the unprofessional and careless way she implies.* It is therefore impossible to assess in any meaningful way the accuracy of her claim. Geoff Mulgan, always one of the most richly enjoyable of New Labour ideologists, likewise insisted that there is 'a lack of a strong ethic of searching for the truth in much of the media . . . For many it doesn't much matter whether what they print is true.'[6] By this stage in his career Mulgan was showing signs of recovery from his attack of postmodernism, the doctrine with which he flirted as a young Blairite intellectual in the mid-1990s (see page 138). He was beginning to discover that good,

---

* The kind of slackness she describes is rare in my experience, but does happen. It is much more common in broadsheet newspapers, which tend to use cheaper and more poorly trained staff, than tabloids like the *Sun* and the *Daily Mail*. Indeed the kind of looseness she alleges – for instance the reporting of rumour as fact – would be a sackable offence on either of these two highly professional operations.

old-fashioned objective reality had something to be said for it after all. He wrote:

> Commercial communication, like political communication, indirectly promotes the idea that there are no truths, only strategies and claims (a view which has indirectly had such a huge influence on the academic study of communication).
>
> In all of this I don't want to posit a simplistic view that we live in a world made up of unproblematic objective truths. Rather my argument is that we should want institutions – governments as well as media – to place a high value on the search for truth and objectivity, even if this ideal is never quite attainable.[7]

Mulgan, like O'Neill and Lloyd, failed to provide empirical evidence for his claim that the press didn't care whether what it printed was true. Of course, this failure by critics of the British media to substantiate their very provocative and arresting arguments does not in itself mean that what they are saying is false. Indeed, it seems intuitively likely there is at least some element of validity in their claims. But there is clearly a need for caution before accepting their central proposition that the British media are a uniquely noxious vehicle for distortion and fabrication.

Pro-government critics of the British media have failed to note that the largest deceptions have rarely come when newspapers take issue with government accounts of the truth. On the contrary, the most serious misreporting has often occurred when newspaper reporters have believed what ministers and government spokesmen have told them.

The list of victims who have been suckered in by government

disinformation is too numerous and embarrassing to dwell on for long. It includes all those unlucky journalists who were deluded into hyping the imaginary sport of Surfball, those newspapers (almost all of Fleet Street) which at first swallowed without question New Labour claims about health and education spending, and those papers which credulously accepted government claims ahead of the Iraq War.

The *Observer*, for example, deluded its readers when it tamely accepted the protestations from a Foreign Office spokesman and changed its story that the British government had had fore-knowledge of the botched coup in Equatorial Guinea (see pages 84–5.) (This decision followed a lively argument between that faction of the *Observer* which believed that the government was trustworthy, and the faction which takes a more sceptical view. The first faction won.) It deluded its readers again when it accepted the credentials of Downing Street's dodgy dossier in February 2003 and presented the world with the blazing but misleading headline: 'How Saddam Hides Illegal Weapons Sites'. The *Sun* and the *Evening Standard*, which gave front-page promi-nence to the false claims that Saddam Hussein was ready to release his celebrated 'weapons of mass destruction' within forty-five minutes, were doing their readers no favours. Indeed, Onora O'Neill's strictures about the press quoted above – that newspapers 'publish, circulate and promote material without indicating what is known and what is rumour, what is derived from a reputable source and what is invented, what is standard analysis and what is speculation, which sources may be knowledgeable and which are probably not' – are very similar to the criticisms mounted by the Butler Inquiry into the September 2002 dossier on Iraq's weapons of mass destruction.

It would be extremely naive to accept too readily the numerous protestations from New Labour and its allies that it is horrified by the mendacity of the media. What New Labour wants is favourable coverage, and its accuracy or otherwise is of little interest. During the Kosovo War, Downing Street went to extreme lengths to undermine the credibility of the seasoned BBC foreign correspondent John Simpson, who was reporting from the Serb capital Belgrade. In private briefing it accused him of 'falling short of the standards of a leading journalist' and 'swallowing Serb propaganda'.[8] The real objection to Simpson was not that he was reporting lies, but inconvenient truths. Likewise during the Afghan war the full weight of the Downing Street machine was turned on another BBC correspondent Rageh Omaar, one of a handful of journalists reporting from inside Kabul. Once again, Downing Street alleged that Omaar was being 'duped' by the Taliban, but the real reason for the anger at his brave and measured reporting was that he could not be readily controlled by Number 10.*

As with the attacks on the BBC, there are grounds for caution before accepting at face value the New Labour explanation that it despises the *Daily Mail* because the newspaper systematically lies and distorts the facts. When Downing Street issued powerful assurances that there was not an ounce of truth in the story that the conman Peter Foster had given financial advice to Cherie Blair, its

---

* Alastair Campbell rang the BBC Head of News Richard Sambrook at home on 10 November 2001. 'What the fuck's going on with this Rageh Omaar report?' bellowed Campbell. 'You're being duped by the Taliban.' Sambrook replied: 'Rageh's report was very careful and measured. He made it clear that he could only show what the Taliban were showing him. Our people on the ground know what they are doing, Alastair.' See Peter Oborne and Simon Walters, *Alastair Campbell*, p. 281.)

account was credulously accepted by most newspapers. But it was the *Daily Mail* who then published the e-mails that proved he had done precisely that. When the Home Secretary David Blunkett promised that there had been no impropriety over the visa obtained by the nanny to his lover Kimberly Fortier, it was the *Daily Mail* which showed that his office had indeed helped to 'fast-track' the visa. The refusal of the *Daily Mail* and its sister paper the *Mail on Sunday* to collaborate lazily with the lies and equivocations from the Downing Street machine is, as much as anything else, the reason why those papers have earned the undying hatred of Tony Blair and his inner circle.

New Labour – like all governments and ruling groups – deeply dislikes the way newspapers and the media have a habit of placing in the public eye new and difficult facts which contradict the official version of events. This is beginning to lead to a new and startling doctrine: that there are truths that the public is not fit to see. One interesting manifestation of this proposition came from the columnist Polly Toynbee in the wake of the resignation of David Blunkett. Toynbee wrote that nothing that Blunkett had done 'was really a sacking offence in itself'. She then went on: 'But through Britain's lack of privacy laws and grossly prurient press, aided by unfettered chequebook journalism buying up nannies to spill beans, we know far more than we ought to. Once it's known, we can't unknow it. Like it or not it undermines a home secretary's dignity. It shouldn't – which is why the press should be reined in – but inevitably it does.'[9]

Toynbee assumed that the press coverage, not David Blunkett's use of power to pursue private ends, forced the Home Secretary to quit. She is making the striking argument that the Home Secretary's conduct should be tolerated. For her the greater villain is the British press, the agent which brings the facts to light, causing us to 'know far more than we ought to'. Onora O'Neill employs a similar argument, suggesting that 'some sorts of openness and transparency may be bad for trust'.[10] It is the kind of argument favoured by ruling classes everywhere, not that distant from Plato's notion of an elite class of guardians and a wider population sustained by necessary myths.

New Labour's Appropriation of the Truth

Nevertheless it must be accepted that critics of the media have a great deal of wisdom on their side. The strongest point made by Onora O'Neill, John Lloyd, Geoff Mulgan and others is the devastating political and cultural effects that have been produced because of the detachment of the British press from civil society. Onora O'Neill sensibly warns that 'A free press is not an unconditional good. Press freedom is good because and insofar as it helps the public to explore and test opinions and to judge for themselves whom and what to believe and trust.'[11] John Lloyd asks, in the peroration to his book:

Can we imagine a journalism which is civic? One which defies its own natural instincts – to make celebrities of itself; which acts as an adjunct to activity and reflection; which presents to its audience first drafts of history which are absorbing and subtle, strong on narrative but attentive to the complexity and context of every story; which is not struggling with political power, but struggling, together with that power's best instincts, to make the contemporary world at once comprehensible and open to the participation of its citizens.[12]

It is scarcely possible to fault a word of this vision. Over the past few decades the British media has gained an unhealthy social, cultural and political importance at the expense of other public institutions including parliament and the political parties. The media, with its false values, its structural preference for the short and not the long term, for the synthetic and not the real, for sentimentality and not compassion, for the dramatic and not the mundane, can rarely create anything original and good.[13] But it does possess an awesome destructive force. Lloyd's call for a civic journalism is timely and refreshing.

The weakness of this analysis is the failure to acknowledge the necessity for its corollary – a civic government. Central to the argument of John Lloyd, Geoff Mulgan, Alastair Campbell, Denis MacShane and others is the proposition that government is by and large truthful and honest. Indeed Lloyd postulates that the government has become the victim of a kind of media conspiracy to show 'that politics is a dirty game, played by devious people who tell an essentially false narrative about the world and thus deceive the British people'.[14]

It is at this point that his argument falters. This book has demonstrated beyond doubt that Britain has a lying government, which systematically and as a matter of routine falsifies the facts; it has shown that political mendacity is as shameless and as systemic as anything alleged – let alone proven – against the British media. Yet it is even more devastating in its effects. Though media lying always causes great harm, government lying directly undermines authority and the structures of the state. Government lying amounts to a horrifying assault on civil society, the main reason that mendacity is always embedded in totalitarian regimes.

Yet New Labour itself, and its wider circle of supporters, refuses to accept that the problem even exists. This is very mysterious. Several years ago I remarked to David Miliband, a rising star in the Tony Blair government, that it was a pity that New Labour lied. He looked at me askance, and told me to 'be careful in your use of words'. I once offered David Goodhart, the editor of the thoughtful and intelligent and broadly Blairite magazine *Prospect*, an article on government lying. Goodhart turned down the offer on the basis that the thesis was uninteresting, or so he said. John Lloyd, an extremely experienced journalist, vehemently levels the charge of mendacity at the press. But he acquits New Labour of serious lying. Not only that, he goes to the length of quoting consummate and scheming liars like Alastair Campbell and Peter Mandelson with sympathy and respect.

There is an interesting collective psychology at work here. Publicly, New Labour is emphatic that it does not lie. In private conversation, however, I have found that New Labour ministers and their supporters are occasionally capable of acknowledging that leading figures in the government deceive, dissimulate and lie. In my experience they rarely show much worry or concern, accepting this as something that has to be done, of no importance. Illuminating examples of this tolerant attitude can be found in two major sympathetic New Labour biographies: Donald Macintyre's book on Peter Mandelson and John Rentoul's life of Tony Blair. Rentoul fastidiously records examples of Blair mendacity before moving briskly on to other things. Macintyre takes the same approach with Peter Mandelson. This absence of comment by both authors, each of whom is properly sympathetic to their subject, is very telling.

Macintyre's fine book is marred by this one omission: Peter Mandelson is one of the most profligate liars in British public life. Many people who have had dealings with Mandelson know this perfectly well. Indeed Macintyre is far too scrupulous a writer not to describe some of those lies himself. Yet he passes by Mandelson's mendacity unobtrusively, in the muted, matter-of-fact tone of a bank manager drawing embarrassed attention to a bounced cheque. For instance Macintyre reveals how, during the Ecclestone affair in which it was alleged that the government had changed a policy as a result of a political donation, 'Mandelson replied, not strictly accurately, that by the time the *Sunday Telegraph* made its first enquiry, "the Prime Minister had decided that the original donation should be returned and that the further donation should not be accepted."'[15] (The phrase 'not strictly accurately' does not do full justice to the out-and-out mendacity that Mandelson employed on this occasion.) Macintyre's thorough book, rightly regarded as an outstanding political biography and a key to understanding the New Labour movement, fails to give anything like proper attention to the grave difficulty his admired subject found in telling the truth. And yet habitual deceit is one of Mandelson's defining characteristics, like Asquith's drinking or Ramsay MacDonald's fondness for duchesses. Macintyre's failure to give more than a passing glance at the elephant in the drawing room suggests either that he did not notice, or that he took it for granted that Mandelson was an habitual liar but felt the trait unworthy of exploration, or simply regarded lying as just one of those things that happen.

Rentoul is open to the same line of criticism. Take for instance, the following passage in his biography of Tony Blair, describing the secret role of Peter Mandelson in Blair's bid for the party leadership:

> The extraordinary fact about Mandelson's role in the campaign is that, officially, he did not exist. The official campaign team had been unveiled on the day of Blair's announcement. Mo Mowlam and Jack Straw were joint campaign managers. The campaign committee consisted of Peter Kilfoyle, Andrew Smith, the fraternal delegate from Gordon Brown's Treasury team, Barry Cox, the television executive and only member from outside Westminster, who was responsible for fundraising, and Anji Hunter, head of Blair's office. The committee met every morning, but the decisions that mattered – about media strategy and speeches – were taken elsewhere.
>
> The central figure in the 'real' Blair campaign was Mandelson. The transparent fiction that Mandelson was 'not involved' was deemed necessary because Mowlam and Kilfoyle were two of many who told Blair that they would not work for him if Mandelson had anything to do with the campaign. It meant an elaborate deception had to be maintained.[16]

There are two points to be made about this piece. The first is that Rentoul is far too honest a writer to cover up the details of Tony Blair's deceit. It is set out in full in an exemplary piece of reporting. It is notable, however, that Rentoul expresses no anger, moral criticism or even surprise at Blair's duplicity. And his claim that Mo Mowlam and Peter Kilfoyle's hostility towards Mandelson 'meant an elaborate deception had to be maintained' is simply wrong. Mowlam and Kilfoyle's hostility to Mandelson meant nothing of the sort. It meant there was a problem, that was all. It was a problem that could have been resolved by hammering out the issue in the open. Blair could have confronted Mowlam and Kilfoyle, bluntly told them that Mandelson was part of the deal, and they could like it or lump it. Alternatively he could have admitted defeat and informed Peter Mandelson he was not wanted. Those are the two courses that an honest man would have adopted.

But Tony Blair resolved on neither. Instead he chose secrecy and deception. The lie did not, as Rentoul's language suggests, flow as a matter of course from Mowlam and Kilfoyle's hostility. Quite the reverse. An alternative course of action was to hand. Blair could have told the truth. Indeed it would have been much better if he had. But Rentoul, perhaps forgivably in a biographer, enters a fraction too readily into the mindset of a politician who, when confronted with a problem, feels he has no choice but to deceive two of his closest supporters.*

In a way it is unfair to single out Rentoul and Macintyre. They are two of the most well-informed, honest and fair-minded of New Labour sympathising journalists. But it is their very fair-mindedness that makes each of their cases so telling. The fact that even the most honourable and relatively detached pro-government writers show such little curiosity or alarm at the mendacity of their respective subjects is important. It shows the extent to which mendacity is tolerated among even the most attractive and thoughtful apologists for the New Labour culture.

---

* Rentoul does criticise Tony Blair for later publicly thanking 'Bobby', his code name for Peter Mandelson, once he had secured the leadership. But here he criticises Blair for bringing the deception to a wider public, and thereby demonstrating 'an arrogance and a disdain for many in the Labour Party', and not for the original deception.

There is a very important disproportion at work here. New Labour endlessly claims to feel a deep and powerful moral revulsion at the alleged lies uttered by its opponents, whether the Tories or the tabloid press. But in their own ranks they tolerate – or fail to notice – mendacity on an awesome scale. New Labour figures like the remarkable Denis MacShane have no hesitation in uttering the most flagrant lies themselves, yet constantly make the charge of lying at the opponents, quite often with no justification.

This presence of a group of shameless, habitual liars at the centre of power is an amazing state of affairs, without precedent in modern British history. It is responsible for a widening abyss in standards of integrity between government and the wider world of British public life. New Labour standards of truth and falsehood are not merely far shoddier and less demanding than those of the population at large. They are also quite different in kind.

Over the past few years New Labour has smashed the established dividing line between truth and falsehood, and put another in its place. Peter Mandelson and Alastair Campbell, Tony Blair's two propaganda chiefs, have converted truth into an instrument of power. They have privatised the truth, rather as the Conservative Party took the utilities, telecoms and rail industries out of public ownership in the 1980s and 1990s. In an act of grand larceny, truth and falsehood have been removed from the public sphere, and put to the particular use of New Labour. The motive may well have been virtuous, but the consequences are hateful. Attempts to appropriate the truth are always very dangerous. Governing parties from time to time make these claims to ownership of the truth. Historical precedent shows they can be a prelude to an assault on the freedoms of the citizen, the rule of law, and political stability. The remainder of this book will examine ways in which the truth can be reclaimed from the political elite, and restored to the common domain.

11

HOW TO REBUILD PUBLIC TRUTH

'Democracy is about conceding power to those with whom you disagree, not to those with whom you agree' – Jack Straw, 25 April 1995

In this last chapter I set out a handful of modest ideas that are intended to restore the values of truthfulness, accuracy, integrity and scruple to British public life. The intention is not to make political debate less vigorous, passionate or purposeful. Still less are these proposals designed to establish an advantage for a particular political party. On the contrary, they will bring clarity to debate. They will ensure that, whatever else the parties dispute, they can at any rate agree about the facts.

If implemented, these proposals will help eradicate the bitter disputes about process and manipulation that disfigure all modern election campaigns. They will remove much of the need for the bitter personal attacks and the accusations of bad faith. Instead politicians will be liberated to have more profound, intellectually honest debates about the great issues of our time. These proposals will help lift the curse of cynicism and deceit from British politics and replace it with decency and hope. They will indirectly bring back voters to the polling booths, and help to restore our democracy to vigorous health.

'FactCheck'

Statements by politicians of all parties contain lies, deceptions and distortions of the facts. Sometimes journalists bring these false-hoods to public attention, but much more often they fail to do so. Most of the time the reason for this neglect is simply that reporters are too ignorant, stupid, lazy or just occasionally too busy to spare the time to pay careful attention to the veracity of what a politician is saying. In a significant number of occasions this failure springs from more venal motives. The journalist does not want to offend the spin-doctor or minister who provides him with his best stories and access, so he chooses not to bring his informant's mendacity and moral turpitude to public attention.

There is a crying need for a body to bring back integrity to the political process by monitoring the statements of politicians of all parties. A model for this is the FactCheck.org website, which cov-ered the US presidential election for the first time in 2004.

FactCheck confined itself to a specific aim: monitoring the pres-idential candidates, their party spokesmen and their advertisements (a much larger feature of American than British politics) for lies and deceptions. To take a random example: on 18 October 2004 FactCheck examined a John Kerry ad that claimed 'Bush has a plan to cut Social Security benefits by 30% to 45%'. The FactCheck diag-nosis was taut and brief: 'That's false. Bush has proposed no such plan and the proposal Kerry refers to would only slow down the growth of benefits, and only for future retirees.'The same treatment was handed out to the Bush campaign. Anyone wishing to get a fuller flavour of the work the organisation does should visit the FactCheck.org website.

FactCheck has only been in operation since December 2003. At the start of the presidential campaign FactCheck was practically unknown, yet by September 2004 there were an average of 29,000 visitors per day to its website. Then, during the vice-presidential debate, Dick Cheney made a reference to FactCheck, calling it in aid to dispel a lurid allegation made against him about his connection with the construction giant Halliburton. FactCheck's profile immediately shot up. It took more than 100,000 visitors per day during the final two weeks of the campaign, and came to be quoted as an authority on the press and TV. FactCheck was able to enter the fray as a neutral arbiter when campaign rows blew up, for instance sifting fact from fiction during the Swift Boat Vets allegations.

Towards the end of the campaign FactCheck was coming to fill an important gap in public space by bringing integrity to the notoriously mendacious US election struggle. It is important to understand the sources of its authority. The first crucial factor was its utter impartiality between the two election candidates. It treated them both with equal scepticism. The second was its financial independence. FactCheck's three-person staff is funded by the Annenberg Family Foundation. The third factor was its nous.

The genius behind FactCheck is a journalist named Brooks Jackson, who has many years' experience on the *Wall Street Journal* and with CNN behind him. 'Basically you've got to be a journalist who's been lied to a few times to do this job,' he told me in October 2004 when I talked to him in his unostentatious office in the

National Press Building, not far from the White House. He says that politics produces so much paper, so many press releases, so many policy documents, that it is impossible to check every statement. This means that a sixth sense for the false and misleading is essential. .'Politicians are incorrigible,'Jackson told me.'It's in their blood. They don't look at the facts in the way that you and I and other journalists do. They look at facts as a weapon.'[1]

There is a burning need today for a comparable organisation in Britain to monitor the mendacities put out by the three main parties. It should not merely focus on the lies of government. Mendacious assertions put out by Tories about government policy, or the lies which Liberal Democrats famously tell during by-election campaigns and elsewhere, should fall within its remit.

Once a British 'FactCheck' is established, it should be able to reclaim a great portion of public space for the straightforward, objective truth. The sources and bases of its judgements must always be transparent and open to challenge and, if need be, correction. Its only interest must be to establish the facts. The interpretation it will leave to others. In due course it may well take its place as one of the British public institutions that sanction and protect civil society.

There are already several model organisations that enjoy independence and therefore public integrity. The Bank of England, for instance, now enjoys the sanctity that derives from independence. Its job is not to decide policy. It leaves that task to ministers, acting through parliament. But in its own very narrow sphere – the implementation of monetary policy to meet the various targets laid down for it – the Bank of England is sovereign and no longer open to political manipulation. The National Audit Office, based on statute and responsible to parliament rather than ministers, brings massive confidence to British public accounts.

Other guardians of British public truth are less grand yet no less impressive. The most relevant example, specialising in the narrow though vital field of economic policy, is the Institute for Fiscal Studies. Economic policy-making by the political parties is probably the single area where there is greater rigour today than thirty years ago. When parties lay out their economic manifestos they no longer make the inflated growth and other assumptions that were common practice three decades ago. These deceptions of the electorate are no longer possible in part because of the presence of the IFS, which makes publicly available its dry, candid, disinterested analysis of the economic statements of the political parties.

It is worth pausing a moment to reflect on the origins of this remarkable organisation. It has its origins in what would now be called civil society. Four professional people from the City – a banker, an investment trust manager, a stockbroker and a tax consultant – were appalled by the way that the 1965 Finance Act was introduced.[2] The four men agreed on the need for an independent research institute to procure a more rational tax system. It came from outside the political process, and has proved a powerful force for good. Like the Bank of England it has brought back candour into British policy making.

'MediaCheck'

Independent monitoring of statements issued by politicians and the party machines would be a powerful factor in bringing trust back into the political process. There is an equally strong argument for disinterested, fact-based analysis of political coverage in the media. As Onora O'Neill said in her Reith Lectures:'Our present culture of suspicion cannot be dispelled by making everyone except the media trustworthier. To restore trust we need not only trustworthy persons and institutions, but also assessable reasons for trusting and for mistrusting.'[3]

Dame Onora's observation is true in the most profound sense. Politicians and governments mainly talk to voters through newspapers and the airwaves. They have no choice. This has not always been the case. At an earlier, and in many ways happier, stage of democratic evolution politicians talked to voters directly. The political parties, which only half a century ago had vast membership bases of one million and upwards, could send activists out door-to-door and use direct, face-to-face contact in a way that is out of the question today.

Meanwhile newspapers held back from interpretation of political speeches. Instead they printed them in full, and they were avidly read by a politically literate electorate hungry for knowledge and understanding. Real political oratory flourished. The arrival of a government minister at a local constituency would raise a crowd of hundreds. The great orators could command tens of thousands, coming from miles around. Historians record that Gladstone drew crowds of over 100,000 in his Midlothian Campaign.'Shouters'were stationed at outlying vantage points. Their job was to absorb Gladstone's thunderous message, delivered without notes and full of magnificent biblical imagery, and pass it as best they could to those beyond direct hearing range. In the best attended events, yet more distant shouters were employed to relay the words to the most outlying parts of the audience.

Today's media have taken on the role of Gladstone's shouters. But unlike them, they no longer seek to deliver the message from the politician direct. They interpret it, highlighting parts and omitting others. They rarely soften a politician's message. Instead they can brutalise it, cheapen, distort and sometimes falsify it. According to Onora O'Neill we now live in a world where media conglomerates have 'unrestricted rights of free expression, and therefore a licence to subject positions for which they don't care to caricature and derision, misrepresentation or silence'.[4]

O'Neill's remarks show that it is vital not merely that voters should feel able to trust their political leaders, but also the media through which they learn about our politics. It is almost as important that politicians themselves should feel trust in the media, rather than the furious hatred, contempt and suspicion that – to give the most potent example – defined the relationship between the Labour Party and the British press in the 1980s. The jibe made by the Conservative prime minister Stanley Baldwin at the British newspaper barons in 1931, drafted by his cousin Rudyard Kipling, that 'power without responsibility is the prerogative of the harlot' is apposite today.

Those within government who call for the media to play a role in widening rather than narrowing British public life, and making the democratic process more generous and creative, are completely right. The media must not belong to a private world with their own rules and mechanisms, estranged from the events they report, and the consequences of the way they report them. The media too have their huge responsibility to the truth. They, just like politicians, can thieve it from the public domain. No political journalist can look back with ease at the way that the Labour leader Neil Kinnock, a substantial politician and a figure of enormous public legitimacy, was victimised and converted into a caricature by the press. The treatment of Kinnock was an abuse of media power.

Everybody knows what John Lloyd means when he quite correctly attacks the media for a tendency to 'polemicise the world, rather than seek an understanding of it'.[5] The modern British media have the ability to make the world a nastier and meaner place, and can use that power with horrible effect. It is right that they should be made much more accountable. The only real question is how.

The most practical suggestion to have emerged so far comes from the Geoff Mulgan, former head of policy at Downing Street. 'There might be value to apply validation to the media themselves,' he said in his 2004 LSE lecture:

> There is no question of the state having any role in this. But it is entirely plausible that civil society, perhaps with the universities, could play a much more active role in assuring standards, investigating errors, and holding to account individual journalist and media outlets against a strong ethic of truth and accuracy, just as they should hold governments to account too.[6]

There are hazards to Geoff Mulgan's proposition. Its objectives might have to be clearly defined. Academia – his suggested vehicle – rarely shows any sophistication about how the media works, or what it is for. But Mulgan's notion is at bottom an attractive one. It is reassuring that he understands that government can play no role in a monitoring body.

As is so often the case with this most engaging figure, he has sketched out few details. Once again, however, the IFS and

FactCheck.org models are relevant. In order to act as a powerful force for good, 'MediaCheck' would need to obtain the authority that the IFS already possesses in the economic field in the UK or FactCheck.org has been starting to acquire in American political discourse. MediaCheck would need to be formally independent of government and political parties. There would be no reason at all, however, why ministers, opposition spokesmen and MPs should not bring as many cases as they want to the attention of MediaCheck.

If it is to restore integrity and trust to British political coverage, MediaCheck's judgements need to be respected and feared by newspaper editors and reporters. As with the IFS, this authority can only come from independence, impartiality and an austere dedication to the truth. MediaCheck must never concern itself with interpretation, but only with accuracy. The motto of the website would be drawn from the famous article by C. P. Scott, editor of the *Manchester Guardian*, published on 5 May 1921: 'Neither in what it gives, nor in what it does not give, nor in the unclouded face of presentation must the unclouded face of truth suffer wrong. Comment is free but facts are sacred.'

This website would provide a sharp, well-written daily commentary on the factual accuracy of the political reporting of Britain's newspapers and broadcasting stations. Its job would be to cause the maximum possible aggravation to newspapers and broadcasters that tell lies and distort the facts, and in so doing debase and damage our public life. As a secondary benefit, it would rescue the British media and help return them to civil society.

Trusting Statistics

The most creative and benign act of reform carried out by the New Labour government remains the first: the announcement by Chancellor Gordon Brown that he was giving independence back to the Bank of England. There were many obscurantist critics, above all in the Tory party, who attacked the move. They argued that it was wrong because it took economic policy-making away from political control. In practice the move granted a massive new integrity to a crucial area of economic policy, boosted public confidence, and played a part in sustaining economic stability over the past seven years.

Today there is an equally compelling case that the British government should renounce control of public information, just as in 1997 it renounced control of interest rates. Successive governments – not just the present New Labour administration – have manipulated statistics for political ends. They have converted public information from being a neutral, common resource and converted it into a weapon of political debate.

Though in the short term the conversion of information into a political tool has always helped governments to make their case, in the long term it has created suspicion and distrust. The classic statement of this point of view came from Jack Straw, when he protested against manipulation of statistics by John Major's Tory government.

Straw's important but under-reported protest was made in a speech to the Royal Statistical Society on 25 April 1995. The speech was delivered at a delicate point in British politics. The collapse in economic policy which led to the ERM debacle of September 1992, along with the series of 'sleaze' revelations concerning Conservative MPs, had led to what was regarded at the time as a crisis in public trust. Straw's arguments deserve close attention. They are even more relevant today than they were then:

> In any democracy the public should have a healthy scepticism about the claims, and practices, of politicians. But there can come a point where the cynicism goes so deep that it corrodes the foundations of our political system, leading to a wholesale lack of confidence in the system, and to a detachment between the governed, and what is perceived to be the governing class – in which I include MPs of all parties. I believe that we are dangerously close to that position today.

Straw went on to make a subtle and interesting point:

> In the last six years, every serious newspaper has abandoned its straight reporting of parliament. One consequence of this is that the allegedly factual report has replaced the speech as a key political weapon. Those of us who have spent as long as I have in opposition know that a statistically based report on this or that will command far greater attention, than ever a speech will. In turn this has placed an ever higher political premium on the nature and availability of official statistics.

This meant, as Straw said earlier in his speech, that 'Information, statistics, has become the hard and brittle currency of politics. The nature of that information, its collection, dissemination, and control, has become key to the partisan battle for the hearts and minds of the electorate.'[7]

Straw hastened to add that he was not criticising the integrity of government statisticians. His worry was a broader one: what ministers were doing with the raw data. He suggested that it was too susceptible to manipulation by government, and not accessible enough to opposition parties. Straw cited a number of abuses that he believed the Tory government had committed, including manipulation of the employment figures and fragmentation of health statistics so that they cease to create a meaningful picture. The Tory and Liberal Democrat oppositions today would also cite plenty of examples.* In a remarkable passage, Straw called for change: 'Democracy is about conceding power to those with whom you disagree, not to those with whom you agree; and about ensuring that every citizen has a similar access to the information on which decisions are made and governments are judged.[8]

Straw's solution was extremely audacious. He called for the creation of a new, independent National Statistical Service. In many ways he anticipated what Gordon Brown would do to the Bank of England. Jack Straw pledged a 'Governance of Britain Act' that would take the new strengthened statistical office out of the control of ministers, give it statutory independence, and place it in the same relation to parliament and the government as the National Audit Office already enjoyed.

The incoming New Labour government pledged to bring about

---

* In late 2004 shadow chancellor Oliver Letwin brought forward proposals for changes to the statistical service that bore a close similarity to those suggested by Jack Straw. (See his National Statistics Draft Bill, published on 31 January 2005.) Its purpose is to 'free national statistics from political interference and make them the most accountable and transparent in the world'. In an accompanying press release Letwin promised to introduce the bill within three months of winning a general election, stating that 'national statistics must serve, and be seen to serve, the interests of the country, not the ruling party'. The problem is that proposals made in opposition to liberate public information rarely look so good in government.

this reform in the 1997 manifesto.[9] Once Labour obtained power the promise was broken, and government statistics were left under ministerial control, with the miserable consequences which Jack Straw outlined in 1995.* It is time to dig up Jack Straw's proposal on official statistics again. It would be an important step forward towards returning truth to the common domain.

Rebuilding the Distinction Between Party and State

For more than a century the British civil service has been regarded as the most honest in the world. It has stood for an ethic of fastidious, disinterested public service. In recent years this reputation has been grievously undermined. Though this process accelerated sharply under New Labour, the Tory governments led by Margaret Thatcher and, to a less striking extent, John Major led the way. Indeed nothing illustrates the contemporary confusion between the party and the public domain more poignantly than the role of Margaret Thatcher's foreign affairs adviser Charles Powell.

In theory Charles Powell was a civil servant who, while faithfully serving the government of the day, should have remained detached from party interest. Charles (now Lord) Powell was, however, careless at observing the distinction. He allowed himself to become deeply embroiled in party politics, as the following entry in the Alan Clark diaries illustrates:

---

* 'The service is still fragmented. The code of practice is defective. It places far too great a reliance on administrative sources. Ministers continue to be able to manipulate the presentation of data . . .'

I couldn't get home as there was a little dinner at Lyall Street. Just Aspers [John Aspinall, gambler and zoo-keeper], Jimmy Goldsmith and Charles Powell. The 'guest' was Conrad Black [then *Daily Telegraph* proprietor], the purpose to see to what extent he was amenable to being leant on, in the gentlest manner of course, to steer Max [Hastings, *Daily Telegraph* editor] away from plugging Heseltine so much.[10]

It was quite improper that Charles Powell should have been any-where near this conspiratorial little gathering. Powell was going down a path that would in due course be followed by his younger brother Jonathan Powell, 'chief of staff' to Tony Blair, more egre-giously by Alastair Campbell, and by various others. Charles Powell was an early but very important example of a demeaning contem-porary trend: the public servant who no longer grants his primary loyalty to the state and cedes it instead to the ruling party.

This transgression of boundaries is one of the important reasons for the rise of political lying. Civil servants should be disinterested guardians of the truth. Instead they have allowed it to be lifted out of the public domain and put to private political use. As we have seen, those civil servants – like Sir Richard Wilson – who objected to this theft of the public truth were partially frozen out. The effects of this ugly new practice were seen most famously in the Iraq dossiers of September 2002 and February 2003, but also in scores of less newsworthy cases, a number of them cited in this book.

Civil servants have been made accomplices to political deceit. This has happened because the constitutional settlement that emerged from the Gladstonian Reforms of the 1850s has started to come under threat and even to collapse. But it is essential that the principles that lay behind that settlement should be restated in a new Civil Service Act that will re-establish the dividing line between party and state. The Blair government has promised this legislation on a number of occasions but always reneged. It is urgently needed.

Parliament Must Regain Its Role

It is for the most part legal for a politician to lie and deceive the British people. Yet political lying pollutes the public sphere. It is a form of non-violent assault upon the electorate, because it deprives voters of their right to make a balanced and well-informed choice at election time.

Until recently there was a well-established mechanism to deal with politicians who failed to tell the truth. It was called parliament. The worst offence a politician could commit was to mislead parliament, while the most grievous solecism an MP could commit inside the Commons chamber was to cast doubt upon the good faith of a fellow MP by calling him a liar.

Yet this parliamentary sanction has weakened sharply in recent years. There are two reasons for this. The first is a consequence of the declining power of parliament, and the rising importance of the media. Politicians now spend far more time than they used to speaking directly to voters, either in television studios, in press conferences or elsewhere. Policy statements are now made outside the Commons chamber, so ministers cannot so readily be held to account by colleagues, and made subject to the very substantial disciplinary powers of the Parliament.

The second reason is just as concerning. It remains the case that parliament continues to enforce the strict rule that prohibits one MP from accusing another of misleading the House. In this respect it is more vigilant than ever. But it has become ever more lax about enforcing its own laws regarding good faith and honesty. An early and worrying manifestation of this change in attitude came with the Arms to Iraq affair at the end of the long Tory period in office. Though Sir Richard Scott's inquiry found Conservative ministers had misled the House of Commons, not one felt obliged to resign.

Seven years of New Labour have done nothing to restore standards of integrity. It has now become quite common for the prime minister and others to breach ministerial codes of conduct with impunity. Section one of the Ministerial Code insists that 'it is of paramount importance that ministers give accurate and truthful information to Parliament, correcting any inadvertent error at the earliest opportunity.'

It looks as if some select committees have lost the will or ability to pursue those who mislead them. In November 2004 there was a sad little debate as the government abolished the old House of Commons Sessional Orders that the Speaker would read out at every state opening of parliament. The purpose of these orders was in part to reiterate the grave importance of telling the truth to parliament. The language was old-fashioned, but its meaning was unequivocal as it stated that tampering with witnesses who appear before the Commons 'Is declared to be a high crime and misdemeanour; and this House will proceed with the utmost severity against such offender.'

The language had stood for hundreds of years, but was casually washed away as part of the latest modernisation proposals. The move was briefly debated in an almost empty chamber late on a

Wednesday afternoon. Only a few MPs noticed, and only a tiny number, led by the Labour MP Andrew MacKinlay, protested. Six months earlier the Foreign Affairs Committee, after a brief discussion, decided not to mount a proper investigation into the sharp contradictions between the evidence given by the prime minister's director of communications Alastair Campbell to the Foreign Affairs Committee, to the Intelligence and Security Committee and to the Hutton Inquiry.

Make Political Lying a Crime

British MPs and ministers used to be renowned through the world for their high standards of probity and integrity. Although there are notable individual exceptions, including quite a number in Tony Blair's cabinet,* that general sense of redoubtable honesty that was such an enviable element of British government has in general vanished. It used to be widely felt that British public life abided by comfortably higher standards of integrity than those that existed in private business. Now that situation has reversed.

One of the reasons for this is the toughening up of company law and financial regulation that has taken place in the past few decades. Company directors who make misleading statements can now be prosecuted and, in extreme cases of dishonesty, jailed. In the City of London the old system of self-regulation, based on the

---

* To give just a handful of examples, I have come across no cases of Charles Clarke, John Reid, Patricia Hewitt, Tessa Jowell, Peter Hain, Margaret Beckett, Alan Milburn, Hilary Benn, Hilary Armstrong, Paul Boateng or plenty of other ministers lying or deceiving the public in a serious way.

attractive but outdated idea that 'my word is my bond', has been replaced by statutory regulation. The tougher regime, and the threat of jail facing business people who tell lies, has led to a restoration of standards and public trust after the succession of financial scandals in the City in the 1980s.

Those who doubt whether it is right to impose the same punitive sanctions on politicians might care to embark upon the following thought experiment: imagine that a famous British company decided to raise substantial funds on the stockmarket. Imagine that a very few months after the flotation it emerged that everything claimed in the prospectus was false. Imagine that the assets it had boasted of simply didn't exist, and that the profit streams were a fabrication.

Imagine the outcry as investors lost all of their money. Imagine the fury in parliament, and the angry denunciations of City corruption from Labour MPs and ministers. Imagine Tony Blair's scathing condemnation of corporate incompetence at Prime Minister's Questions. Imagine the Conservative Party leader eagerly joining in. Imagine the prim announcement from the Trade and Industry Secretary that there would be a public investigation.

Imagine that the enquiry was carried out by Lord Butler, the former Cabinet Secretary. Imagine that at the conclusion of his work he was able to show that the accountants who provided the raw material had warned that the figures were speculative and uncertain, but this warning had never been passed on to the investing public. Not only that, but Lord Butler had demonstrated that other material information, which cast the flotation in an unfortunate light, had been withheld from the investors. The fraud squad would likely have been brought in, and collars felt.

In the case of a fraudulent company prospectus, only money goes missing. The September dossier was a fraudulent prospectus for war, and it led to the deaths of tens of thousands of Iraqis, and scores of British soldiers. And yet not a soul in government lost his job, and the individual who controlled the dossier was later promoted. It would be an excellent idea if the threat of criminal prosecution made politicians, like company promoters, hesitate before making extravagant and false claims.

Conclusion

The six suggestions above would help. But what Britain really needs is not just a change in the law, but a change of heart. We face a choice. We can do nothing, and carry on cheating, and deceiving each other, and wait for the public anger, alienation and disgust that will follow. We can watch the gradual debasement of decent democratic politics, and the rapid rise of the shysters and the frauds and – before very long perhaps – something nastier by far.

Or we can try and act once more as moral human beings. It's a common effort. It affects us all, politicians, journalists, citizens. But there is hope. Britain has a magnificent tradition of public integrity and civic engagement, which can all be reclaimed. It could even be better than before.

Appendix One

Independent
25 November 1992

How Ministers Hide the Facts by Telling the Truth

Anyone privileged enough to have read the sheaves of Whitehall documents disgorged to the Old Bailey during the Matrix Churchill trial will know that there are lies, damn lies and parliamentary answers, says Anthony Bevins.

Take just three replies given by ministers in the wake of press'speculation'that ministers had connived with machine tool manufacturers to encourage the export of arms-related equipment to Iraq in the late 1980s.

On Wednesday 5 December 1990, at a meeting of the Western European Union, Sir Russell Johnston, a senior Liberal Democrat MP, had the brass neck to ask Alan Clark, then Minister for Defence Procurement, whether he'was aware of and connived at sales from the United Kingdom to Iraq of equipment which could be used for military purposes?'

Mr Clark replied: 'I have a complete and total answer to these allegations, which are rubbish, trash and sensational, and in the fullness of time that answer will be presented . . .'

It was Mr Clark's evidence in the Old Bailey case – presenting a diametrically different answer – that brought the trial to a close.

But there are other techniques for skinning the inquisitive cats of the Commons. On 18 December 1990, a Labour MP asked Peter Lilley, then Secretary of State for Trade and Industry: 'What advice was given by his department to exporters of sensitive material to Iraq in the late 1980s?'

The truthful answer would have been that Sir Geoffrey Howe, Foreign Secretary, had published guidelines on arms-related exports to Iraq and Iran in October 1985. Those guidelines had been 'amended' in December 1988, and the Old Bailey papers showed that not only the wording, but the application of the guidelines had been relaxed – along with a deliberate decision not to disclose the changes to Parliament.

So Mr Lilley said in his written Commons reply: 'Guidelines on sensitive exports to Iraq were published in October 1985.' That was true. But far from the whole truth, and Mr Lilley knew it.

Finally, take a question and answer from Sir David Steel to Mr Major on 31 January 1991. Sir David asked the Prime Minister if he would consider setting up an inquiry 'into the acquisition by Iraq of British arms and technology'.

Mr Major said: 'There is a considerable degree of sensitivity about the supply of arms and equipment . . . for some considerable time we have not supplied arms to Iraq for precisely that reason.' In the first sentence, the Prime Minister dealt with the two issues raised by Sir David – 'arms and technology'. In the second sentence, which Sir David this week politely called 'an elision', the Prime Minister did not mention technology or equipment. If he had said that Britain had not supplied arms and equipment to Iraq, he would have been telling a lie.

Every scandal provides such a pattern of carefully-crafted Whitehall duplicity – from the 1986 Westland affair to last month's pit closure programme.

After the *General Belgrano* had been torpedoed during the 1982 Falklands conflict, John Nott, Secretary of State for Defence, told the Commons that the Argentinian cruiser 'had been closing on elements of our task force . . . from a distance of some 200 nautical miles'. Tam Dalyell, Labour's most obsessive parliamentary sleuth, asked what course she had been on when she was attacked. In a written Commons reply on 29 November 1982, he was told that when the *Belgrano* was torpedoed, she was on a course of 280 degrees – almost due west.

Mr Dalyell realised that there was something dreadfully wrong. If the *Belgrano* was 200 miles from the task force, and was 'closing on' it on a course of 280 degrees, then, given her position when she was torpedoed, the task force must have been sailing about somewhere on the South American mainland. At that point, the government lies began to become unstitched.

Any honest autobiography will expose the nature of the game. Take Nigel Lawson's recent *View from No 11*, in which he reveals the extent of his disputes with Margaret Thatcher – the same Margaret Thatcher who in May 1989 dismissed speculation that Mr Lawson and Sir Geoffrey Howe were for the chop in a July reshuffle, saying: 'Do you know how much hurt you do to them, to their families, to their children? It is wounding. You wound . . .

'Nigel is a very good neighbour of mine, and a very good Chancellor. Geoffrey is a very good Foreign Secretary.' She then added: 'I am not going any further.'

But Mrs Thatcher did go further in her July reshuffle, when she shunted her very good Foreign Secretary from the Foreign Office into the relative backwater of the Commons leadership. Mr Lawson resigned the following October.

But not all of the duplicity of government is disclosed in the words that politicians speak. Mr Lawson also revealed that before the English poll tax legislation had been published, he had naturally been asked, as Chancellor, to be one of its sponsors.

With some satisfaction, he wrote that neither the press nor the Labour Opposition noticed, but he declined. His name was not on the Bill because he regarded the effects of the tax to be 'insupportable'.

So silence, too, is a golden rule of Whitehall. After the 1985 Howe guidelines had been amended in December 1988, William Waldegrave, then Minister of State at the Foreign Office, said in a letter to Mr Clark: 'The form of words we agreed to use if we are now pressed in Parliament over the guidelines was the following: "The guidelines on the export of defence equipment to Iran and Iraq are kept under constant review, and are applied in the light of prevailing circumstances, including the ceasefire and developments in the peace negotiations."'

That, too, was true, as far as it went – while not disclosing that the guidelines had been rewritten.

But no one ever asked, no one was ever told, and to this day, Mr Waldegrave has kept his mouth shut. Which presumably makes him an eminently-qualified minister with responsibility for open government.

Appendix Two

Observer
13 March 1994

Pork Pies and Political Pickles

A Labour leader lied, says a Government Minister. The Tories do very little else, says Anthony Bevins.

Last week's allegation that James Callaghan lied to the Commons was rich coming from a Tory, but it was by no means the first time the former Labour Prime Minister had been defamed for peddling falsehoods.

At the height of the 1979 election campaign, a devastating *Daily Mail* front page accused Labour's politicians of telling '12 big lies' they hoped would save their necks.

'The big lie is the last refuge of the desperate politician,' the *Mail* thundered. 'And Mr Callaghan is very desperate.'

Offering help to a bamboozled electorate, not to mention Opposition leader Margaret Thatcher, the *Mail* detailed charge and defence: contrasting each of Labour's 'dirty dozen' lies with a Tory truth.

Prime Minister Callaghan had said: 'To pay for income tax cuts the Tories would have to double VAT on clothing, shoes, essential kitchen goods, furniture, cars and so on.'To which the *Mail* replied: 'TRUTH: "We will not double it" – Mrs Thatcher.' Nor, indeed, did they. The lower VAT band was jacked up from 8 per cent to 15 per cent soon after the Thatcher victory, but it took John Major to double it.

Other supposed Labour 'lies' included allegations that the Tories were threatening to 'hive off chunks' of British Airways, and, according to Denis Healey, that the Tories planned to sell off the Government's majority stake in BP. Those were the days.

The boot has stayed on the same Tory foot ever since. But in more than fourteen years of power the crude lie has been turned into a fine art.

Take an early example; the sinking of the *Belgrano* during the 1982 Falklands war. With a forensic deployment of Commons questions, Labour's Tam Dalyell discovered that when the Argentine cruiser had been torpedoed, she had not been a threat to British forces.

The Defence Secretary, John Nott, told the House: 'At the time that she was engaged, the *General Belgrano* and a group of British warships could have been within striking distance of each other in a matter of some five to six hours.'

Noting the 'could', Mr Dalyell asked for the ship's position and course when she was sunk, and found she could only have been a threat if British war ships had been sailing on the Argentine mainland.

But when Mr Dalyell pressed home his attack on Mrs Thatcher, she went under cover of dense Whitehall smoke: 'The precise courses . . . were incidental to the indications we possessed of the threat to the Task Force.' Truth, too, had become incidental.

Mrs Thatcher had a much narrower escape over the 1986 Westland affair, during which Leon Brittan, Trade Secretary, leaked highly selective quotes from a law officer's confidential advice – to smear Michael Heseltine, Defence Secretary, his Cabinet opponent. The question was whether Mrs Thatcher had been told what was going on, and when. A select committee investigation asked, 'Did Mr Brittan have the Prime Minister's prior authority for the disclosure?' and, 'Why did Mr Brittan not tell the Prime Minister he had authorised disclosure?'

But it was unable to come up with the answers because Leon Brittan QC played each ball with a deadpan dead bat; a refusal to respond. It was left to a 1987 hagiography on Mrs Thatcher's subsequent election victory to disclose that on 27 January 1986, the day the critical Westland question had been debated by the Commons, 'Mrs Thatcher confided to a close associate that she might have to resign'.

The attempted suppression of Peter Wright's *Spycatcher*; the sale of arms-related equipment to Iraq; the 'entanglement' of arms and aid in the Pergau dam project; talks with the IRA – the catalogue of deceit and deception is too thick to staple.

A thousand schools to close? 'Honest John Patten', the Education Secretary, says he is going to get rid of 700,000 surplus pupil places by closing fewer than 100 schools. A political settlement in Ireland? Nothing will be agreed until everything is agreed. But then they add, 'but not necessarily agreed by everybody'.

Lies and the manipulation of red tape have turned Whitehall into an impenetrable jungle. But Tory duplicity over taxes at the last election could yet put paid to any lingering traces of Conservative credibility.

Fighting an election campaign targeted on the threat of Labour's tax 'bombshell', Mr Major denied any plans of his own to increase the tax burden. Question: 'Can you give a pledge that the tax burden will not increase?' Major: 'We have brought direct taxation down and will continue to do so.' VAT? Major: 'I've said ad nauseam that I have no plans and see no need to increase it.'

Chancellor Norman Lamont said before the election, that under Labour 'the tax burden borne by ordinary taxpayers – not just the better off – would rise by the equivalent of at least an extra 10 pence in the pound'. Chancellor Kenneth Clarke calculates that, so far, he and Mr Lamont have managed the equivalent of seven pence in the pound.

Things have reached such a pass that earlier this year, in a faint echo of its 'dirty dozen' coup, the *Daily Mail* carried an analysis contrasting some of Mr Major's more fanciful statements with the actualite.

Relish the delicate touches of the Tory press as it deferentially asks: 'Did you really say these things, Prime Minister?' Adding: 'In the interests of fair play the *Mail* records Downing Street's "fabrications".'

Major: 'It is not our expectation that the tax burden would have to increase.' (24.3.92) *Mail*: 'From 6 April, families will be handing over up to twice as big a chunk of their earnings . . . as under Labour's last Chancellor, Denis Healey.'

Major: 'Face-to-face talks with the IRA "would turn my stomach" – 1 November 1993, after the Shankill Road bombing which killed ten.' *Mail*: 'Prime Minister authorised sending of secret messages to the Republicans.'

Major: 'There is going to be no devaluation, no realignment.' (10.9.92) *Mail*: 'Pound devalued after withdrawal from ERM on 16 September 1992.'

Lord Callaghan should issue a libel writ against William Waldegrave, the Minister who characteristically refuses to apologise for his accusation that the former Chancellor lied to the Commons over his plans for sterling devaluation in 1967. The so-called Minister for open government should be sued for every penny he has.

The pity is, we have sunk so low that the Treasury would probably indemnify him.

Twentieth-century cherry-tree factor: the response of the British politician: the art of political lying is to be indirect. A phrase should convey the impression that something is true, when in fact it is an outrageous porkie, and yet leave scope for reinterpretation when the truth emerges. Here are some of the great practiners:

– We have no plans to . . . , meaning 'yes, that is exactly what we are going to do, but we don't want you to know' – John Major during the last election, on the extension of VAT.

– I have not even begun to contemplate Cabinet changes, meaning 'I'm going to sack the Chancellor in a fortnight' – John Major in May last year.

– It would turn my stomach to . . . , meaning 'I am doing it, but it would turn my stomach if you found out' – John Major when his Government was secretly talking to the IRA.

– I cannot foresee the circumstances . . . , meaning 'I'm just waiting to grab the first chance that comes along' – Michael Heseltine on speculation that he would run for the Tory leadership against Mrs Thatcher.

– X is unassailable, meaning 'X and I are at daggers drawn and I'm out to make his life impossible' – Margaret Thatcher on Nigel Lawson, just before he quit.

– Economical with . . . as in 'economical with the truth' meaning 'not' – Cabinet Secretary Robert Armstrong during the *Spycatcher* affair.

Notes

Introduction

1. House of Commons Select Committee on Culture, Media and Sport, 'The Millennium Dome', Minutes of Evidence, 2 December 1997.
2. Nicholas Watt, 'Mandelson casts himself as saviour of Millennium Dome', *The Times*, 3 December 1997.
3. *Evening Standard*, 19 December 1997.
4. Colin Brown, 'Mandy gives birth to baby Dome', *Independent*, 23 February 1998.
5. Quotes from Jim Fitzpatrick, Gerry Steinberg, Claire Ward and Stephen Wallace taken from John Hind, 'Mandelson wants to play. But no one can find the ball', *Observer*, 24 May 1998.
6. House of Commons Select Committee on Culture, Media and Sport, Minutes of Evidence, Examination of Witnesses (Questions 140–159), Wednesday 8 July 1998, Mr Robert Ayling and Ms Jennie Page.
7. Stephen Bayley, *New Labour Camp*, p. 109.
8. John Lloyd, *What the Media are Doing to Our Politics*, p. 205.
9. Robert Peston, *Brown's Britain*, p. 349.

Chapter 1: The Origins of Contemporary Political Lying

1. Peter Oborne, 'Minister: Our right to lie', *Evening Standard*, 8 March 1994.
2. Agence France Presse, 9 March 1994.

3. *Evening Standard*, 8 March 1994.
4. Chris Moncrieff, 'Derisive Smith slates Major's 'clapped out' government', Press Association, 12 March 1994.
5. This section is in part based on two articles by the late Anthony Bevins: 'Pork pies and political pickles', *Observer*, 13 March 1994; 'How ministers hide the facts by telling the truth', *Independent*, 25 November 1992. These two articles are published in full as appendices to this book on p. 265.
6. I am relying for my account of this affair in part on the useful article by Martin Linton, *Guardian*, 9 October 1984. Linton went on to become the Labour MP for Battersea.
7. Magnus Linklater and David Leigh, *Not With Honour*, p. 166.
8. Quoted in Bevins, 'Pork pies'.
9. John Major, speech to Scottish CBI, Glasgow, *Hansard*, 24 September 1992.
10. *Observer*, 28 November 1993.
11. The Scott Report: Enquiry into the Export of Defence Equipment and Dual Use Goods to Iraq and Related Prosecutions, 15 February 1996.
12. See Bevins, 'How ministers hide the facts'.
13. Richard Norton-Taylor, *Truth is a Difficult Concept*, p. 154.
14. Scott Report, D4.12.
15. See Stephen Castle, 'It's not over yet: Despite a brilliant damage-limitation operation the tide may turn against the government', *Independent on Sunday*, 18 February 1996.
16. See Castle, 'It's not over yet'; Leading article, 'Scott has the final word', *Guardian*, 27 February 1996; Donald Macintyre and John Rentoul, 'Ministers distorted my words, says Scott', *Independent*, 23 February 1996. See also the brilliant speech by Robin Cook on 27 February 1996, *Hansard*.
17. Tony Blair, 'Pathetic evasions of a weak government', *Sunday Telegraph*, 25 February 1996.
18. Quoted in Matthew Parris and Kevin Maguire, *Great Parliamentary Scandals*, p. 421.

19. *The Times*, 11 April 1995.

20. John Lloyd, *What the Media are Doing to our Politics*, p. 207. This quote is taken from a long interview with a 'cabinet minister' carried out by John Lloyd at the end of his book. For discussion of this interview, and health warning, see page 9 in the Introduction.

21. John Rentoul, *Tony Blair*, p. 18.

22. Conversation with the author, April 2000.

23. Rentoul, p. 238.

24. Ibid., p. 239.

25. Ibid., p. 264.

26. Tony Blair, Labour Party Conference, 1994.

27. Ibid.

28. Stephen Bates, 'We are on your side, Blair tells voters', *Guardian*, 5 October 1994.

29. Donald Macintyre, *Mandelson*, p. 87.

30. See Lloyd, p. 209.

31. Michael White, 'Let go of official statistics to regain trust, Blair urged', *Guardian*, 19 January 2004.

32. *The Times*, 24 November 1987, quoted by Rentoul, p. 146.

33. Introductory section, 1997 Labour Party manifesto. Note the striking similarities with Michael Howard's 'timetable for action' speech at Conservative Party conference 2004.

34. Tony Blair, *Evening Standard*, 14 April 1997; Robin Cook, Press Association, 2 October 1997.

35. *Guardian*, 3 October 1996.

36. See John Kampfner, 'Blair's business bandwagon backs up party change', *Financial Times*, 21 September 1995.

37. Press Association, 1 August 1996.

38. Draft manifesto, 'New Labour, New Life for Britain', 1996.

39. See *Hansard*, 27 April 1999.

40. *Forbes Magazine*, May 2001.

41. See World Economic Forum Global Competitiveness Reports, 1998 and 2004.

42. Tony Blair, *Hansard*, 16 November 1994.

43. BBC Radio 4 *Today* programme, 7 September 2004.

44. Alison Little, 'Treasury draws up plan to privatise welfare state', Press Association, 16 July 1996.

45. Peter Riddell, 'Clarke's kids were doing the right thing', *The Times*, 18 July 1996.

46. Draft manifesto, 'New Labour, New Life for Britain', 1996.

47. Here and in the paragraphs that follow I am relying very heavily on a series of articles by the economic consultant Keith Marsden in the *Wall Street Journal*. They are 'New Labour, old tools, *Wall Street Journal Europe*, 13 April 1995; 'Britain is no loser', *WSJ Europe*, 9 November 1995; 'Messrs Blair and Brown: Stop denying Britain's success', *WSJ Europe*, 12 January 1996; 'The Tories may lack taste, but Labour lacks truth, *WSJ Europe*, 23 August 1996.

48. See Keith Marsden, 'Miracle or Mirage? Britain's Economy Seen from Abroad', Centre for Policy Studies, 1997. Introduction by Lord Parkinson.

49. Tony Blair interview, 'We'll see off Euro-dragons', *Sun*, 22 April 1997.

50. Tony Blair, *Sun*, 17 April 1997.

51. Paul Dacre, interview with the author.

52. Lloyd, p. 209. But see my health warning in Introduction, page 9.

53. Anthony Bevins, 'Why Tony Blair is the greatest', *New Statesman*, 17 January 2000.

54. Anthony Bevins, 'The Gospel according to Tony', *Daily Express*, 15 June 2000.

55. Polly Toynbee, *Guardian*, 27 November 1996.

Chapter 2: New Labour in Power

1. *The Times*, 3 May 1997.
2. Phil Murphy, Press Association, 7 May 1997.
3. Tony Blair, *Hansard* written answers, 31 July 1997.
4. *Guardian*, 8 July 1998.
5. Alison Little and Roger Williams, 'Reprieve' for Britannia', Press Association, 2 August 1997, usefully lists these papers in a Saturday night news wrap-up.
6. Paul Routledge, 'Britannia may be saved in £50 million refit', *Independent on Sunday*, 3 August 1997.
7. Andrew Grice,'Patten faces prosecution in MI6 probe', 3 August 1997.
8. Jon Sopel, interview with the author, February 2005.
9. *The Times*, 4 August 1997.
10. Kevin Marsh, interview with the author, February 2005.
11. Chris Patten, interview with the author, February 2005.
12. Chris Patten, interview with the author, February 2005.
13. 'Britain boosted by Chancellor's spending spree', *Daily Mirror*, 15 July 1998;'Brown goes on a summer spree', *Daily Mail*, 15 July 1998.
14. Celia Hall,'Brown presents £9 billion NHS rise as £18 billion', *Daily Telegraph*, 15 November 1999; David Hughes, 'Where is the money?', *Daily Mail*, 17 July 1998.
15. Hughes,'Where is the money?'
16. Sion Simon, 'Labour's unhealthy fibs', *Daily Telegraph*, 15 November 1999.
17. See Andrew Grice,'Public go cold on Labour's reheated promises', 19 February 2000; Gaby Hinsliff, 'Same again!', *Daily Mail*, 18 February 2000.
18. 'Straw gives money for 5,000 more policemen', *Daily Telegraph*; 'Long arm of the Straw: 5,000 more cops', *Sun*, taken from'Labour's tap-dance round the truth', *Scotsman*, 22 October 1999.
19. Quoted in Andrew Grice, 'Straw knew vow on new police was misleading', *Independent*, 18 October 1999.
20. Ibid.

21. Dawn Primarolo: 'Personal tax and benefit measures introduced since 1997 have lifted 1.2 million children in the UK out of poverty', *Hansard*, 27 November 2001; Labour Party Manifesto 2001, p. 24:'In this Parliament, over one million children have been lifted out of poverty'; Treasury press release and the Chancellor of the Exchequer:'I can say today that having taken 1.2 million children out of poverty during this Parliament, the Government now propose in the next Parliament to take the second million children out of poverty', quoted in *Daily Mail*, 12 April 2002.

22. See Households Below Average Income Report, published 11 April 2002.

23. Quoted in *The Times*, 12 April 2002.

24. See, for instance, *Guardian*, 28 February 2002.

25. Danny Dorling, Heather Eyre, Ron Johnston and Charles Pattie 'A good place to bury bad news', *Political Quarterly*, 2002, pp. 476–92.

26. Ibid., p. 479.

27. Ibid., p. 480.

28. Ibid.

Chapter 3: From Truth to Falsehood

1. *Hansard*, 23 October 2000.

2. See Jack Malvern, *The Times*, 27 February 2002.

3. Angela Frewin, 'Hospitality looks to new minister for tourism boost', *Caterer and Hotelkeeper*, 26 June 2003.

4. Taken from the profile of Rt Hon. Richard Caborn, Minister for Sport and Tourism, DCMS website, afternoon of 13 January 2005.

5. Tony Bevins, 'Straw misled the Commons in jury debate', *Daily Express*, 25 July 2001.

6. See, for instance, Paul Waugh,'Irish fury at UK handling of farm crisis', *Independent*, 12 March 2001 and *Breakfast with Frost* transcript, http://news.bbc.co.uk/1/hl/programmes/breakfast_with_frost/1214453.stm

7. Sky News, Sunday 11 March 2002.

8. Iain Anderson 'Foot and Mouth Disease', p. 9.

9. Melissa Kite, 'Wheels drop off No 10's single currency double act', 11 August 2003.

10. AFX News Limited, 30 September 2004.

11. *Guardian*, 8 February 2000.

12. Rachel Sylvester, 'Euroscepticism encourages Britain's dark streak of racism says minister', *Daily Telegraph*, 7 August 2004.

13. See BBC Radio 4 *Today* programme, 10 August 2004.

14. See *Hansard*, Minutes of Evidence, 24 March 2004, *Hansard*, 29 October 2003 and *Hansard*, 30 March 2004.

15. See BBC News Online: http://news.bbc.co.uk/vote2001/hi/english/main_issues/sections/facts/newsid_1203000/1203475.stm

16. See Ben Webster, Transport Correspondent, *The Times*, 6 June 2002.

17. See Charles Clover, 'Prescott in a jam over failure to meet promise on car journeys', *Daily Telegraph*, 6 June 2002.

18. Press Association, 6 June 2002.

19. See Patrick O'Flynn, 'Asylum: Scandal of huge cover-up', *Daily Express*, 27 August 2002.

20. See David Hughes, 'Election wins mean voters back the euro claims Straw', *Daily Mail*, 28 August 2002. See also James Lyons and Leigh Arnold, 'Straw plays down fears over EU Constitution', Press Association, 27 August 2002; Hamish MacDonnell, *Scotsman*, 28 August 2002.

21. Joe Haines, *Mail on Sunday*, 1 September 2002.

22. Jack Straw, quoted in *Mail on Sunday*, 1 September 2002.

23. Denis MacShane, quoted in John Kampfner, 'The Minister for Europe', *New Statesman*, 13 December 2004.

24. Denis MacShane, quoted in Kevin Brown, 'Business rejects currency link to job losses', *Financial Times*, 2 February 2001.

25. Denis MacShane, quoted in *Evening Standard*, 16 November 1999. According to the *Evening Standard* report, MacShane 'backed scrapping the pound to join the euro' in debate with Michael Portillo.

26. Denis MacShane, quoted in *Independent*, 11 November 1998; *Mirror*, 11 November 1998.

27. Richard Norton-Taylor, conversation with the author.

28. Max Hastings, conversation with the author, January 2005.

29. Peter Mandelson, quoted in David Hughes, *Daily Mail*, 23 December 1998.

30. Oonagh Blackman, 'I'm Mandy . . . don't fry me', *Daily Mirror*, 17 October 2000.

31. Piers Morgan, quoted in Andy McSmith, 'Mandelson disputes his Mirror image', *Daily Telegraph*, 18 October 2000.

32. Trevor Kavanagh, 'Weapon of deceit', *Sun*, 21 April 1999.

33. Donald Macintyre, *Mandelson*, p. 431.

34. Oborne, Peter, *Alastair Campbell*.

35. Taken from Simon Hoggart's account of the Peter Mandelson interview with Alastair Campbell on Channel 5 Television, *Guardian*, 6 July 2004.

36. Ibid.

37. A transcript can be found on the vote-no.com website, press centre, news archive, 25 November 2004.

38. I have relied for this account on Fraser Nelson, 'Denis MacShane denies making remarks and then backtracks', *Scotsman*, 4 December 2004. Also Fraser Nelson, conversation with the author, December 2004.

39. See Peter Oborne, 'What made Jack Straw tell the truth about the botched coup in Equatorial Guinea', *Spectator*, 24 November 2004.

40. Rory Godson, 'Byers adviser misled Sunday Times writer', 14 October 2001.

41. Tony Blair, BBC Radio 4 *Today* programme, 14 May 2001.

42. John Deane and Andrew Woodcock, 'Blair and Cook defend Vaz', Press Association News, 14 March 2001. See also Nigel Morris, 'Former minister regularly defended by Blair', *Independent*, 9 February 2002.

43. Brian Groom, 'Blair defends Vaz as Tories demand Hinduja questions', *Financial Times*, 27 January 2001.

44. Transcript of Stephen Byers speaking on ITV's *Jonathan Dimbleby* programme; also reported by the Press Association, 24 February 2002.

45. Press Association, 24 February 2002.

46. Estelle Morris speaking on BBC1 *Question Time*, 28 February 2002.

Chapter 4: The Lies, Falsehoods, Deceits, Evasions and Artfulness of Tony Blair

1. Quoted by Piers Morgan, 'The Insider', *Daily Mail*, 28 February 2005.

2. John Rentoul, *Tony Blair*, p. 102. Rentoul hints that Tony Blair's words may have been strictly true in the sense that he could have submitted contributions to the famous Labour supporting paper that had never been printed.

3. Ibid., p. 442.

4. Andrew Pierce, *The Times*, 19 December 1996.

5. Rentoul, p. 16.

6. *Evening Standard*, 15 September 1994.

7. See letter, Michael Heseltine, *The Times*, 24 September 1994.

8. Jon Sopel, *Tony Blair*, p. 65. See Rentoul, p. 252 for a similar account.

9. Tony Blair speaking on BBC1 *Question Time*, 8 July 1999.

10. Tony Blair speaking on BBC Radio 4 *Today* programme, 1 October 1999.

11. Tony Blair speaking on BBC1 *Breakfast News*, 26 July 1999. The bill referred to was the Michael Foster bill.

12. Tony Blair speaking on BBC1 *Question Time*, 8 July 1999.

13. Lobby briefing, 11 a.m., Monday 20 October 2003, Number 10 Downing Street website: 'Asked to confirm that yesterday was the first time the Prime Minister had suffered from the medical condition in question, the PMOS said yes.'

14. For a full account of President Clinton's remarks see *Daily Mirror*, 27 October 2003.

15. Lobby briefing, 11 a.m., Monday 27 October 2003, Number 10 Downing Street website.

16. See Paul Waugh, 'Clinton reveals Blair heart scare details', *Independent*, 26 February 2004.

17. See *Evening Standard*, 20 November 2003.

18. See *Evening Standard*, 20 November 2003. See also Lobby briefing, 3.45 p.m., Thursday 20 November 2003, Downing Street website.

19. BBC2 *Newsnight*, 16 May 2002.

20. Anthony Howard, *The Times*, 21 May 2002.

21. Patrick Wintour, 'The Prime Minister talks to Patrick Wintour about becoming a father at 46, Ken Livingstone and peace in Northern Ireland', *Observer*, 21 November 1999.

22. See http://news.bbc.co.uk/1/hi/uk_politics/649571.stm for this report.

23. John Rentoul, *Tony Blair*, pp. 562–3.

24. Tony Blair, speech to the Fabian Society, July 1995, quoted by Francis Wheen, 'A great feat of ballot-rigging', *Guardian*, 23 February 2000.

25. Tony Blair, *Hansard*, 19 December 2001.

26. See Transport, Local Government and the Regions Select Committee, 8th Report, 10 Year Plan for Transport, 27 May 2002. Minutes of Evidence, 6 February 2002.

27. Julian Glover, 'Tony the straightest guy in town', *New Statesman*, 30 October 2000, p. 7.

28. Simon Walters, interview with Tony Blair, *Mail on Sunday*, 14 November 1999.

29. See http//www.scottishlabour.org.uk/pmspeechtuc/ for speech extracts. See also Kevin Maguire, 'Blair in new spin row after dinner speech', *Guardian*, 11 September 2003, for reaction from trade unionists.

30. See, for instance, Andrew Grice, 'Blair refuses to withdraw "wreckers" attack', *Independent*, 5 February 2002.

31. Written Answers, 8 October 2003, House of Lords 4399.

32. Both quotes are to be found in Iain Dale, *The Blair Necessities*.

33. See, for instance, Paddy Ashdown, *The Ashdown Diaries, Vol. 2*, pp. 124, 223.

34. James Naughtie, *The Rivals*, pp. 72–3.

35. Robert Peston, *Brown's Britain*. The quotes, however, are taken from the *Sunday Telegraph* serialisation of the book on 9 January 2005.

36. See Tom Baldwin, 'What next for the TBGB Show?', *The Times*, 12 January 2005: 'The Chancellor has repeatedly refused to deny claims in a book written with Treasury cooperation that he told Mr Blair: "There is nothing you could say to me now that I could ever believe."'

37. Polly Toynbee, *Guardian*, 8 December 1999. Author's emphasis.

38. Author's emphasis. Quoted in Rentoul, p. 553.

39. Andy McSmith, *Faces of Labour*, p. 17.

40. See Donald Macintyre, *Mandelson*, Chapter 12.

Chapter 5: Why Politicians Lie

1. Anonymous, *Primary Colors*, p. 364.

2. Plato, *The Republic*, p. 81.

3. Quoted in Ronald Bailey, 'Origin of the Specious, Why do Neoconservatives doubt Darwin?', *Reason Magazine*, July 1997. I am indebted to Ronald Bailey for the help he has given me in the preparation of this chapter.

4. For a lucid summary of George Bush's lies and falsehoods, see David Corn, *The Lies of George W. Bush*.

5. I have relied heavily on Perez Zagorin's essay, 'The Historical Significance of Lying and Dissimulation – Truth-Telling, Lying and Self Deception', *Social Research*, Fall 1996, for this survey of religious arguments for and against dissimulation.

6. Dr Martin de Azpilcueta, known as Dr Navarrus, quoted in Zagorin, ibid.

7. See Thaddeus Holt, *The Deceivers*.

8. See Anthony Eden, *Hansard*, 20 December 1956; William Russell, 'Enduring legacy of Empire's last stand,' *Glasgow Herald*, 26 July 1996.

9. Arthur Ponsonby, *Falsehood in Wartime*.

10. Colin Crouch,'Coping with Post Democracy', p. 17. The paragraphs that follow are inspired by Crouch's elegant and persuasive analysis.

11. Ibid., p.13.

12. See James Moore and Wayne Slater, *Bush's Brain*, for how Rove creates the truth on behalf of George Bush.

13. See Bryan Appleyard,'Don't believe a word you say about them', *Sunday Times*, 18 May 2003.

14. *Observer*, 30 July 2000.

15. Bernard Williams, 'Truth, Politics and Self-Deception', *Social Research* 63, 1996.

Chapter 6: Construction of the Truth

1. Leading article, *Guardian*, March 1994.

2. Tony Blair, Hutton Inquiry, hearing transcripts, 28 August 2003.

3. Quoted by George Jones and Michael Kallenbach,'Saddam torture claim"Contradicts Evidence"', *Daily Telegraph*, 5 December 2002.

4. See, for instance, Alison Little and Michael Clarke, 'Cook Denounces"Evil" Saddam', Press Association, 19 December 1998. Ironically Cook was later to become one of the most astringent critics of British government myth-making in Iraq.

5. Dalyell pronounced himself unhappy with the prime minister's response. 'Prime ministers should not be cavalier with the truth,'he said later.'Small inconsistencies can reveal larger inconsistencies. Small lies are often part of larger lies.' See James Lyons and Chris Moncrieff, 'Blair "Cavalier with Truth" in Iraq Dossier', Press Association, 4 December 2002.

6. Joseph A. Schumpeter, *History of Economic Analysis* (New York:

Oxford University Press, 1954), quoted in Thomas Sowell, *A Conflict of Visions*, p. 59.

7. Sissela Bok, *Lying*, p. 6.

8. Roy Jenkins, interview with Donald Macintyre, *Independent*, 23 September 2002.

9. Quoted in Rory Bremner, 'The real Tony Blair', *New Statesman*, 27 September 2004.

10. Ron Suskind, 'Without a Doubt', *New York Times* magazine, 17 October 2004.

11. Quoted in David Corn, *The Lies of George W. Bush*, p. 278.

12. Matthew Parris, 'Lies, damned lies and Blair's brand of pure showmanship', *The Times*, 2 October 2004.

13. See for instance Matthew d'Ancona's political column in the *Sunday Telegraph*, and Anthony Seldon, *Blair*.

14. Michel Foucault, 'Truth and Power', 1977.

15. I am grateful to my friend Peter Swaab, senior lecturer in English Literature at University College London, for guiding me through this perilous territory.

16. Tristram Hunt, 'Why do all politicians now need a "narrative"?' *New Statesman*, 25 June 2001. I am indebted to Dr Hunt's groundbreaking essay. Hunt was the first political writer to note the significance of the emergence of the word 'narrative' in common political speech. It has been lazily accepted without inspection or assessment by most commentators.

17. Geoff Mulgan, *Guardian*, 13 April 1994.

18. Geoff Mulgan and Charles Leadbeater, *Guardian*, 13 July 1994.

19. Peter Mandelson, interview with Katharine Viner, *Guardian*, 9 August 1997.

20. Reply from Peter Mandelson, 29 May 2002.

21. Lord Donoughue, *Hansard*, 21 November 1996.

22. Patricia Hewitt: House of Commons Social Security Committee, 3 June 1998. Joyce Quin: *Hansard*, 1 May 1996. Angela Eagle: *Hansard*, 24 July 2000. Douglas Alexander: BBC *Newsnight*, 12 March 2002.

23. Alastair Campbell, lobby briefings from Number 10 website on the following dates: 18 September 2000, 4 December 2000, 7 January 2001, 10 January 2001, 11 January 2001.

24. H. W. Fowler, *Modern English Usage*, pp. 684, 562.

Chapter 7: Constructing a Culture of Deceit

1. See Peter Oborne and Simon Walters, *Alastair Campbell*, pp. 151–6.

2. 'Ducking the Truth, Government Instructions to Civil Servants on Answering Parliamentary Questions', Liberal Democrat internal document. See also Marie Wolf and Andrew Grice, 'Civil servants told to investigate MPs', *Independent*, 11 June 2002.

3. Mulholland asked whether he would ever lie 'to get the best possible coverage for the Labour Party'. Campbell answered, 'No.' *Guardian*, 17 February 1997.

4. Alastair Campbell, interview with Robert Crampton, *The Times* magazine, 10 January 2004.

5. Roy Greenslade, *Guardian*, September 2003.

6. Alastair Campbell, evidence to House of Commons Public Administration Committee, 11 May 2004.

7. Ibid.

8. Alastair Campbell, Press Association, 9 November 2001.

9. Alastair Campbell interview, 'Shooting the Messenger', 16 April 2003, www.abc.net.au

10. Alastair Campbell, 'It's time to bury spin', *British Journalism Review*, Vol. 13, No. 4, 2002, p. 23.

11. Alastair Campbell, *Today*, 17 February 1994; *Today*, 30 May 1994.

12. Alastair Campbell, evidence to the House of Commons Intelligence and Security Committee, 17 July 2003.

13. Alastair Campbell, quoted in *Private Eye*, February 1999.

14. Oborne and Walters, p. 68.

15. Ibid., pp. 71–2.

16. See ibid., pp. 213–14. After the 1997 general election David Bradshaw, author of the erroneous article, was hired to work in Downing Street.

17. Ibid., p. 28.

18. *The Times*, Diary, 10 September 1994.

19. Nicholas Jones, *Soundbites and Spin Doctors*, pp. 164–5.

20. Colin Brown, *Fighting Talk*, p. 255.

21. These two stories are taken from Oborne and Walters, pp. 212–13.

22. Robert Shrimsley, 'Caught in a media trap by suspicious minds', *Financial Times*, 28 July 2003; Robert Peston, quoted in Peter Oborne, *Alastair Campbell: New Labour and the Rise of the Media Class*, p. 189.

23. For a fuller account of this episode, see Oborne, pp 192–3.

24. See Matthew Parris, 'Another voice', *Spectator*, 26 October 2002. Parris concludes generously: 'I do not think Alastair threatened me dishonestly. I expect he had no recollection of our in-car conversation, realised this was long before Euan went to the Oratory and concluded I must have made it up.'

25. 'Blair wants to send son to Tory flagship opt-out school', *Daily Express*, 21 June 1994.

26. See Matthew Parris's own illuminating analysis of this subtle point: 'Campbell: the Blair that dare not speak its name', *The Times*, 26 July 2003.

27. Anthony Howard column, *The Times*, 17 June 2003.

28. *Daily Telegraph*, 9 November 2002.

29. See *Daily Telegraph*, 7 November 2002; *Independent*, 10 November 2002; *Daily Telegraph*, 10 November 2002.

30. See Joy Copley, 'Blair goes back into battle with crackdown on crime', *Scotsman*, 8 January 1999; Copley, 'Blair promises a wind of change for British prices', *Scotsman*, 9 January 1999.

31. *The Times*, 24 December 1998.

32. See the account in Anthony Seldon, *Blair*, pp. 166–7, which quotes Price extensively.

33. Interview with Lance Price, March 2005.
34. Lobby briefing, 11 a.m., 22 January 2001, Number 10 Downing Street website. See also Sir Anthony Hammond KCB, QC, 'Review of the Circumstances Surrounding an Application for Naturalisation by Mr S. P. Hinduja in 1998', 5.94, p.33.
35. Lobby briefing, 11 a.m., 23 January 2001. See also the account in Hammond, 'Review', 5.108, p.36, and Hugo Young, 'It was Alastair Campbell who led an iniquitous panic', *Guardian*, 30 January 2001. Young wrote that 'it was only when Campbell told journalists on Monday that Mandelson had had no personal involvement whatever – a statement the minister had never made, either publicly or privately – that the world was substantively misled.

   The stark claim was then followed by an equally stark contradiction, again through Campbell, to the effect that Mandelson had, after all, personally called O'Brien . . .'
36. Oborne, p. 191.
37. See, for instance, Bob Roberts and James Hardy, 'No. 10: We did call Kelly "A Walter Mitty", *Daily Mirror*, 5 August 2003.
38. Conversations with Joe Murphy, now political editor of the *Evening Standard*, and Liam Halligan, now economics editor of Channel Four News.
39. Press briefing,10.30 a.m., 22 January 2003, Number 10 website.
40. Charles Reiss, *Evening Standard*, 22 January 2003.
41. Michael White, Andrew Meldrum and Paul Kelso, 'Britain agrees deal to let banned Mugabe attend Paris summit', *Guardian*, 23 January 2003.
42. See, for example, Philip Smucker, Sarah Womack and David Graves, 'Sphinx reveals secret of Blair family break', *Daily Telegraph*, 28 December 2001; Patrick O'Flynn and Guy Saville, 'For some the war goes on', *Daily Express*, 28 December 2001; Marie Wolf, 'Blairs take surprise holiday amid the pyramids', *Independent*, 28 December 2001.
43. Nicholas Watts, 'Blair faces tax bill for holiday at Egypt's expense', *Guardian*, 6 April 2002.

44. See Gavin Cordon, 'Downing Street denies Campbell role in Ferguson knighthood', Press Association, 19 March 2004.

45. Alastair Campbell quoted in David Hughes, 'I fixed Alex's gong', *Daily Mail*, 20 March 2004.

46. See, for example, Lord Falconer's denial when questioned by Viscount Goschen, *Lords Hansard*, 10 April 2001. See also Number 10 website, 11.30 a.m. lobby briefing, 25 October 2001:'Asked if he was emphatically denying that anyone from Downing Street had ever told the *Sun* the Election date, the Prime Minister's Official Spokesman said yes.'

47. 'Mr Price disclosed details of the leak to 200 academics, journalists and spin-doctors at General Election 2001: Campaign Decision Makers' Conference, run by the Corporation of London in July': see James Hardy,'A spin too far', *Daily Mirror*, 25 October 2001.

48. Lobby briefing, 11.30 a.m., 25 October 2001, Number 10 website.

49. Quotes from *Guardian* Unlimited website.

50. Lobby briefings, 11 a.m. and 4 p.m., 11 February 2002, Number 10 website.

51. See, for example, Marie Wolf and John Lichfield,'Blair comes under new pressure on Garbagegate', *Independent*, 14 February 2002. Downing Street has still not revealed who made the change, or why it was made.

52. Lobby briefings, 11 a.m. and 4 p.m., 11 February 2002, Number 10 website.

53. As reported in the *Daily Mail*, 14 February 2002.

54. *Bucharest Business Week,* Vol. 5, No. 28, 23 July 2001.

55. Lord Paul, quoted in David Hughes,'Mittal and the four lies of No. 10', *Daily Mail*, 14 February 2002.

56. Lobby briefing, 11 a.m., 13 February 2002, Number 10 website.

57. I am relying for these quotes on the *Daily Mail*, 14 February 2002.

58. *Sunday Mail*, 23 December 2001, *Sunday Express*, 23 December 2001, *The Times*, 24 December 2001.

59. Kamal Ahmed and Gaby Hinsliff, 'Blair Baby "has had" MMR jab', *Observer*, 23 December 2001; Simon Walters, 'At last Blair admits Leo has had jab', *Mail on Sunday*, 23 December 2001.

60. Andrew Grice, 'Blair's baby given MMR vaccine only last week', *Independent*, 2 February 2002.

61. Anthony Barnett, 'The Campbell Code', OpenDemocracy, 29 January 2004.

62. Sissela Bok, *Lying*, p. 23.

Chapter 8: Iraq

1. Quoted in Ronald Bailey's *Reason Magazine*, July 1997. This quote is widely attributed to Irving Kristol.

2. Quoted in *Hutton and Butler: Lifting the Lid on the Workings of Power*, ed. W. G. Runciman, p. 128.

3. Anthony Barnett, *The Campbell Code*, 29 January 2004 (www.open-democracy.net).

4. Alastair Campbell, evidence to House of Commons Foreign Affairs Committee, 25 June 2003.

5. Tony Blair, quoted in *The Times*, 4 March 2002.

6. Tony Blair, interview for NBC, 4 April 2002 (www.number-10.gov.uk/output/Page1709.asp).

7. Butler Report, HC 898, 14 July 2004 pp. 164–7.

8. Ibid., pp. 64–5.

9. House of Commons Intelligence and Security Committee, Iraqi Weapons of Mass Destruction – Intelligence and Assessment, paras 126–7.

10. Tony Blair, speech given in Sedgefield, 5 March 2004.

11. Tony Blair, *Hansard*, 24 September 2002.

12. ISC: par 65, p. 21.

13. ISC: par 110, p. 31.

14. Tony Blair, press conference with Vladimir Putin, 11 October 2002.

15. Tony Blair, 2 June 2003 (available at www.number-10.gov.uk/output/Page3803.asp).
16. Wells Evidence to Hutton: 14 August, 16: 8ff.
17. See http://news.bbc.co.uk, 29 May 2003; *Daily Mail*, 30 May 2003.
18. See Hutton Inquiry website (www.the-hutton-inquiry.org.uk). Evidence, Alastair Campbell, letter to Greg Dyke, 26 June 2003, BBC/5/0092 (evidence referred to 28 August 2003).
19. See Hutton Inquiry website: www.the-hutton-inquiry.org.uk/content/cab/cab_1_0154to0155.pdf.
20. The minute was submitted to the Hutton Inquiry as MOD/22/0001. See also Butler Report, p. 137.
21. Hutton Inquiry, 25 September 2003.
22. See Hutton Report, pp. 46 and 347.
23. Hutton Inquiry, 1 September 2003.
24. See http://www.royal.gov.uk/output/Page496.asp.
25. Tony Blair, Hearing Transcript, Hutton Inquiry Website, 23 August 2003.
26. ISC Report, paragraph 134.
27. Puzzlingly dated 24 June, the day before his FAC hearing. It must have been sent later.
28. See Hutton Inquiry website (www.the-hutton-inquiry.org.uk)., Hearing Transcripts, Alastair Campbell, 22 September 2003.
29. See Paul Waugh, 'MPs attack Campbell over "Inconsistent" WMD evidence', *Independent*, 19 March 2004.
30. Intelligence and Security Committee, Iraqi Weapons of Mass Destruction – Intelligence and Assessment, para. 132.
31. Government response to the Intelligence and Security Committee Report on Iraqi Weapons of Mass Destruction – Intelligence and Assessments, 11 September 2003, presented to parliament February 2004.
32. *Sunday Telegraph*, 8 June 2003; www.bbc.co.uk, 8 June 2003.
33. See Colin Brown, 'Gunfight at the BBC corral', *Sunday Telegraph*, 29 June 2003.

34. Sir David Manning memo, quoted in *Daily Telegraph*, 18 September 2004.

35. Sir Christopher Meyer memo, quoted in ibid. I am very grateful to Dr David Morrison for guiding me through this territory.

36. Gary J. Schmitt and Abram N. Shulsky, 'Leo Strauss and the World of Intelligence (by which we do not mean nous)', Quoted in Eric Alterman, *When Presidents Lie*, p. 306.

Chapter 9: Political Lying and the Threat to Trust

1. Glen Newey, Full Report of Research Activities and Results available at www.regard.ac.uk/research_findings/R00022315/report.pdf.

2. 'Politicians Being Economical with the Truth is the Price of a Healthy Democracy', ESRC Press Release, 18 May 2003.

3. See also Polly Toynbee, 'A simple man seduced by scoundrels', *Guardian*, 16 December 2004.

4. William Waldegrave, *Hansard*, 19 February 1993.

5. See Sissela Bok's magisterial analysis on this point. Bok, *Lying*, pp. 12–13.

6. As the philosopher Onora O'Neill notes, 'Deceivers do not treat others as moral equals; they exempt themselves from obligations that they rely on others to live up to.' Onora O'Neill, *A Question of Trust*, p. 71.

7. Bok, p. 173.

8. Foot and Mouth Disease 2001: Lessons to be Learned, Inquiry Report, p. 81.

9. Ibid.

10. Neal Lawson, 'This is the party of the living dead', *Guardian*, 8 January 2005.

Chapter 10: The Role of the Media

1. See Peter Oborne, 'A flea in the government's ear', *British Journalism Review*, Vol. 13, No. 4, 2002, p. 33.

2. Onora O'Neill, *A Question of Trust*, p. 98.
3. See Brett Arends, 'Howard is talking tough', *Daily Mail*, 3 April 2003.
4. See *Daily Mirror* and *Independent*, 5 January 2005.
5. O'Neill, p. 95.
6. Geoff Mulgan, LSE Lecture, 4 May 2004.
7. Ibid.
8. *The Times*, 16 April 1999.
9. Polly Toynbee,'A simple man seduced by scoundrels', *Guardian*, 16 December 2004.
10. O'Neill, p. 68.
11. Ibid., p. 95.
12. John Lloyd, *What the Media are Doing to Our Politics*, p. 203.
13. For a fuller discussion, see Peter Oborne, *Alastair Campbell: New Labour and the Rise of the Media Class*, pp. 112 –20.
14. Lloyd, p. 20.
15. Donald Macintyre, *Mandelson*, p. 279.
16. John Rentoul, *Tony Blair*, pp. 238–9.

Chapter 11: How to Rebuild Public Trust

1. Peter Oborne, *Independent*, 1 November 2004.
2. This account is taken from Bill Robinson,'The First Five Years', IFS Thirtieth Anniversary Pamphlet.
3. Onora O'Neill, *A Question of Trust*, p. 98.
4. Ibid., p. 94.
5. John Lloyd, *What the Media are Doing to Our Politics*.
6. Geoff Mulgan, LSE Lecture, 4 May 2004.
7. Jack Straw, speech to the Royal Statistical Society, 25 April 1995.
8. Ibid.
9. Labour promised'open government' and an'independent National Statistical Service'. See 1997 Labour Party Manifesto available at www.labour-party.org.uk/manifestos

10. Alan Clark, *Diaries: In Power, 1983–92*, entry for Sunday 3 March 1990. To his credit, as the Clark diary makes clear, Conrad Black resisted these entreaties. This dinner somehow came to the attention of the Labour MP Tam Dalyell, who put down a memorable Early Day Motion in the House of Commons in protest. Dated 3 April 1999 it'notes that the non-party role of civil servants is further undermined by the participation of Charles Powell, one of the Prime Minister's private secretaries, at a recent dinner with Mr Aspinall, Sir James Goldsmith, the honourable member for Plymouth, Sutton, and Conrad Black, owner of the *Daily Telegraph*, held for the specific purpose of putting pressure on Mr Black to show greater support for the leader of the Conservative Party in her current difficulties, in the columns of his newspaper; welcomes the refusal of Mr Black to succumb to the blandishments of two-known Conservatives and a senior Whitehall official; and calls on the civil servant to take the only honourable course, retire from public service, and apply for more appropriate employment with Conservative Central Office.'

Bibliography

Alterman, Eric, *When Presidents Lie: A History of Official Deception and its Consequences* (New York: Viking, 2004)

Anonymous, *Primary Colors: A Novel of Politics* (London: Vintage, 1996)

Ashdown, Paddy, *The Ashdown Diaries: Volume I* (London: Allen Lane, 2000)

——, *The Ashdown Diaries: Volume II* (London: Allen Lane, 2001)

Bayley, Stephen, *New Labour Camp* (London: Pan Books, 1999)

Beckett, Francis and Henke, David, *The Blairs and Their Court* (London: Aurum Press, 2004)

Best, Joel, *Damned Lies and Statistics: Untangling Numbers from the Media, Politicians, and Activists* (Berkeley: University of California Press, 2001)

Blair, Jayson, *Burning Down My Master's House: My Life at the New York Times* (Beverly Hills: New Millennium Press, 2004)

Bok, Sissela, *Lying: Moral Choice in Public and Private Life* (New York: Vintage, 1999)

Bower, Tom, *Branson* (London: Fourth Estate, 2001)

——, *Gordon Brown* (London: HarperCollins, 2004)

Brown, Colin, *Fighting Talk: The Biography of John Prescott* (London: Simon & Schuster, 1997)

Campbell, Jeremy, *The Liar's Tale: A History of Falsehood* (New York: W.W. Norton & Company, 2001)

Clark, Alan, *Diaries: In Power 1982–1992* (London: Weidenfeld & Nicholson, 1993)

——, *The Last Diaries: In and Out of the Wilderness* (London: Weidenfeld & Nicholson, 2002)

Cook, Robin, *The Point of Departure* (London: Simon & Schuster, 2003)

Corn, David, *The Lies of George W. Bush: Mastering the Politics of Deception* (London: Random House, 2003)

Crick, Michael, *The Boss: The Many Sides of Alex Ferguson* (London: Simon & Schuster, 2002)

Curtis, Mark, *Web of Deceit: Britain's Real Role in the World* (London: Vintage, 2003)

Dale, Iain, *The Blair Necessities: The Tony Blair Book of Quotations* (London: Robson Books, 1997)

Dyke, Greg, *Inside Story* (London: HarperCollins 2004)

Elliot, A. Larry and Schroth, Richard J., *How Companies Lie: Why Enron is Just the Tip of the Iceberg* (London: Nicholas Brealey, 2002)

Flynt, Larry, *Sex, Lies and Politics: The Naked Truth about Bush, Democracy and the War on Terror* (London: Aurum, 2004)

Fowler, H. W., *Modern English Usage* (Oxford: Oxford University Press, 1965)

Franken, Al, *Lies (and the Lying Liars Who Tell Them): A Fair and Balanced Look at the Right* (London: Penguin, 2004)

Fritz, Ben, Keefer, Bryan and Nyhan, Brendan, *All the President's Spin: George Bush, the Media and the Truth* (New York: Simon & Schuster, 2004)

Gould, Philip, *The Unfinished Revolution: How the Modernisers Saved the Labour Party* (London: Abacus, 1998)

Hanks, Mark and Garrett, Ben, *The Book of Political Bollocks* (London: Metro Publishing, 2004)

Hastings, Max, *Editor: An Inside Story of Newspapers* (London: Macmillan, 2002)

Havel, Vaclav, *The Power of the Powerless* (New York: M. E. Sharpe, 1990)

Holt, Thaddeus, *The Deceivers: Allied Military Deception in the Second World War* (New York: Scribner, 2004)

Jones, Nicholas, *Soundbites and Spin Doctors: How Politicians Manipulate the Media – and Vice Versa* (London: Orion, 1996)

Kampfner, John, *Blair's Wars* (London: The Free Press, 2003)

Kerr, Philip (ed.), *The Penguin Book of Lies* (London: Viking, 1990)

Knightley, Philip, *The First Casualty: The War Correspondent as Hero, Propagandist and Myth-Maker from the Crimea to Iraq* (London: Andre Deutsch, 2003)

Koss, Stephen, *The Rise and Fall of the Political Press in Britain* (London: Fontana, 1990)

Liddle, Roger and Mandelson, Peter, *The Blair Revolution: Can New Labour Deliver?* (London: Faber & Faber, 1996)

Linklater, Magnus and Leigh, David, *Not With Honour: The Inside Story of the Westland Scandal* (London: Sphere Books, 1986)

Lloyd, John, *What the Media are Doing to Our Politics* (London: Constable, 2004)

Macintyre, Donald, *Mandelson: The Biography* (London: HarperCollins, 1999)

MacShane, Denis, *Using the Media: How to Deal with the Press, Television and Radio* (London: Pluto, 1979)

McSmith, Andy, *Faces of Labour: The Inside Story* (London: Verso, 1996)

Milosz, Czeslaw, *The Captive Mind* (London: Penguin Classics, 2001)

Moore, James and Slater, Wayne, *Bush's Brain: How Karl Rove made George W. Bush Presidential* (New York: John Wiley & Sons, 2003)

Morrison, David, *Iraq: Lies, Half-truths and Omissions* (London: Athol Books, 2003)

Mowlam, Mo, *Momentum: The Struggle for Peace, Politics and the People* (London: Hodder & Stoughton, 2002)

Naughtie, James, *The Rivals: Blair and Brown – The Intimate Story of a Political Marriage* (London: Fourth Estate, 2001)

Norton-Taylor, Richard, *Truth is a Difficult Concept: Inside the Scott Inquiry* (London: Fourth Estate, 1995)

Nutting, Anthony, *No End of a Lesson: The Story of Suez* (London: Constable, 1996)

O'Neill, Onora, *A Question of Trust* (Cambridge: Cambridge University Press, 2002)

Oborne, Peter, *Alastair Campbell: New Labour and the Rise of the Media Class* (London: Aurum, 1999)

Oborne, Peter and Walters, Simon, *Alastair Campbell* (London: Aurum 2004)

Parris, Matthew and Maguire, Kevin, *Great Parliamentary Scandals: Five Centuries of Calumny, Smear and Innuendo* (London: Robson Books, 2004)

Peston, Robert, *Brown's Britain* (London: Short Books, 2005)

Plato, *The Republic* (London: Penguin Classics, 2003)

Pollard, Stephen, *David Blunkett* (London: Hodder & Stoughton, 2005)

Ponsonby, Lord Arthur, MP, *Falsehood in War-Time* (London: Allen & Unwin, 1940)

Rangwala, Glen and Plesch, Dan, *A Case to Answer* (Nottingham: Spokesman Books, 2004)

Rawnsley, Andrew, *Servants of the People: The Inside Story of New Labour* (London: Penguin 2001)

Rentoul, John, *Tony Blair: Prime Minister* (London: Little, Brown, 2001)

Richards, Paul (ed.) *Tony Blair: In his Own Words* (London: Politico's Publishing, 2004)

Runciman, W.G. (ed.), *Hutton and Butler: Lifting the Lid on the Workings of Power* (The British Academy 2004)

Seldon, Anthony, *Blair* (London: The Free Press, 2004)

Short, Clare, *An Honourable Deception?: New Labour, Iraq and the Misuse of Power* (London: The Free Press, 2004)

Slessor, Tim, *Ministries of Deception: Cover-ups in Whitehall* (London: Aurum, 2002)

Smith, Michael, *The Spying Game: The Secret History of British Espionage* (London: Politico's Publishing, 2004)

Sopel, Jon, *Tony Blair: The Moderniser* (London: Penguin 1995)

Sowell, Thomas, *A Conflict of Visions: Ideological Origins of Political Struggles* (New York: Basic Books, 2002)

Sparrow, Andrew, *Obscure Scribbler: A History of Parliamentary Journalism* (London: Politico's Publishing, 2003)

Thorpe, D.R., *Eden: The Life and Times of Anthony Eden* (London: Pimlico, 2004)

Williams, Bernard, *Truth and Truthfulness: An Essay in Genealogy* (Princeton: Princeton University Press, 2002)

Woodward, Bob, *Plan of Attack* (London: Simon & Schuster, 2004)

Articles

Bailey, Ronald, 'Origin of the specious: Why do neoconservatives doubt Darwin?', *Reason Magazine*, July 1997 (http://reason.com/9707/fe.bailey.shtml)

Chomsky, Noam, Jay, Martin, Le Carré, John, Moorehead, Caroline and Solzhenitsyn, 'The lying game' (Index on Censorship, Volume 33, No. 2, April 2004, Issue 211)

Crouch, Colin, 'Coping with post-democracy' (Fabian Society, 2000)

Dorling, Danny, Eyre, Heather, Johnson, Ron and Pattie, Charles, 'A good place to bury bad news?: Hiding the detail in the geography on the Labour Party's website' (*Political Quarterly*, 2002)

Ebeling, Richard, 'Living a life of the lie: Part 1' (*Freedom Daily*, May 1993)

Hayes, John, MP, 'Tony B. Liar: PMQ Report', Undated

Lloyd, John, 'Law on trial: Media power' (Index on Censorship, Volume 32, No. 4, October 2003, Issue 209)

Newey, Glen, 'ESRC report: Full report of research activities and results' (www.regard.ac.uk)

Newey, Glen, 'Political lying: A defence' (*Public Affairs Quarterly*, Volume 11, Number 2, April 1997)

Newey, Glen, 'Truth and deception in democratic politics: Summary of research results, 2003' (www.regard.ac.uk/cgi-bin/regardng/show Reports.pl?ref=R000223151)

Perez, Zagorin, 'The historical significance of lying' (*Social Research*, 22 September 1996)

Simmons, Jon, 'Crime in England and Wales 2001–2'

Suskind, Ron, 'Without a doubt' (*New York Times* magazine, 17 October 2004)

Thaler, Paul, 'The lies that bind' (*New York Times* magazine 140, 9 June 1991)

Williams, Bernard, 'Truth, politics and self-deception' (*Social Research* 63.3, Fall 1996)

Other Materials

Anderson, Iain (forward by) 'Foot and Mouth Disease: Lessons to be Learned Inquiry' (Report HC888 2002 http://archive.cabinetof-fice.gov.uk/fmd/nav/report.htm)

Ambitions for Britain, Labour Party Manifesto, 2001

Blair, Tony, 'Speech by the Prime Minister: Why the Dome is Good for Britain', 24 February 1998 (www.number-10.gov.uk/output/page1158.asp)

Blair, Tony, Party Conference speeches, 1994–2004

Butler, The Rt. Hon Lord, 'Review of Intelligence on Weapons of Mass Destruction: Report of a Committee of Privy Counsellors', 14 July 2004, (HC 898)

Campbell, Alastair, extracts of evidence given to the ISC, 17 July 2003 (Restricted, ISC/1/0036)

Campbell, Alastair, letter to John Scarlett, 17 September 2002 (CAB/11/0066)

Conservative Party Manifesto, 1992

Conservative Research Department Campaign Guide, 2001

Economic & Social Research Council (ESRC), Press Release, 'Politicians Being Economical with the Truth is the Price of a Healthy Democracy' 18 May 2003, (www.esrc.ac.uk/ESRCContent/news/may03–9.asp)

'Gambling Bill, The: Bill 163 of 2003–04', 28 October 2004 (Research Paper 04/79)

'Government's Annual Report, The, 1999–2000'

Hammond, Anthony, 'Review of the Circumstances Surrounding an Application for Naturalisation by Mr S P Hinduja in 1998'

HM Treasury Financial Statement and Budget Report, 1998 (Red Book)

HM Treasury Financial Statement and Budget Report, 2000 (Red Book)

HM Treasury Pre-Budget Report, November 1999

HM Treasury Pre-Budget Report, November 2000

House of Commons Culture, Media and Sport Select Committee, 'Examination of Mr Robert Ayling and Ms Jennie Page', *Minutes of Evidence*, 8 July 1988

House of Commons Culture, Media and Sport Select Committee, 'Marking the Millennium in the United Kingdom', *Minutes of Evidence*, 12 July 2000

House of Commons Foreign Affairs Committee, 'Ninth Report: The Decision to go to War in Iraq', 7 July 2003

House of Commons Foreign Affairs Select Committee, 'Second Report: Sierra Leone', 9 February 1999

House of Commons Public Administration Select Committee, 'Sixth Report: The Government Information and Communication Service', 6 August 1998

House of Commons Standards and Privileges Committee, 'Tenth Report: Complaint against Mr Geoffrey Robinson', 20 January 1998

House of Commons Standards and Privileges Committee, 'Ninth Report: Complaints against Mr Peter Mandelson', 1 July 1999

House of Commons Standards and Privileges Committee, 'Third Report: Complaint against Mr Keith Vaz, Proceedings and Appendices', 12 March 2001

House of Commons, Foreign Affairs Committee, 'Ninth Report of Session 2002–03: The Decision to Go to War in Iraq' (HC 813–1, 7 July 2003)

Hutton Evidence, Hearing Transcripts, 19 August 2003

Hutton Inquiry Hearing Transcript, Tony Blair MP, Prime Minister, 28 August 2003

Hutton Evidence, Hearing Transcripts, 22 September 2003

Hutton, Lord, Report of the Inquiry into the Circumstances Surrounding the Death of Dr David Kelly C.M.G. 28 January 2004 (HC 247)

Interview with M. Jacques Chirac, President of France, French Ministry of Foreign Affairs, 10 March 2003, (http://www.iraqwatch.org/government/france/mfa/france-mfa-chirac-031003.htm)

'Iraq, its Infrastructure of Concealment, Deception and Intimidation', February 2003. Often referred to as the 'dodgy dossier'.

'Iraq's Weapons of Mass Destruction: The Assessment of the British Government', September 2002. Sometimes called the 'WMD dossier'.

Labour's Business Manifesto (*Economist* Print Edition, 10 April 1997)

'Ministerial Code of Conduct: A Code of Conduct and Guidance on Procedure for Ministers', (Cabinet Office, July 2001)

National Audit Office, 'The Millennium Dome', HC 936, 9 November 2000

'New Labour Because Britain Deserves Better', Labour Party Manifesto, 1997

Scott, Richard, 'The Scott Report: Enquiry into the Export of Defence Equipment and Dual Use Goods To Iraq and Related Prosecutions', 15 February 1996

Taylor, The Rt Hon Ann, MP (Chairman), 'Intelligence and Security Committee: Iraqi Weapons of Mass Destruction – Intelligence and Assessments' September 2003 (Cm 5972)

'Saints and Cynics', *British Journalism Review*, (Vol.13, No. 4, 2002)

Scarlett, John, letter to Alastair Campbell, CAB/11/0070

Tory Betrayals Since 1992, Labour pamphlet

Treaty of Amsterdam

Treaty of Maastricht

UNMOVIC, 'Unresolved Disarmament Issues: Iraq's Proscribed Weapons Programmes', 6 March 2003 (http://www.un.org/Depts/unmovic/new/documents/cluster_document.pdf)

Index